On the Waterfront

On the Waterfront comprehensively examines one of the most important films of the Hollywood canon. Providing the historical context for the film, this volume emphasizes film making as a collaborative process rather than an "auteurist" approach, although it does highlight individual contributions to the film and the political controversy generated by the cooperation of Kazan and Schulberg with the House Un-American Activities Committee. Included are essays specially commissioned for this volume, analyzing the screenplay, Kazan as director, Schulberg as screenplay writer, the score by Leonard Bernstein, and the reception of the film in classrooms. Collectively they demonstrate how and why this film has been an enduring favorite among cineastes and movie buffs alike. A foreword by Budd Schulberg, contemporary reviews, and stills round out the volume.

Joanna Rapf is Professor of English and Film & Video Studies at the University of Oklahoma, Norman. She is the author of *Buster Keaton: A Bio-Bibliography*, and has contributed to journals such as *Literature/Film Quarterly, Film Quarterly,* and *Journal of Popular Film & Television.*

THE CAMBRIDGE UNIVERSITY PRESS FILM HANDBOOKS SERIES

General Editor: Andrew Horton, *University of Oklahoma*

Each CAMBRIDGE FILM HANDBOOK is intended to focus on a single film from a variety of theoretical, critical, and contextual perspectives. This "prism" approach is designed to give students and general readers valuable background and insight into the cinematic, artistic, cultural, and sociopolitical importance of individual films by including essays by leading film scholars and critics. Furthermore, these handbooks by their very nature are meant to help the reader better grasp the nature of the critical and theoretical discourse on cinema as an art form, as a visual medium, and as a cultural product. Filmographies and selected bibliographies are added to help the reader go further on his or her own exploration of the film under consideration.

On the Waterfront

Edited by

JOANNA E. RAPF
University of Oklahoma

Foreword by

BUDD SCHULBERG

PUBLISHED BY THE PRESS SYNDICATE OF THE UNIVERSITY OF CAMBRIDGE
The Pitt Building, Trumpington Street, Cambridge, United Kingdom

CAMBRIDGE UNIVERSITY PRESS
The Edinburgh Building, Cambridge CB2 2RU, UK
40 West 20th Street, New York, NY 10011-4211, USA
477 Williamstown Road, Port Melbourne, VIC 3207, Australia
Ruiz de Alarcón 13, 28014 Madrid, Spain
Dock House, The Waterfront, Cape Town 8001, South Africa

http://www.cambridge.org

First published 2003

Printed in the United States of America

Typefaces Stone Serif 9.5/13.5 pt. and Gill Sans   *System* LaTeX 2_ε [TB]

A catalog record for this book is available from the British Library.

Library of Congress Cataloging in Publication Data
On the waterfront / edited by Joanna E. Rapf.
     p.   cm. – (The Cambridge University Press film handbooks series)
    Includes bibliographical references and index.
    ISBN 0-521-79079-4 – ISBN 0-521-79400-5 (pbk.)
    1. On the waterfront (Motion picture).   I. Rapf, Joanna E.   II. Cambridge
film handbooks series.
PN1997.O43 O52   2003
741.43′72 – dc21   2002034958

ISBN 0 521 79079 4 hardback
ISBN 0 521 79400 5 paperback

For Budd and Maurice

" AEYBF"*

as ever your best friend

Budd Schulberg and Maurice Rapf at Fenway Park, Boston in 1999. (Courtesy of Joanna E. Rapf)

Contents

Acknowledgments

This book, like its subject, *On the Waterfront*, has been a collaborative endeavor. First of all, without the six contributors there would be no book. Their enthusiasm for this project, hard work, patience, and insights embody what the creative process is all about.

We have had invaluable help along the way from Leith G. Johnson at the Wesleyan University Cinema Archives in Middletown, Connecticut, the Kazan family, the Schulberg family, Ned Comstock of the USC Cinema-Television Library, the staff at the Academy of Motion Picture Arts and Sciences Margaret Herrick Library, Kristine Krueger at the National Film Information Service, Mary Corliss at the Museum of Modern Art Film Stills Archive, the Reference and Interlibrary Loan librarians at Baker Library, Dartmouth College in Hanover, NH, and of course, our editor at Cambridge University Press, Beatrice Rehl.

I am personally grateful to Mark Williams of the Department of Film & Television Studies and Susan Bibeau of Humanities Resources, both at Dartmouth College, and Dottie Moody and Scott Hale, both at the University of Oklahoma, for help with this manuscript. And finally, I want to thank Andy Horton, the editor of this Series, for his inspiration, guidance, friendship, and spirit of carnival.

— Joanna E. Rapf

Contributors

JON BURLINGAME is one of the nation's most widely published writers on the subject of music for motion pictures and television. He writes regularly for both *Daily Variety* and the *Los Angeles Times* and has also covered the field for *The Washington Post, Newsday, The Hollywood Reporter,* and *Premiere* and *Emmy* magazines. He is the author of three books: the newly published *Sound and Vision: 60 Years of Motion Picture Soundtracks; TV's Biggest Hits;* and *For the Record.* He also teaches film-music-history at the University of Southern California.

JEFFREY CHOWN is a Professor and Director of Graduate Studies at Northern Illinois University. He is the author of *Hollywood Auteur: Francis Ford Coppola* (1988) and director of an award-winning documentary, "Barbed Wire Pioneers." He is currently at work on another documentary, "John Peter Altgeld: The Eagle Forgotten," funded by the Illinois Humanities Council.

DAN GEORGAKAS has been an editor of *Cineaste* since 1969. His work has appeared in numerous film publications, most recently in *Film Quarterly, Journal of Modern Greek Studies, Moviemaker, New Labor Forum,* and of course, *Cineaste.* He is co-author of *In Focus: A Guide to Using Film,* and coeditor of *The Cineaste Interviews* and the forthcoming *Cineaste Interviews II.* His writing has been anthologized in a score of collections. He has contributed regularly to film annuals published by Salem Press, Gale Publishing, and Ozer Publications. He has helped organize film festivals in New York City and he has commented on film for the *History Journal*, MTV, the Voice of America, Pacifica, and the Canadian Broadcasting System. He currently teaches at New York University.

LANCE LEE is an author, teacher, and conservationist. His work contributed to the establishment of a state park system in the Santa Monica Mountains of southern California. He has taught at USC, UCLA, and California State University, Northridge, variously creating or helping to revise and build undergraduate and graduate programs in playwriting and screenwriting. His books on film include *The Understructure of Writing for Film and Television* with Ben Brady (1988) and *A Poetics for Screenwriters* (2001). Also in 2001 his selected plays, *Time's Up and Other Plays,* were published along with his first novel, *Second Chances.* As a poet he has published in this country and England; "Wrestling With The Angel" appeared in 1990, and "Becoming Human" in 2001. His family is split between Los Angeles and London, England.

BRIAN NEVE teaches political science and film in the Department of European Studies, University of Bath, England. His books include *Film and Politics in America: A Social Tradition* (Routledge, 1992), and (edited with Philip Davies) *Cinema, Politics and Society in America* (Manchester Univ. Press, 1981, 1986). He has contributed to various books, journals and magazines, and is an associate editor of *Cineaste.*

JOANNA E. RAPF is a Professor of English and Film & Video Studies at the University of Oklahoma and a frequent Visiting Professor at Dartmouth College. She has published *Buster Keaton: A Bio-Bibliography* (Greenwood 1995) and film-related essays in numerous books and journals. Her current projects are a book on Sidney Lumet and another on her grandfather, MGM producer Harry Rapf.

DAVID THOMSON'S books include *Movie Man* (1967), *A Biographical Dictionary of Film* (3 editions), *America in the Dark* (1976), *Overexposures* (1981), *Suspects* (1985), *Warren Beatty and Desert Eyes* (1987), *Silver Light* (1990), *Showman: The Life of David O. Selznick* (1992), *Rosebud: The Story of Orson Welles* (1996), and *Beneath Mulholland* (1998). He regularly contributes to *Film Comment, Sight and Sound, American Film, Esquire,* and *The New Republic.* He has been a member of the selection committee of the New York Film Festival and the Board of Advisors for the Telluride Film Festival. Between 1977 and 1981 he was Director of Film Studies at Dartmouth College.

Foreword

Fifty years ago I was down on the New York waterfront, drawn to the cause of the longshoremen, the most exploited working men in America, hoping to put a film together for Elia Kazan. Urging me out of my self-imposed exile from film writing by saying his mission was to do a film of social content in the East, he had overcome my resistance by promising to treat my work with the same respect he would accord Arthur Miller's and Tennessee Williams's in the theater. Although raised in the film business, where my father had run a major studio for many years, I had chosen to live the free life of a novelist on a farm in eastern Pennsylvania. I resented the way writers – even the William Faulkners and Scott Fitzgeralds – were shuffled like cards in Hollywood, where producers, directors, and even egocentric stars presumed to have the last word, and where the lowly writers weren't even allowed on the set.

The subject we had chosen, labor racketeering and corruption in New York Harbor, was not exactly what Hollywood was looking for in the Eisenhower Fifties. When a maverick independent producer, Sam Spiegel, with a spectacular flop on his hands, *Melba*, raised $800,000 for Kazan to knock the picture off in thirty-five days, all we were hoping for was to get the picture to the screen. We had no illusions about a "hit." We simply had our hearts set on getting it made. When doubters would ask us "Do you really think people are going to like this picture?" all we could answer was "We have no idea. All we know is, we like it."

It had been strictly antiestablishment all the way. Yes, once Spiegel seduced a reluctant Brando into playing Terry Malloy, Columbia's honcho, Harry Cohn, had begrudged us that $800,000. But we had made it completely on our own terms, in subzero Hoboken in the winter of 1953–4, without a single set being built. The grungy rooftops and coldwater flats, the weather-beaten nineteenth-century piers and the hoary, mahogany bars of River Street had been our studio. From the time we started shooting, there had been no communication from Hollywood. We were orphans, which was fine with us. The only messages from Sam Spiegel signaled his alarm that Kazan was not shooting fast enough. Because Sam was afraid of Kazan's anger, and because he knew Kazan and I were close, he would call me at midnight or one o'clock in the morning, to urge me to push Kazan to go faster. I would try to reason with him that Hoboken was a fierce place in which to work with the bitter cold and hostile conditions. I'd reassure him that Kazan was performing miracles to adhere that closely to what was essentially a B schedule. Sam had known what it was to live from hand to mouth ever since he escaped the Nazis, and now he lived with the fear that if we ran out of money on the project, there would be no one to bail us out.

Spiegel's relentless breathing down Kazan's neck about staying on schedule provoked an exchange, the memory of which still makes us laugh. During the arduous script preparation, each time I thought we finally had the work pinned, Sam would follow up next day with "Why don't we open it up one more time?" In truth, I had started with a broader canvas, wanting to tell not only Terry Malloy's personal story, but the waterfront priest's, and to set it all in social perspective. I wanted to define the pecking order, right up to the Mayor and the "Mr. Big" who owned him. To give Spiegel his due, he hammered for tighter structure, and stronger (and what came to be total) focus on my main character. Precious scenes that added texture and complexity were jettisoned to the purpose of keeping it moving. The film asks "And then? And then? And then?" Often with a pang of regret I had to admit that in the interest of relentless storytelling, my pet sidebars had to go.

Sam Spiegel didn't give a damn about the cause of the longshoremen, and I resented that. But I had to admit, thinking pure *movie* now, Spiegel's insistence on *structure* was making for a better script.

But I finally dug my heels in when Spiegel wanted to cut drastically the scene in the hold when Father Barry delivers a fighting sermon over the body of Runty Nolan, the feisty little gadfly in the dock boss' ointment. I had lifted the speech almost bodily from one the "Waterfront Priest," Father John Corridan, had given on the docks, an incredible challenge to the lethal dock bosses in which he invoked Christ in the shape-up, holding a union card and being passed over unless He kicked back part of His miserable wages to the mobbed-up hiring boss. The speech had fascinated me, and I had worked hard to get it right. It ran six pages and Spiegel insisted it had to be slashed to a page, arguing that what might work in the theater or in a book could not be done in a film. This time I reminded Spiegel and Kazan of our unusual agreement by which the writer had final word on the script. But that didn't stop Sam. Next morning, in that disingenuous way he had, when we were to begin discussion of the following scene, Sam said, "Wait a minute, first I'd like to hear the cuts you made in the priest's scene." And when I told Sam through gritted teeth that I thought I had told him I wasn't changing a word of that scene, Sam looked truly hurt. "But Budd, I thought you said yesterday you finally agreed to cut it."

I blew up. "That's it, I'm finished, I'm quitting!" My nerves were raw. I had been on this project for more than two years now, mostly on what we called "spec," and things had been so lean that I actually had had to mortgage my farm. A $5,000 advance against my quixotic financial interest in the film had been postponed from month to month. To head off this crisis, Kazan suggested we take a walk around the block. The main thrust of his argument was "Look, Sam can be maddening, he can drive you crazy, even if sometimes he's right. But never forget, he was the only one we could find who would do our picture. Spiegel saved our ass."

That stopped me. I had to agree and so back to Sam's expensive suite at the St. Regis (charged to our picture) we went. Finally, with a late-in-the game assist from Kazan, I got my way and Father Barry's six-page "sermon" in the hold stayed in the script.

The shoot began with the scenes on the rooftop, very rough work since all the equipment had to be dragged up a four-floor walkup, and the wind chill had everybody's teeth rattling. In fact, Marlon's remark was classic: "It's so fucking cold up here there's no way we could overact." But the technical problems kept mounting and near the second day Sam Spiegel arrived to protest that production was already half a day behind schedule. Now it was Kazan's turn to blow up. If this was the kind of producer interference he was facing, to hell with it, he was quitting! I said "Gadg, let's take a walk around the block," and when we walked away from the set, I echoed Kazan's words after my blowup with Spiegel: "Look, he may be a pain in the butt, but never forget he was the only one we could find who would do our picture. Spiegel saved our ass." Kazan's wrath turned to laughter, and he climbed back to the roof and got back to work.

Our sense of alienation from mainline Hollywood continued when Kazan ran the rough cut for Harrry Cohn in his private projection room at the studio. I was waiting at the farm for Cohn's reaction. How a studio launches a film is usually vital to its success. How many prints? How much advertising? Any press tours?

The call came in at 1 A.M.: "Budd, I don't know what to tell you. I'm still in shock. I just came out of the projection room. Just the two of us, well three, Harry had this Latin c____ with him. I sat right behind them. They were all over each other all through the picture. When the lights came on they just got up and walked out. Never even looked back. Never even said good night. I think he hates the picture."

Another reason for the cold shoulder, we learned, is that the in-house Oscar contender was his *The Caine Mutiny*, a major production starring Humphrey Bogart. The toughest of all the moguls wanted to play down his own competition. So when our picture opened unheralded one morning at the Astor, Kazan and I went down to see if anybody was going to show up. To our amazement, the line went on into the next block. Father Corridan and my longshoremen friends were with us and we reasoned that with twenty-five thousand longshoremen on the books, and that many more involved in the work of the harbor, plus all the mob guys, naturally they'd all turn out opening day. So we still thought it was a one-day phenomenon. It was not until *The New York Times* came out next day with a rave and nonwaterfront people came lining up that it began to dawn on us that it might be more than a one-day wonder. Even when it remained a hot ticket at the Astor all week long, we dismissed our success as a local phenomenon. This was a New York City movie after all. Beyond the Hudson River, where we shot the film, we still feared Zanuck's dire prophecy: "Who's gonna care about a lot of sweaty longshoremen?" So we were amazed when moviegoers flocked to it in Georgia, Michigan, Kansas, Texas . . . and when we won all those foreign festival awards. Fifty years later, as this book goes to press, that same sense of surprise at its success has never left us. We still remember our saying to each other, "All we know is, we like it." That it would one day be included in the American Film Institute's all-time top ten and become an icon of thumb-to-nose independent filmmaking seemed as long a shot as betting that Henry Wallace would be the next president of the United States.

It winning all those Oscars, and wiping out Cohn's pet *Caine Mutiny*, didn't soften our hearts toward the Hollywood establishment. We remained our curmudgeonly selves by refusing to attend the Academy's snooty postaward Governor's Ball. Instead, we threw our own bash at a favorite Chinese restaurant, The House of Chan, with some of the cast, all of the crew, the core group of rebel longshoremen, and the ex-fighters I knew and had brought in to play the racketeer union goons. Strictly blue collar all the way. Even that night, in the glow of sweet revenge, Kazan and I would not have believed that our film would be remembered, even revered into the next millennium.

Why the film has never gone away is open to many interpretations. There is, of course – so perfectly serving the story and the theme – the haunting quality of the acting, the directional energy, the low-key but unforgettable photography, Leonard Bernstein's first-time-ever score, and the gorgeously unpretentious look of Hoboken itself, a nineteenth-century town where the Italians and the Irish were duking it out every day for control and survival on the docks.

Elsewhere I've described the ideal motion picture as a horse race in which all the entries get their noses to the finish line in a dead heat. It's a small miracle when two of them make it, and when every element is there at the wire it's a *Lord of the Rings* miracle.

Of course I realize not every critic sees it that way. While most of the contributors to this book analyze the film in terms of its virtues, there are a few that see it through a darker glass. Some of the negative comments are, to my mind, so perverse that I confess to having had moments when I wondered if I could write this Foreword. One contributor thinks it has no relevance today because it is so completely and narrowly of its own time. He finds a very different reaction from that of the many young audiences with whom I have viewed it. I think they react so positively because – despite the old-fashioned black-and-white look and union labor battles that may be ancient history – this is essentially a theme that will be relevant as long as the human mind is a hive of conflicting passions, loyalties, ideals. "Wherein I'll catch the conscience of the king." The conflict is universal, to be or not to be, to do or not to do. In particular, we were telling what I saw as the true story of exploitation of the dock workers in the harbor of New York. We were telling a story I could document scene by scene as to how a racketeer waterfront local held its browbeaten membership in thrall, parceling out the jobs four hours at a time, demanding fat kickbacks from their measly wages, breaking their legs if they protested and whacking them if they persisted. But in general we were after something we all face every day of our lives. Our waterfront story could be retold today whenever the haves give it to the have-nots. Instead of Johnny Friendly's easy money boys, we've got the Enron hundred-million-dollar high flyers saying like the unreconstructed Terry Malloy, "Do it to them before they do it to me." And we've got the whistle blowers whose hearts are with the thousands of innocent employees seeing their pensions and their life savings blown away.

Among some effective essays here, including the editor's knowledgeable and lively introduction, are some ivory tower aberrations that pass for academic criticism. One of them questions why the dock boss, Johnny Friendly, chooses Terry's brother Charley to warn Terry to dummy up – or else! – when facing the Waterfront Crime Commission. Apparently reality has no bearing on highbrow preconceptions. Otherwise, it should be obvious that Terry's brother is the logical if not the only choice to beg the kid to stay "D 'n D" and save his life. If there's anyone who could persuade Terry not to testify against the Friendly mob, it's his only brother, who loves him even as he uses him. This critic then crawls further out on his shaky limb by suggesting that a better film would be based on Terry's brother, "Charley the Gent." Terry isn't quite Hamlet, but I found myself wondering if this critic would have suggested that Shakespeare should have elevated Ophelia's brother to the main character in *Hamlet* and changed the title to "Laertes."

Another off-the-wall response to the film, echoing the Stalinoid ideologues Lindsay Anderson and John Howard Lawson, is the accusation that the ending is "fascist" because one man, Terry Malloy, leads the embattled longshoremen onto the pier, breaking the hold of the dock boss. As a lifelong member and advocate of organized labor, I would think it obvious that there is no conflict between democratic unions and strong leaders. One need only think of Harry Bridges and the west coast longshoremen, Walter Reuther and the Automobile Workers Union, Dubinsky and his Ladies' Garment Workers Union ... dominant men, yes, but at regular intervals willing to take their chances in democratic elections, as contrasted with the Jimmy Hoffas and the Tough Tony Anastasias. 180 degrees from "fascism," the waterfront ending was influenced by the courageous behavior of Johnny Dwyer who dared stand up to the "pistols" of Local 895 on the west side of Manhattan. One day, most dramatically, they refused to go in to work when the mob *gauleiter*, Eddie Thompson, blew the whistle. Only when the stevedore finally turned to Dwyer and asked him to blow it, would the men "vote with their feet" by following him into work. I described that turning point in another article I wrote for *The New York Times Magazine* (Sept. 27, 1953), "How One Pier Got Rid Of The Mob." Later I drew on this unique event for the ending of our film. I would have thought that academics would have researched that article, along with the many others I did for various magazines when Father Corridan asked for my help in bringing to public attention the plight of the longshoreman, until then an untold story.

Perhaps most vexing of all the negative comments is the academic fixation that Terry's denouncing the "Pistol Local" to the Waterfront Crime Commisssion is an apology and a metaphor for the House Un-American Activities Committee hearings on Communism in Hollywood. That is not what Elia Kazan asked me to do when he came to see me, and in no way was that my motivation for wanting to write this film. What disturbs me most about this aspersion – repeated in film schools across the country until it's become academic gospel – is that if you think of the longshoremen as merely stand-ins or surrogates for the Hollywood testifiers, you trivialize the ordeal of the actual longshoremen who had to overcome their terror in order to testify against the lethal thugs who ran the ILA. I remember the many nights in the St. Xavier Church basement when Father Corridan urged the frightened rebels to testify, and later I watched them under fire while attending all forty days of the hearings. One who helped the research and became a friend, Tommy Bull from Hoboken, had to ship out all the way to Australia to save his life. Tony Mike diVincenzo, the Hoboken dock boss who came over to the side of the angels, was also in danger, and so were other St. Xavier rebs in fear for their lives. I had written an earlier *Waterfront* without Terry's testimony. It was only when I monitored those incredible hearings that I became convinced that the real waterfront was writing our ending for us. That's the true reason why the testimony scene is in the film and keys the climax.

But despite all these detours from reality one might expect from professors, scholars, or critics with their own hard-nosed agendas, I commend the editor for putting together what I believe to be the first comprehensive study of our film. How to get all those horses' noses to the finish line in a dead heat deserves the attention of every true believer in making and watching films that don't merely entertain but seek to stir our social conscience and make a difference.

Brookside
February 20, 2002

JOANNA E. RAPF

Introduction: "The Mysterious Way of Art"

Making a Difference in *On the Waterfront*

On August 3, 2000, at the Frank Sinatra Amphitheater on the Hoboken waterfront where *On the Waterfront* was shot, screenwriter Budd Schulberg was honored for his work on that film and for his contributions to the cultural life of this now beautiful and thriving community. A plaque has been placed where the piers once stood, marking the location of the filming of this landmark motion picture. With the gray light over the New York skyline as a backdrop, the play, *On the Waterfront*, adapted by Budd Schulberg and Stan Silverman from the film and novel, was given a staged reading to a largely local audience that included some people who had been on hand almost fifty years ago when cast and crew endured cold weather and a hostile waterfront environment to create the work that is the subject of this book.

On the Waterfront won eight Academy Awards in the spring of 1955 (it was nominated for eleven): Best Picture, Screenplay, Direction, Cinematography, Editing, Art Direction, Actor (Marlon Brando), and Supporting Actress (Eva Marie Saint). One of the awards it did *not* receive was for Leonard Bernstein's remarkable score, as Jon Burlingame discusses in his essay in this volume. Both Kazan and Schulberg have expressed some reservations about the music. "It put the picture on the level of almost operatic melodrama here and there. That's the only thing I object to" (Young 183).*

---

* References cited may be found in the section Selected Critical Bibliography at the end of this book.

1A. The Advertisement for the Theatrical Staged Reading of *On the Waterfront* in Hoboken, New Jersey, Thursday, August 3, 2000.

The film is number eight on the American Film Institute's greatest 100 American films of the 20th century, and even people who have not seen it recognize such lines as "I coulda been a contender." Many reviews at the time it opened [some included in this volume]

1B. Budd Schulberg speaking at the event. (Courtesy of Joanna E. Rapf)

recognized its greatness. *The Saturday Review* began quite simply: "Let me say right off that *On the Waterfront* (Columbia) is one of the most exciting films ever made in the United States" (25). The *New Yorker* described it as "galvanic" (52), while *Newsweek* got to the heart of its intensity as "a story of violence, of the hand and of the heart, that moves with the uncomfortable beat of a rising pulse. It is melodrama that transcends itself, its violence set off against striking depictions of love, corporal and spiritual" (78).

Although the auteur theory has led to the unfortunate habit of talking about a movie in terms of its director, this *Handbook* will stress the fact that making motion pictures is a collaborative art. *On the Waterfront* is a film that beautifully illustrates not only the importance of direction, but of script, cinematography, acting, art direction, editing, sound, music, and of that intangible, essential quality behind all great films: having something to say.

In putting this book together, I have been inspired not only by the brilliant collaboration that produced an undisputedly great film, but also by the fact that the screenwriter of this film is still a fervent fighter for social causes, including recognition of the writer who is too often hidden as only a name on a rolling list of credits where the director takes the possessive. My personal connection is reflected in this book's dedication to Budd Schulberg and to my father, Maurice Rapf, his best friend and Emeritus Director of Film Studies at Dartmouth College. Budd and Maurice grew up together in Hollywood during the 1920s as studio brats, one the son of Paramount executive and producer, B. P. Schulberg, and the other the son of MGM vice-president and producer, Harry Rapf. The bosses' sons were inseparable. With the studios as their playground, they had access to costumes, sets, and a world of make-believe that was the stuff of dreams. They raised racing pigeons together (a hobby later incorporated into *On the Waterfront*), and as young men began a lifelong enthusiasm for sports, especially the opportunity to wager on college football in the fall. They even ended up at Dartmouth College together, and took a memorable trip to the Soviet Union in 1934. Both became outspoken leftists. After graduation, they began careers as writers, initially sharing the difficulties of working on the script of *Winter Carnival* (1939). In Hollywood, they participated in Marxist study groups, and Budd began the novel that was to become one of the great American books about a movie producer, *What Makes Sammy Run?* (1941). In his testimony to the House Un-American Activities Committee on May 23, 1951, he says his break with the Communist Party was triggered when John Howard Lawson and others associated with the Party in Hollywood told him that he could be released from his weekly assignments only if they approved the plan of the novel and oversaw its writing. This insistent pressure on his freedom as a writer was an anathema.

> I decided I would have to get away from this if I was ever to be a writer. I decided to leave the group, cut myself off, pay no more dues, listen to no more advice, indulge in no more political literary discussions, and to go away from the Party, from Hollywood, and try to write a book, which is what I did.[1]

Ultimately, it was his testimony before the HUAC that also caused a painful break with my father who, although he never testified, was blacklisted and remained a committed leftist. Happily, the two men reunited in the 1960s when their sons enrolled at their alma mater, Dartmouth College, and they renewed a friendship that lasts to this day. Budd, a "liberal anticommunist," and my dad, an "unrepentant reactionary Communist," show that ultimately labels don't matter. Shared roots, a love of family, over eighty years of memories create a bond of friendship that transcends the vagaries of politics and human frailty.

Although Schulberg became disillusioned with the Communist Party, especially over its treatment of writers in the Soviet Union, he has remained a "leftist," committed to social causes, to making this world a better place, to fighting injustice, bigotry, racial intolerance. Perhaps his greatest legacy, besides his novels and the screenplay for *On the Waterfront*, will be the Watts Writers' Workshop in Los Angeles and the Frederick Douglas Creative Arts Center in New York where disadvantaged young people are supported in their creative work. He truly has changed people's lives and contributed significantly to the social, cultural, and literary wealth of the 20th century.

In the foreword to this *Handbook,* he writes about the importance of films that do not merely entertain, but "seek to stir our social conscience and make a difference." Obviously, *On the Waterfront* is such a film, as all the contributors to this volume agree. However, their perspectives are various, and not all flattering. Scholars, living above the trenches, sometimes have the reputation of being disconnected from the blood and guts of making a film. Schulberg is refreshingly critical of some of the essays in this book, and his perspective allows us to reflect on the difference between the way an author thinks of his work and the way we receive it.

Unlike Schulberg, who came from Hollywood royalty, the other man who might be termed an "author" of *On the Waterfront,* Elia Kazan, was an immigrant's son. He was four when his Greek parents came to this country from Turkey and settled in New York where his father became a successful rug merchant. He tells of this background in *America, America* (1963), based on his own largely autobiographical novel. A year after graduating from Williams College, and a stint at the Yale School of Drama, Kazan joined the Group Theatre in New York which had been founded by Harold Clurman, Lee Strasberg, and Cheryl Crawford in 1931 (for the history of Kazan and the Group, see the essay by David Thomson). During the Great Depression the Communist Party was attractive to artists and intellectuals looking for a better world. Kazan became a member in the summer of 1934. For the House Un-American Activities Committee in 1952, he explained his reasons this way:

> ... it seemed to me at that time that the Party had at heart the cause of the poor and unemployed people whom I saw on the streets about me. I felt that by joining, I was going to help them, I was going to fight Hitler, and, strange as it seems today, I felt that I was acting for the good of the American people.
>
> (Bentley 486)

Like Schulberg, Kazan has always had a social conscience. In the early 1930s he had hoped for social revolution and admired Franklin Delano Roosevelt. In hindsight, he now feels progress comes about "through resolution of dissension. When a problem is resolved, there's a tiny step forward" (Young 177). His disillusionment with the Party came when he was "tried" for refusing to follow orders to instigate a strike in the Group Theatre. Although for many years after he says he still believed in the ideals of Communism, he wanted nothing more to do with American Communists, and he left the Party in the spring of 1936. Then the Stalin – Hitler pact shattered any idealism he had about the USSR.[2]

By 1950, Kazan was probably the most influential stage director in New York, with productions of Arthur Miller's *All My Sons* in 1947 and *Death of a Salesman* in 1949, and Tennessee Williams's *A Streetcar Named Desire* in 1947. In 1947 he cofounded the Actors Studio with Lee Strasberg, bringing the Stanislavski-based "Method" to the forefront of American theater. The Method, as Kazan sees it, involves "turning psychology into behavior.... You have to show what is being felt through behavior" (Young 150, 161). A number of the actors later to appear in *Waterfront* were students of Kazan's, including Marlon Brando, Eva Marie Saint, Lee J. Cobb, and Rod Steiger. He was "the white-haired-boy director," walking Broadway with a swagger, the king of the great white way.[3]

He also had a successful career in films, having directed a sensitive rendition of Betty Smith's novel, *A Tree Grows in Brooklyn*, in 1945. Three films he did for Darryl F. Zanuck at 20th Century-Fox stand out even today for their courage in dealing with difficult and controversial issues: *Boomerang!* (1947), a look at what happens when a man is unjustly accused of murder; *Gentlemen's Agreement* (1947), about anti-Semitism; and *Pinky* (1949), about racism. Kazan had a well-deserved reputation for caring about issues of morality, social justice, responsibility, and conscience. And it is because of this reputation that his cooperation with the House Un-American Activities Committee during its probe into Communist infiltration in the entertainment industry was so surprising to many (see the essays by Neve and Thomson). But he clearly acted out of conscience, a belief – perhaps stronger for his immigrant roots – that he was doing what he should as a "citizen." He explores these ideas fully in his autobiography, *A Life*.

With both the writer and director of *On the Waterfront* having "named names," Schulberg in 1951 and Kazan in 1952, it is inevitable that their film has been "read" as a defense of their actions. All the essays in this book touch on this issue in one way or another, but the consensus remains that if you did not know about the personal backgrounds of Schulberg and Kazan, it would be a stretch to see *Waterfront* as a commentary on testimony before the HUAC. As Lance Lee stresses in examination of the screenplay, "it is the work that counts," comparing *Waterfront*'s greatness as a script to the greatness of Shakespeare's plays. In both cases, their significance need not have anything to do with the lives of the men who wrote them.

Both Schulberg and Kazan had been working on waterfront stories before they testified, and for Schulberg especially, his focus was clearly on combating corruption on the New York/New Jersey waterfront. Kazan, on the other hand, *has* drawn a parallel between himself and Terry Malloy and the issue of testifying. In his autobiography, *A Life* (1988), he writes quite openly: "*On the Waterfront* was my own story; every day I worked on that film, I was telling the world where I stood and my critics to go and fuck themselves" (529). Yet in spite of this, the primary importance of the film is *not* that it's a reflection of the political turmoil of postwar America, but that it is, simply, a great film, a work of art. One of the aims of the essays in this volume is to explain why.

If we look at the film's preproduction history as a road map, there are two distinct paths that converge and lead to the collaboration of Schulberg and Kazan. First there is Malcolm Johnson's Pulitzer Prize – winning series of articles for the *New York Sun*, "Crime on the Waterfront," exposing union corruption on the docks of New York. In 1950 the articles appeared as a book and Budd Schulberg was asked by fledgling film producer Joseph Curtis, a nephew of Columbia's Harry Cohn, to write a script based on the material. Robert Siodmak tentatively agreed to direct. The resulting script, also called *Crime on the Waterfront*, was finished in the spring of 1951. Schulberg describes doing research for the script in his *New York Times* article, "*Waterfront:* From Docks to Film," also included in this volume. He writes of hanging out in waterfront bars, drinking with, and gaining the confidence and respect of, the local longshoremen by talking boxing, a sport he loved and knew well (he had not only written a novel about boxing, *The Harder They Fall* (1947), but had comanaged a fighter). He learned first-hand about corrupt unions, run by mob bosses who hobnobbed with New York politicos, about "the shape-up," the bribery, the code of "D 'n D" ("I don't know nuthin', I ain't seen nuthin', I'ain't sayin' nuthin'"), the fear, the violence. In cities like Hoboken it was hard to tell where politics ended and the rackets began. It was a system based on a three-way collusion of corrupt unions, the racketeers, and the shipping companies, all greasing the hands of local politicians. And Schulberg met the waterfront priests who championed the rights of the downtrodden longshoremen in whose bars he drank and whose homes he visited. He focuses in particular on Father John Corridan of the lower West Side, who became the model for Father Barry in the film. He describes him this way in the *New York Times* piece: "I got to know Father Corridan, a rangy, fast-talking, chain-smoking West Side product who talks the darndest language I ever heard, combining the gritty vocabulary of the longshoremen with mob talk, the statistical findings of a trained economist and the teachings of Christ."[4]

With a writer's ear, Schulberg picked up the language of the waterfront from the priests to the workers to the mob, and incorporated it into the dialogue of his script. But due to financial problems, this initial version of the waterfront story was never made, and the rights to Johnson's book, *Crime on the Labor Front*, reverted to Schulberg (see Georgakas for a full account).

The second path begins with Arthur Miller. In 1949 he was looking for a new project and became interested in the on-going waterfront struggles. He undoubtedly read Malcolm Johnson's articles, but Miller researched and wrote about the mob killing of a man named Peter Panto who tried to organize longshoremen in Brooklyn's Red

Hook district in the 1930s and whose body was dumped in the East River.[5] Because of their common interest in such social problems as union corruption, Miller talked to his friend Kazan about collaborating on a film. The resulting screenplay called *The Hook* was drafted between February of 1949 and the summer of 1950.[6] The title refers both to the Red Hook district of the Brooklyn waterfront, the setting for the film, and the longshoremen's hook. But like Schulberg's first script, this one too was never made. Miller pulled out when Harry Cohn of Columbia Pictures, on the advice of Roy Brewer of the Motion Picture Alliance for the Preservation of American Ideals, suggested that it would be politically expedient to turn the waterfront mobsters into communists. In Ciment,[2] Kazan says he got a phone call from Miller saying he didn't want to do the picture" (102). He told Jeff Young, "I asked why, and he said he couldn't tell me. He never explained it" (125), but in *A Life*, Kazan elaborates the story in detail (410–415), and both Georgakas and Thomson discuss it in their essays in this volume.

In *A Life* Kazan credits his wife, Molly, with the idea of contacting Budd Schulberg (486). Kazan had fallen out with Arthur Miller. *The Hook* had just been the first straw; Kazan's friendly testimony before the HUAC was the last. Schulberg had not met Kazan before when he got a phone call from him in the spring of 1952 at his Bucks County Pennsylvania farm. They spent a weekend together, discussing possible projects, and decided on the waterfront subject since they had a common interest there and Schulberg had his unproduced screenplay and the rights to Malcolm Johnson's book.

Schulberg began by continuing his on-site waterfront research that he describes as "a year-long experience that I shared with Kazan" ("Afterword" to the script of *On the Waterfront* 145). All during this time he was also writing articles for *Commonweal*, *The New York Times Magazine*, and *The Saturday Evening Post* about the longshoremen and their fight against the corrupt bosses who controlled their lives. He was their advocate; their cause became his cause. When Budd was ready to sit down and write the script, Kazan took a break from the project and went to work with Tennessee Williams on *Camino Real*, a successful production that reestablished him professionally. He came out of it, he says, "with a full tank of gas; my energy was back" (*A Life* 506).

The script went through at least eight drafts. Even the shooting script which Kazan annotated as he was preparing the film (dated June 28, 1953 in the Archives at Wesleyan) is still called "The Golden Warriors," and many of the characters do not yet have their final names – Johnny Friendly, for example, is still Mickey Friendly. Initially, the script was rejected by Darryl Zanuck at 20th Century-Fox, to whom Kazan still owed a picture. It is Zanuck who reputedly said, "Who's going to care about a lot of sweaty longshoremen?" ("Afterword" 147). Then Warner Brothers said no, followed by Paramount and MGM. This is 1953, the height of anticommunist hysteria in this country, and a script that some now see as a justification for informing was, paradoxically, seen by the studios as "pink," prolabor, prounion, maybe even "red."

Sam Spiegel, maverick independent producer who still went by the pseudonym "S. P. Eagle," came to the rescue and took on the project, eventually getting Columbia Pictures to distribute it. A fugitive from Hitler's Germany in 1933, he had just done *The African Queen* with John Huston and the British production, *Melba*, directed by Lewis Milestone. Spiegel was an expert at wheeling and dealing in Hollywood. After Marlon Brando initially returned the *Waterfront* script, turning down the role of Terry Malloy, Kazan had contacted Frank Sinatra for the part – "He spoke perfect Hobokenese" (*A Life* 515) – but Spiegel managed to maneuver Marlon Brando into reconsidering. At the time, Brando was a much bigger star than Sinatra and that would help with financing. He had made *A Streetcar Named Desire* (1951) and *Viva Zapata* (1952) with Kazan, but said that because of the HUAC testimony he now would not work with him. Spiegel convinced him otherwise and today his Oscar-winning performance of a mumbling, touching, anguished, lonely orphan, a fighter whose swagger covers inner doubt, is the most memorable aspect of this film. Kazan has written "If there is a better performance by a man in the history of film in America, I don't know what it is.... what was extraordinary is the contrast of the tough-guy front and the extreme delicacy and gentle cast of his behavior" (*A Life* 517).

The "Eagle," as he was known, was a stickler for script, a "bear for structure," who found *Waterfront* long and discursive ("Afterword" 141). The seemingly endless rewrites infuriated the screenwriter who, at one point, walked out. Draft number 6, simply titled "Waterfront," contains this notation in Schulberg's handwriting: "Revised script as of approx. Oct. 1, following Spiegel – Kazan suggestions for 'substantial reconstruction of continuity line'."[7] In *A Life*, Kazan comments, "the script kept improving – growing shorter and tighter," until it became "a model screenplay, a near perfect piece of work" (518). Lance Lee's essay in this volume explains why.

The film was shot during the winter of 1953–54 with Boris Kaufman as cinematographer (see Chown's essay for a discussion of the decision to shoot the film in black and white and for Kaufman's contributions). Brother of Dziga Vertov and Mikhail Kaufman, both filmmakers and cameramen, he learned his craft with his brothers as part of the Soviet Kino – Pravda group. But in 1928 he went to France with his parents. There, he collaborated with Jean Vigo on all three of that cult figure's films (*A propos de Nice* [1930], *Zéro de conduite* [1933], and *L'Atalante* [1934]) before coming to the United States in 1942. He gained a reputation as an artist with b&w cinematography. He liked the soft shadows of early morning and late afternoon light, clear days for long shots and cloudy days for close-ups when diffuse light helps to bring out facial features. In an interview in this volume he talks about the problems of maintaining uniformity in the visuals while shooting this film for two-and-a-half months on the docks of Hoboken, New Jersey during the "worst months of the year – with rain, fog, and sunshine." Kazan says simply:

> When we were filming *Waterfront*, one premise I set with him right away was that I didn't want to make the skyline of New York picturesque. Don't stress it. He gave me some real beauty, the kind of beauty that we like. He had a lot of guts, in the cold with a rebellious crew. He did a terrific job, and I admire him.
>
> (Young 181–182)

Kazan's enthusiasm for this project was, from the start, related to his personal situation – "It was my reply to the beating I'd taken" (*A Life* 488) – but for Budd the film was an ongoing crusade against waterfront corruption. He followed the Senate Committee hearings headed by Senator Estes Kefauver on the corruption of the International Longshoremen's Association, hearings that eventually forced Governor Dewey, who had, like other politicians, been in thick with crooked longshore-union officials, to set up the New York State Crime

Commission. Every day, for forty days in 1953, Schulberg attended these hearings which revealed in graphic and sickening detail the sordid conditions on the New York waterfront. As he told Kazan, "I felt that life was writing the end of our film" (*Tikkun* Interview 9). There is a difference between being an informer, a "stool pigeon," a "rat" – and being a "whistle blower," as Jeff Chown discusses. It is clear that for Schulberg, the kind of testifying demanded of his character, Terry Malloy, was absolutely essential to cleaning up the hellish conditions under which the longshoremen worked on the New York waterfront.

Although *Waterfront* is Terry's story – and this was Kazan's affinity, as discussed below – Schulberg's interest was, from the start, the waterfront priest, Father Corridan in real life, Father Barry in the film, the "fast-talking, chain-smoking" man of God for whom the New York docks become his parish. He went on to write a novel, *Waterfront* (1955), and the play mentioned at the beginning of this essay in which the priest is the main character and Terry dies at the end. In discussing this book, Schulberg highlights his emphasis: " . . . the violent action line of Terry Malloy is now seen for what it is, one of the many moral crises in the spiritual – social development of Father Barry" (*The Saturday Review* 6). His focus is religious in scope, universal in his desire to reveal social injustice and to help to bring about equal opportunity to the workingmen and women of the New York waterfront.

Kazan, on the other hand, individualizes the story of the film: "This is about Terry! A Boy becomes a citizen! A man finds his DIGNITY AGAIN" (PN). Under the heading "Theme" in his Production Notebook, he jotted down for himself: "The Biggest loyalty a man has is to all the people, which in a Democracy, is the state. The Biggest obligation a man has is to be a *citizen*" (PN, italics mine), and for this son of immigrant parents, being a "citizen" means being a "man," but, "A man is not a man without pride and belief in himself" (PN). Describing the character Brando is to play, he writes to the actor that Schulberg's priest, Father Barry, never really comes to like Terry in the story, but Terry himself "goes out to REGAIN his Dignity and self esteem and he does – the HARD way. That is the personal story. A Bum becomes a man. That's it" (PN). And the central action in reclaiming his manhood is his decision to testify, a decision that has a double edge. It is, of course, crucial to the social drama of the film – and to actual waterfront conditions – but it also relates directly to Kazan's own personal drama.

It was in the spring of 1952 that Kazan testified before the HUAC, and he and Schulberg began work on the *Waterfront* project shortly thereafter. There is no question that Kazan believed he did the right thing in testifying; like Schulberg, he wanted to fight the Communist Party's influence in the arts. He talks extensively about this in his autobiography, but admits that for a year after (the year during which *Waterfront* was being prepared), he felt enormous "shame and guilt" (*A Life* 466).

> "I decided to stand alone. . ." (485)
> " . . . the important thing is to fortify
> and uphold one's sense of worth." (820)

His descriptions of Terry in the Production Notebook for *Waterfront* reverberate with these same emotions. For him, the film is "a study of the psychological anatomy of guilt" and of how "shame and guilt are replaced by self-reliance and dignity" (PN). And that key word "dignity" is everywhere in his notes. Terry had allowed himself to be exploited by both his brother, Charley, and his father figure, Johnny Friendly. Kazan explains, "Unconsciously, he is beginning to realize that Friendly and Charley degraded his dignity and castrated his sense of self-worth" (PN). He describes Terry's desperation, and underlines these words: "<u>He wants his dignity Back!</u>" (PN), and a few pages later:

> . . . He wants his dignity back. He wants his
> self-respect back. He's not going to be cowed
> any more. . . . He wants his dignity back. . . .
> He testifies! (PN)

Under the heading "<u>Theme</u>": "This Motion Picture is about one thing only: a Young man who has let his <u>dignity slip away, and regains it!</u>" (PN).

He compares Johnny Friendly (still "Mickey" in this version of the script) to such leaders in the American Communist Party as Jack [John Howard] Lawson and V. J. Jerome, and he sees Terry's rebellion [like his own] as against their authority. And underlined in pencil, with an arrow for emphasis: "What suffers most on the waterfront from the shape-up etc. is an intangible quantity know as the dignity of man! dignity of man! dignity of man!"

The film begins as Terry Malloy (Marlon Brando), ex-boxer, brother of Charley Malloy (Rod Steiger) who is union leader Johnny Friendly's (Lee J. Cobb) right-hand man, is set up as an accomplice to the murder of Joey Doyle. The Union wants to make sure that Doyle doesn't "rat" to the cops on its illegal activities. Terry is stricken with guilt for his part in what he thought was going to be just "a little working over." Joey's sister, Edie (Eva Marie Saint) lashes out at Father Barry for not doing anything about crime on the waterfront – "Was there ever a saint who hid in the Church?" – setting up the arc for the priest's growth into a social activist. Edie meets Terry during the shape-up on the dock when he and her father, Pop Doyle, scuffle over a tab to work, and the first hint of his guilt-induced softening comes as he hands the tab over to Edie for her father. Father Barry, enraged at the system of the shape-up, suggests the longshoremen use the church as a safe meeting place "to talk." Terry is then recruited by his brother Charley to go to this meeting as a "spy" for Johnny Friendly, to give him the "names and numbers of all the players." This is Terry's first mission as a stool pigeon, and he's uncomfortable about it: "You make a pigeon out of me." His brother clarifies the distinction: "Stooling is when you rat on your friends, on the guys you're with." Terry will spend the rest of the film learning who his friends really are.

At the church, Terry rescues Edie from the Mob goons who attack the meeting and he walks her home. Here we have the famous scene where Edie drops her white glove and Terry picks it up and absent-mindedly puts it on his own hand, "suggesting both an intimacy and an awkward experimentation... with a different view of life," as Brian Neve writes in his essay on Kazan. Kenneth Hey is more specific, suggesting that it's "almost as if he were about to 'try out' her moral values. He had worn boxing gloves for the mobsters, and he will now try to fit into the white glove of virtue" (178). This scene may also contain one of the most romantic lines in the history of the movies: "You grew up very nice."[8]

Guilt and the stirrings of tender feelings toward another human being begin to work on Terry. In the Production Notebook, Kazan suggests that Terry's "need for purity and tenderness and love" has, up to this point, had its outlet only in the racing pigeons he raises. Now, he observes "Something's beginning to come to life within Terry." When Kayo Dugan is killed in the ship's hold by the Mob for agreeing to testify before the Crime Commission, Terry's guilt and confusion grow to the point that he turns to Father Barry for help. He has already been served a subpoena, but he's told Edie, "I won't eat cheese for no cops, that's for sure." But as he listens to Father Barry's long "sermon," the one that Spiegel wanted to cut because it was too much talk and that Schulberg and Kazan fought to keep in the film (see Georgakas's essay and Schulberg's foreword), he's deeply affected by such lines as "Every time the mob puts the crusher on a good man – tries to stop him from doing his duty as a citizen – it's a crucifixion." Remember that Kazan wrote in the Production Notebook: "the Biggest obligation a man has is to be a citizen." It is only when Terry finally does "his duty as a citizen" and testifies, that the "Bum becomes a man" (PN).

Terry goes to Father Barry to confess about setting up Joey Doyle. Although the Father says he is not going ask him "to do anything" – "It's your own conscience that's got to do the asking" – he makes it clear that Terry needs to tell Edie and that he needs to testify against Johnny Friendly and his gang.

Edie learns the truth about Terry's role in her brother's death as she and Terry stand in the chill air of the waterfront. Their voices are masterfully drowned out by a ship's whistle, its high-pitched wail an aural echo of the inner anguish of both young people, and in Kaufman's cloudy day close-ups we see the pain on their faces. It's now clear that Terry is on the verge of testifying and the mob is worried. His brother, Charley, tries to convince Johnny Friendly to go easy on him. Friendly tells him to bring Terry to 437 River Street where they'll go over him to find out if he's a "canary" or if he's "D 'n D." The famous cab scene follows, the "I coulda been a contender" scene, the acting in which David Thomson discusses in detail in his essay. The two brothers come to an understanding of each other they did not have before, and Charley lets Terry off. Of course, Charley is killed for it, setting up the strongest motivation of all for Terry "to rat" on his former family.

At first Terry reacts with violence and goes after Friendly with a gun, but Father Barry stops him: "Fight him tomorrow in the courtroom." After Terry's testimony, Jimmy, the young member of the gang he founded, "The Golden Warriors," kills all his pigeons in frustration – "a pigeon for a pigeon" – and Edie tries to convince Terry to leave the waterfront and go away, maybe to a job on a farm. But Terry still has not regained his dignity. He has testified, but he needs to prove he is a man by going back down to the docks to claim what is his: his right to work. Kazan puts it this way in the Production Notebook:

> And again the Father works his shame building and mounting until he can't take it and he explodes. And this time he tells Friendly in front of the whole world that he did right and is not ashamed and that they are enemies to the death and that his great allegiance is to everyone – Terry, at the end, has his dignity back!

The ending of the film, as many of the essays in this volume discuss, has always been problematic. Johnny Friendly has been beaten, but the man the script calls "Mr. Upstairs," the mysterious power behind the mob who is briefly seen watching TV and saying, "If Mr. Friendly calls, I'm out, and you don't know when I'll be back," is still in control. Corruption still dominates the waterfront. One individual has a personal triumph, but as John Howard Lawson argued in his hostile review of the film, it can consequently be seen as "antidemocratic, antilabor, antihuman propaganda" (perhaps a bit extreme?). Terry establishes his right to work "*in spite of*" the union, according to Lawson, and "the unholy alliance of politicians, businessmen and gangsters" who are there at the beginning are still there at the end (4).

Less extreme is Lindsay Anderson's analysis: as inspiring as Terry's final walk is, with Leonard's Bernstein's stirring music swelling our emotions, "this agonized pilgrimage down the quay is pointless."

> The mob has been discredited; Friendly's hold is broken; the dockers have it in their power to be their own masters. Yet, instead of rising to the occasion, they turn like leaderless sheep in search of a new master. . . . To whom are they to turn? To the new strong man, bruised and bleeding though he may be. (128)

The film, he argues, is finally "Fascist." If Schulberg wanted a picture about how "self-appointed tyrants can be defeated by right-thinking people in a vital democracy," the result was quite different. Anderson writes: "Terry is an individualist; his opposition to Friendly is personal; his concern is with himself. 'I was ratting *on myself* all those years'" (127–129, italics Anderson's). The conclusion of *Waterfront* is, in this light, either "savagely ironic" or "fundamentally contemptuous, pretending to idealism, but in reality without either grace, or joy, or love" (128).[9]

Personally Kazan needed to overcome his guilt and regain his dignity; he admits to using *Waterfront* as a channel for his anger, as a means of lashing out at those who had turned on him for testifying. "The films after April 1, 1952, were personal, they came out of me, fired by what I've been describing" (485), he writes in *A Life*, and the result, according to David Thomson, was triumphant: "Kazan's most passionate and impressive works," *Waterfront* and *East of Eden*. *Waterfront* specifically was Kazan's "reply to the beating I'd taken" (*A Life* 488). Describing the aftermath of a dinner with Tony Mike diVincenzo, one of the longshoreman with whom the character of Terry Malloy has affinities,[10] who "named names" before the Waterfront Crime Commission, Kazan notes this moment of epiphany: "This hour at Tony Mike's was the instant of my final commitment, when I saw that, in the mysterious way of art, I was preparing a film about myself" (*A Life* 500). And so he describes Terry's experience in personal terms:

> ... Again here we're approaching a universal value. A man has a right to regain the human dignity that he has unwittingly let slip! A man, who's forfeited his manhood and is the object of abuse and scorn and insult, should turn and strike at his oppressors. (PN)

That the film was a kind of personal catharsis for one of its authors, however, in no way detracts from its "universal value," from its stature as an American "classic," and as a great work of art, "mysterious" in its ways. The English poet John Keats once wrote that "the excellence of any art is in its intensity," while for the German poet Rainer Maria Rilke we know a work of art because it tells us that, in some way, we must change our lives. As the essays in this book show, *On the Waterfront* fulfills both these criteria.

From different perspectives, the authors in this *Handbook* tell the story of this complex and controversial film, of its progress once the two paths had met and joined – Schulberg's which led to the unproduced *Crime on the Waterfront* and Kazan's which led to the fiasco of *The Hook* – a story which takes it from the floor of Schulberg's Bucks County farmhouse in the spring of 1952 to its eight Academy Awards in the spring of 1955. The relevance of *Waterfront* for today's audiences is discussed by Chown in his essay. Schulberg himself has suggested:

> I think it touches a nerve with a lot of people who are conflicted about opposite ways to go in life.... It's outlived the topical interest in the subject matter, racketeering on the dock."
>
> (Lumenick)

The film's legacy is eloquently illustrated in the closing moments of Martin Scorsese's *Raging Bull* (1980) as Jake LaMotta (Robert De Niro), ex-fighter turned overweight entertainer, looks in his dressing room mirror and recites to his image the most famous lines from Schulberg's script (and Brando's performance), the "I coulda been a contender" speech. It is the emotional culmination of LaMotta's life, and our understanding of this life is enriched and complicated when a connection is made back thirty years to Charley and Terry, to Brando and Steiger, to Kazan and Schulberg. A fifty-year legacy adds poignancy to Forest Whitaker's Samurai character in Jim Jarmusch's darkly comic *Ghost Dog* (2000), a misunderstood loner who, like Terry, raises pigeons on a rooftop and deals with and betrays the mob. When his pigeons are killed in revenge, the ravaged coop and dead birds recall Terry's. Ghost Dog dies, as Schulberg wanted Terry to, but in contrast to Christian martyrdom, this death seems to be as meaningless as his life, an urban Samurai warrior whose traditions have passed, whose roots are gone. Fifty years after *Waterfront* there are no social struggles tearing our country apart, no battles of conscience on an epic scale. Terry says to Edie: "Conscience. That stuff can drive you nuts." Perhaps part of the legacy – and greatness – of this film today is to show us the emptiness of life without conscience, without caring, without the passion that drove two men, Elia Kazan and Budd Schulberg, to make a film that makes a difference.

NOTES

1   Schulberg's testimony is quoted in *Thirty Years of Treason*, Eric Bentley, ed. (New York: Viking Press, 1971), 439.
2   This story is told in any number of books on Kazan. See, for example, Michel Ciment, *Kazan on Kazan* (New York: Viking Press, 1974), 22.

3   These self-descriptions come from Kazan's *Waterfront* Production Notebook at the Wesleyan University Cinema Archives. All further quotations from it will be cited as "PN" within the text itself and are with permission of the Kazan Estate.

4   Schulberg tells the story of researching the film in more detail in his "Afterword" to the published script, *On the Waterfront*, 142–5.

5   Panto's story is told in Allen Raymond's *Waterfront Priest*, 65–6.

6   There is a lot of confusion about early drafts of the *Waterfront* script and the genesis and outcome of the Kazan/Miller collaboration. In Thomas Pauly's book, *An American Odyssey*, he credits Kazan with persuading Miller to do a screenplay about the waterfront (182), whereas Kenneth Hey says that Miller contacted Kazan. Regardless of who contacted whom, the screenplay resulting from the Kazan/Miller collaboration, *The Hook*, is located at the Humanities Research Center, University of Texas, Austin.

7   This screenplay is in the possession of the Department of Film & Television Studies, Dartmouth College, Hanover, NH.

8   I must credit my friend and colleague, screenwriter Bill Phillips, for this observation.

9   A more successful American film about the working class, according to Anderson, is John Ford's *Grapes of Wrath* (1940), but that goes back to a time before World War II. A postwar film which shows that social themes can be handled with "integrity and true passion" is Abraham Polonsky's *Force of Evil* (1948), a film which some have compared to *On the Waterfront* in that it deals with two brothers, one smart, one dumb, who must also deal with a situation of political and moral corruption. In this case, it is the dumb brother who is killed and the smart one, with the help of the love of a girl, who comes to realize his shameful behavior and reforms.

10 Schulberg points out that Kazan is mistaken in believing that Terry Malloy is based on Tony Mike diVincenzo. There were, he admits, striking similarities, but when Kazan met diVincenzo in Hoboken he probably related to him so strongly "that he began to feel that Terry was really Tony." Schulberg concludes, "before there was a Tony Mike in my life, there was a Terry Malloy" (Letter to Joanna Rapf, September 7, 2000).

BRIAN NEVE

| The Personal and the Political: Elia Kazan and *On the Waterfront*

INTRODUCTION

The controversy surrounding Elia Kazan's Life Achievement Award at the 73rd Academy Awards ceremony in 1999 revived interest both in the director's work and in his best remembered film. *On the Waterfront* was made at a time when the old Hollywood studios were coming to terms with the postwar decline in audiences, and when new technologies, together with the politics of the time, seemed to discourage work in the social realist tradition. Kazan had been associated with this tradition, but had aspirations at the end of the forties to work on more personal and artistically ambitious films. The controversy surrounding his cooperative testimony before the House Committee on Un-American Activities in 1952, a year after similar testimony by Budd Schulberg, helped fuel a powerful and persistent body of criticism that constructs *On the Waterfront* as a justification of informing. Yet Lloyd Michaels, in his critical survey of Kazan's work, suggests other readings, arguing persuasively that the film is "not, after all, an allegory justifying informing or even an expose of labour racketeering but rather the story of an inarticulate, undirected human being's struggle for personal dignity" (33).[1] Kazan emphasized the importance to him of this personal story in a contemporary letter to Marlon Brando: "A bum becomes a man. That's it."[2] To the extent that reception helps to construct a film in various ways, the text of *On the Waterfront* may be richer for these overlapping circles of interpretation.

Another distinction of the film relates to the casting and the use of a New York – based crew. In addition, the topical theme and semidocumentary aspect ran against the notion at the time that only larger productions and wide screen presentations could help combat the threat of television – an argument that was reflected in the rejection of the Kazan – Schulberg project by the major studios. While Sam Spiegel's last-minute emergence as producer reinforced a number of "Hollywood" practices and norms in the production, there were plenty of more unusual features, from the New York production base, the director's acknowledged respect for his screenplay, and the distinctive cast, in particular reflecting the influence of the Actors Studio that Kazan had helped to found in 1947 (see David Thomson's essay in this volume).

This essay explores Elia Kazan's contribution to *On the Waterfront* with particular reference to his approach to directing. The fifties was the era of the French rediscovery of American cinema and their celebration of a number of key directors as authors of the films on which they worked. Kazan's friend and colleague in many of the artistic and political movements of the thirties, Nicholas Ray, was a particular recipient of such praise and analysis, some time before Andrew Sarris contributed a home-grown auteur theory to the polemical debate on directorial film "signatures." François Truffaut, while still a critic, examined the two collaborations of Kazan and Schulberg, praising *A Face in the Crowd* (1957), but suggesting that the original "antifascist" intentions of the screenplay for *On the Waterfront* had become emasculated, leaving "an unconsciously but nonetheless basically demagogic movie" (113). Truffaut makes implicit reference here to the way that *On the Waterfront* intersects both with previously existing forms of political and artistic expression and with the developing codes of mainstream culture and politics in the Cold War era. Many of these themes and debates can be explored in relation to Kazan's own career and experiences, although one needs to be careful not to distort, as a result of this focus, the collaborative nature of the film. The emergence of a rather uncritical notion of the director as auteur in popular discussion of film if not in film studies has often led to a glib association of Kazan's concerns and experiences with the film.

If there are two major interpretations of Kazan's work – two distinct approaches to trying to create a spine to Kazan's work as a director – one is psychology and the other is politics. In 1947, when rehearsing the stage production of *A Streetcar Named Desire*, Kazan began his private notebook on the production with the thought that "directing finally consists of turning Psychology into Behavior" (Kazan in Cole and Chinoy 296). While Kazan later retreated a little from this focus, arguing that "we went too far in stressing [the] purely psychological nature of acting" (Cook interview), it was for his work with actors that he was most admired: to Nicholas Ray he was "the best actor's director the United States has ever produced" (Wollen 15). The other recurrent frame on Kazan's work is politics. Peter Biskind, writing during the controversy about the Life Achievement award, drew attention to the rarity of "a career fully committed to art and politics, with the politics feeding the work" ("When Worlds Collide" 12). Again, Kazan has played down such an interpretation: "I don't think basically I'm a political animal. I think I'm a self-centered animal. . . . I think what I was concerned about all my life was to say something artistically that was uniquely my own" (Cook interview).

The Stanislavsky tradition stressed, among other things, the need for the actor to "become another person while remaining himself, using his own organic nature, his personality, as material in the creation of a character" (Moore 90). In terms of Kazan's role in *On the Waterfront*, much of the debate concerns the degree to which the intensity of the film is a product of the director's ability to draw on his own life at the time in ways that transferred his own emotion to his performers and characters. Raymond Carney, in his work on Frank Capra, has made comparisons between key method performances of the fifties, including Marlon Brando's in *On the Waterfront*, and the central roles in Capra's films, such as Gary Cooper in *Mr. Deeds Goes to Town* (1936). Here the emphasis is on meaning – and in particular what Carney calls "intense states of passion, dreams, or yearning" – generated not so much by dialogue but in the space between words, by expression, movement, and gesture (327–28).

ELIA KAZAN: THE BACKGROUND

If Elia Kazan was not really a "political animal," his political involvement in the thirties is better seen as a product of his immigrant status, and his sense of alienation from middle-class American life. His most autobiographical film, *America America* (1963), opens with the director's own words: "My name is Elia Kazan. I'm a Greek by blood, a Turk by birth, and an American because my uncle made a journey." Kazan, who was born in Istanbul in 1909, was four years old when his Anatolian Greek father brought him to New York. It was the second generation of immigrants who faced most acutely the problems of adjustment, alienated as they were both from their parents' values and from those of mainstream America. At Williams College, Kazan's experience was of "antagonism to privilege, to good looks, to Americans, to Wasps" (Ciment 12).

It was through the left-wing theaters that ethnic minorities in particular asserted themselves in the Depression years. Kazan discovered his first strong sense of self in America within the "family" of the Group Theatre, and more loosely in the radical social and cultural movements of the time. In his autobiography he writes of the lasting impact on him of the Group, of Lee Strasberg and especially Harold Clurman as father figures (although they were then only in their early thirties), and of his friendship with Clifford Odets. Kazan was an apprentice with the Group, while he also began writing and directing for more radical theaters. In 1934 he wrote the agitprop drama *Dimitroff* with fellow Group actor Art Smith, for a New Theatre League benefit, and the same year he co-directed *The Young Go First*, a play attacking the Civilian Conservation Corps, for the Theatre of Action. The next year Kazan played the strike-leading taxi driver in the most renowned agitprop drama, Odets' *Waiting for Lefty*, his dynamic performance attracting him the label of the "proletarian thunderbolt" (Wendy Smith 214).

An important part of the thirties' legacy is Kazan's marriage in 1932 to Molly Day Thatcher, whose grandfather was president of Yale and father a Wall Street lawyer. While Kazan has been open about his numerous other relationships with women, and in particular actresses, his wife remained a powerful influence for thirty years; in his autobiography Kazan describes her as "my talisman of success and my measure of merit" (*A Life* 569). As a literary editor, play reader, and playwright Molly Kazan was also to influence Kazan's career decisions. Although part of the left culture of the thirties, by the early fifties she had developed a principled critique of the Communist Party that arguably influenced her more pragmatic husband. Kazan reports her early criticism of Arthur Miller's proposals for what would be *The Crucible*, and how her concern that the script for *On the Waterfront* needed yet more work almost created a breach between Kazan and Schulberg.[3]

Kazan later described his outlook during the thirties as "full of anger, silent, unexpressed anger" (Ciment 13). The premise, he remembers, was that "we were outcast, against the current of US life, and we thought the revolutionary and the gangster had qualities that an artist needs in a hostile society" (Ciment 19). The political reflection of this anger was his active membership for eighteen months from 1934 in a Communist Party section within the Group, at a time when the Party predominantly consisted of first- or second-generation immigrants. He left the Party in 1936 when he was called to account for failing sufficiently to press the concerns of the Party within the Group Theatre. Although many of his views and cultural associations remained unchanged, he was later to express a bitterness at the functionaries from Party headquarters on Twelfth Street and the way he was "booted out" (Ciment 84).

During the mid-thirties Kazan also gained his first experience in filmmaking, acting in a collectively produced fantasy short *Pie in the Sky* (1934) – produced by NYKino, the film division of the Theatre of Action, and using Group actors – that satirized the failure of the church and welfare authorities to cope with hunger and poverty. Kazan later assisted the photographer Ralph Steiner in the direction of *People of the Cumberlands* (1937), a production of the Frontier Films documentary group. The result dealt with the lives and families of Tennessee strip miners, and marked the beginning of the director's attested love for the land and people of the American South, despite the prevailing politics of the region.

In terms of acting and acting styles there is a direct line from Kazan's experience in the Group Theatre (with its concern in particular for the work of Stanislavsky) to his co-founding of the Actors Studio in New York in 1947 and his fifties film work. In the period from the reconstitution of the Group Theatre from 1937 to its demise in 1940 Kazan gained recognition for his playing of the racketeer Eddie Fuselli in the Broadway production of Odets' *Golden Boy*. In 1940, the year he gave up acting, Kazan also played small parts, as a street kid and a would-be gangster in two Warner Brothers productions, *Blues in the Night* and the James Cagney vehicle, *City for Conquest*. It was the war years, beginning with the success of Thornton Wilder's *The Skin of Our Teeth*, that saw Kazan's emergence as a successful Broadway director, while in 1944 he signed a contract with Twentieth Century-Fox and directed his first feature, the well-received *A Tree Grows in Brooklyn* (1945).

Kazan learned the craft of filmmaking within the supportive, if restrictive, studio framework. It was the smaller budget, semi-documentary productions (*Boomerang!*, 1947; *Panic in the Streets*, 1950) that gave him greater autonomy, rather than the larger budget "social problem" epics, *Gentleman's Agreement* (1947) and *Pinky* (1949), that Kazan directed with studio head Darryl F. Zanuck as producer. These films were part of a series in the late forties that sought to extend and develop elements of the Popular Front tradition of social criticism. New opportunities for location filming reduced producer supervision, while the popularity of crime melodrama (what would later be termed *film noir*) provided new opportunities for political comment. Politically conscious directors and writers, as well as émigrés from Nazi-occupied Europe, made contributions in these areas, both within the studios and in the expanding independent sector. This liberal strain in postwar film soon came up against fundamental changes in the political and cultural climate, both nationally and internationally, but elements of it survived into the fifties.

At the same time in New York Kazan achieved more distinction with his active involvement as director with the Broadway plays of Arthur Miller (*All My Sons* in 1947 and *Death of A Salesman* in 1949) and Tennessee Williams (*A Streetcar Named Desire* in 1947). The political mood in America began to change after the war, with the waning of antifascist and Popular Front themes and the growing prominence of a Cold War agenda involving notions of an external and an internal Communist threat. It was in 1947 that the so-called "Hollywood Ten," who declined to explain their political associations to the House Un-American Activities Committee, were convicted of contempt of Congress. The Ten, whom at this point Kazan supported, were finally imprisoned for between six months and a year in 1950, when the Supreme Court declined to review the case. Left-wing screenwriter Walter Bernstein remembers visiting the director on the set of *Panic in the Streets* in 1949 and finding that he seemed "to share my politics" (17).

Kazan's cinematic ambitions included the 1951 film version of *A Streetcar Named Desire* (his first film collaboration with Brando), *Viva Zapata* (from a John Steinbeck script), and a collaboration with Arthur Miller. Miller's waterfront script *The Hook* was based on a pre-war case of rank-and-file action against six Brooklyn locals that had long been controlled by notorious criminals, including members of the Anastasia family. When Kazan and Miller submitted the script to Columbia Pictures in 1951 there were political objections that contributed to Miller's withdrawal from the project. In terms of the politics of the early fifties it is arguably *Viva Zapata* (1952), made before Kazan's testimony, that is most revealing. In the film Steinbeck and Kazan present the Fernando character as a Stalinist heavy, while balancing their sympathy for peasant revolution with warnings that the masses should not place too much faith in their leaders. To John Howard Lawson at the time the film's depiction of Zapata, walking away from power because of its effect on him, betrayed the possibility of successful revolution from below (Lawson 38–50). In the early seventies Kazan said that he and Steinbeck, as ex-Communists, were attracted to Zapata's story because it allowed metaphorical comment on "what had happened to the Communists in the Soviet Union – how their leaders became reactionary and repressive rather than forward thinking and progressive" (Young 93). The film is still argued over, and Oliver Stone, another director not easy to define ideologically, has talked of the lasting impact of the film's notion of revolution as an eternal struggle (Biskind, "On Movies" 16).

CONTEXTUAL FACTORS

By the time that the House Un-American Activities Committee (HUAC) had relaunched its hearings on Hollywood in March 1951, the country was in the grip of something like a national panic over the international and domestic threat of Communism. In February 1950 Senator Joseph McCarthy's speech at Wheeling, West Virginia, in which he began his campaign against Communists in the State Department, came in the immediate wake of the conviction of Alger Hiss. Hiss, who had been accused by HUAC in 1948 of passing secrets to a Communist spy ring, had lost his appeal and was beginning a five-year sentence for perjury. To Richard Pells, in his study of the intellectual currents of the time, the conviction of Hiss lent credence to "the theory that all communists should be regarded as potential foreign agents" (272). The Cold War atmosphere, and the pressure on Communists and ex-Communists, was increased by the beginning of the war in Korea, where 25,000 Americans died in the period 1950–53. In the new hearings witnesses who declined to answer questions about their political pasts and associations needed to plead the Fifth Amendment, but such action led to them being blacklisted in the film industry. Schulberg was an early "friendly witness" to the Committee in 1951, citing in particular his visit to the Soviet Union in 1934 and his knowledge of the subsequent fate of many of the writers and artists whom he had met. Schulberg has stoutly defended his position as a "premature anti-Stalinist." Kazan made two appearances before the Committee, and in the second, in April 1952, he named eight communists whom he had known in the Party cell in the Group Theatre.[4]

Much as Kazan could have found ways of publicizing his views on American Communism without enhancing the legitimacy of the Committee and the blacklist, it is difficult to see his motives as entirely determined by self-interest. Rightly or wrongly it seems that Kazan did convince himself, perhaps with his wife's help, that the "reluctance to speak out on Communism increased its current threat," and that he should not sacrifice his film career for a cause that he saw as part of a "worldwide conspiracy" (Pauly 156–60). The emergence over the years of Kazan as the iconic "namer of names" of this period – he gets a chapter to himself in Victor Navasky's key book on the subject – owes something to his prestige and status at the time and more to the *New York Times* advertisement justifying his position, and the self-servingly annotated list of credits that he submitted to the Committee. Lillian Hellman wrote of the special vulnerability of the "children of timid immigrants" to pressures that threatened their hard-won success, and Kazan himself, in his autobiography, admits some of these pressures to demonstrate his patriotism, and his allegiance to the values and symbols of American nationality (Hellman 39 and *A Life* 451). Erik Erikson, himself an immigrant, described his own loyalty oath controversy at this time as "a test of my American identity" (Erikson 747).

"The only way to understand any character," Kazan has said, "is through yourself" (Notebook for *A Streetcar Named Desire* 303). In his Production Notebook for *Waterfront* he draws on his own experiences, and those of friends, in providing keys to Terry's character and relationships. In a letter to Brando in which he explores the differences between the Terry Malloy and Stanley Kowalski characters he argues as follows: "Marlon, this part is much closer to you and to myself too." Kazan also compares Terry's "swagger" early in the story with his own confidence and pride previously, as the "white-haired boy-director." At other points in the Notebook he compares Terry's early relationship with Mickey (Johnny Friendly) with his own relationship with Harold Clurman and with "a Commie who regards Jack Lawson, or V. J. Jerome as *the* authority." While there is no distinctive visual style or *mise-en-scène* that ties this film to Kazan, the striving for autobiographical expression in Kazan's work is arguably first strongly evidenced in *On the Waterfront*. As a child of Stanislavsky, Kazan brings his own "affective memories" to his direction of actors and of the emotional "beats" of the drama.[5] Thus, for all of Schulberg's careful and committed research (some of which Kazan participated in), the film drifts away from the sociological to the personal and even existential.

Budd Schulberg has paid tribute to Kazan's respect for his work as a "screen playwright," arguing that the director treated him and others with the same "artistic respect he accorded to writers in the theater" (Schulberg, Introduction to *On the Waterfront*, ix). The emphasis on individual testimony at public hearings as a way, perhaps the only way, of "fighting back" is in part a product of the events of the New York waterfront during the era of the Kefauver Committee hearings and then the New York State Crime Commission. Schulberg, who attended every day of the Commission hearings, subsequently published a novel where the emphasis is more on Father Barry's conscience than Terry Malloy's, as the priest's urging of longshoremen to testify ends in two men (including Terry) meeting their deaths.[6] Kazan, talking later about criticisms of the film's ending, commented that "Schulberg didn't like my ending either" (Young 122). The tightening of the script, in furtherance of what Schulberg calls the tyranny of "the ninety-minute feature form," is partly responsible for the film's emphasis on Terry Malloy's struggle (Georgakas 8). But Kazan's Production Notebook makes clear that he saw the film from the beginning as Terry's story. Under a heading "Story," he writes simply:

2. Elia Kazan with the script on the set of *On the Waterfront*. From the script, Kazan drew an energy that gradually led him to feel that through the film he was talking about himself. (Courtesy of the Academy of Motion Picture Arts and Sciences)

"This is about Terry! A Boy becomes a citizen! A man finds his DIGNITY AGAIN." In fact, the first page of his annotated shooting script at the Wesleyan Archives contains the handwritten heading, in red ink:

> PHOTOGRAPH
> the Inner Experience
> of **TERRY**
> Don't be Objective! This is not a
>   Documentary
> Be Subjective, Be Terry!

Earlier, longer drafts of the script deal more extensively with water-front issues, and with the lives of other longshoremen; for example, more information is provided about Joey Doyle's efforts at honest unionism.[7]

A crucial decision was taken by director and writer to draw partic-ularly on the experiences of longshoreman Anthony "Tony Mike" diVincenzo, who testified to the New York State Crime Commis-sion in December 1951. What particularly impressed Kazan about de Vincenzo, who later campaigned and organized for the proposed new AFL union that challenged, and nearly replaced the corrupt ILA in a 1954 ballot, was his "primitive" striving to "regain his own position" (PN).[8] Schulberg also supplies some of the potent motifs of the film, from the boxing background that is crucial to Terry's bitterness, to the pigeon coops – Schulberg and his best friend Maurice Rapf had had their own pigeon loft as boys. Kazan, one suspects, while respecting the wider picture, represented in the shape-up and in Father Barry's speeches – derived by Schulberg from the real thoughts of the water-front priests of the day – latched on to the character of Terry Malloy, particularly when reunited with Marlon Brando, as a rich focus for the drama.

While Terry shows little interest in the inequities of the shape-up, and in the kickback system of hiring, (or in Father Barry's take on these issues), he does exhibit guilt about the murder of Joey Doyle, a guilt enhanced by his developing relationship with Joey's sister. What also relates to Kazan's own concerns is Terry's resentment at his older brother, and in particular at the father figure represented – in the absence of real parents – by Johnny Friendly. However much Father Barry mocks Terry's memories of Friendly taking him to the ball park, the breaking away from the world of Friendly and his brother is a painful process, for which Terry needs to reassess his own sense of himself (Kazan himself broke from a father who wanted him to enter the family rug business or some form of commerce, and who con-stantly referred to him a "hopeless case"). Talking of the film, Kazan argued that it was true that "as I worked more and more on that the fuel for it, the energy for it, came from the feeling that I was talking about myself" (Cook interview). He also wrote in his auto-biography that he doubted "that Budd was affected as personally as I was by the parallel of Tony Mike's story." When Terry confronts

3. Tommy [Arthur Keegan] between Terry [Marlon Brando] and Edie [Eva Marie Saint] with a pigeon on the roof. Entrapment is suggested by filming Terry from the other side of the wire net of the pigeon coop. In this shot, the tight two- and three-person framing is maintained. (Copyright Columbia Pictures Corp., 1954. Courtesy of the Museum of Modern Art Film Stills Archive)

Friendly at the film's climax, and shouts at him that he is "glad what I done," there is clearly a reference to the director's personal animus against particular individuals from the Communist Party. In his autobiography, Kazan argues that the "transference of emotion from my own experience to the screen is the merit of those scenes" (*A Life* 500, 529).

Sam B. Girgus has linked Kazan's testimony and the making of *On the Waterfront*, seeing them as marking the director's own public acting out of his change of identity. The argument relates to one powerful but rarely mentioned shot in the film. As Terry Malloy responds to the pain inflicted on him by Tommy, who has killed all his pigeons following his testimony, he looks out toward the Hudson, oblivious of Edie's soothing words. This is not the first time Kazan shows us Terry quietly meditating in his private roof space. But here there is a shot, held for some time, of a liner moving left to right on the Hudson River. Not only does this show us a lyrical aspect of Terry's home and work, and make Edie's suggestion that he retreat inland to a "farm" all the more ludicrous, but it allows Terry time to decide on his final, dangerous course of action. Girgus suggests that the ship is leaving New York for Europe, and links Terry Malloy's new-found commitment to fight for his rights as an American with Kazan's own rejection of elements of his past – his communist politics linked with his immigrant status – and his uncompromised embracing of a notion of American national identity. The year after the release of *On the Waterfront* Kazan made his first return visit to Turkey to search for his "discarded self" (Kazan's phrase), a meditation that led eventually to the film about his own family's immigrant journey, *America America* (Girgus 163, 172),

Kazan was not alone, as the going got tough for ex-Party members – and Kazan had been out of the Party for sixteen years – in weighing the career cost of resisting, but it is by no means impossible that he convinced himself, in the traumatic circumstances of the time, that the moral arguments were not all on one side. Certainly there were relatives and contemporaries who would have pointed this out. Apart from the postwar Albert Maltz case (in which the Communist screenwriter was pressured by the Party to denounce his own writing) and Budd Schulberg's own falling out with the Party over *What Makes Sammy Run* – publicized in his cooperative 1951 testimony – Molly Kazan's own position on the American Communist Party had hardened early on when the Party's cultural section effectively brought the liberal magazine *New Theatre* to a halt in 1940. In the late fifties Molly Kazan wrote *The Egghead*, a play that was performed in New York and reads in part as a wife's questioning of her husband's naivete about domestic communism.[9] Kazan's lawyer, William Fitelson, a man on the left who had become, in Kazan's words, a premature anti-Stalinist, would also have weighed in his advice to Kazan in this period (*A Life* 457).

KAZAN AS DIRECTOR

While some critics see Kazan turning to the psychological from the social after his testimony, in fact this area of interest was already implicit in the thirties experience with the Group Theatre, his co-founding of the Actors Studio, and his deepening collaboration with Tennessee Williams. Kazan's seventies interviews document the approach and method that he brought to his films, with particular reference to his work with actors. Kazan begins with reality, but cannot be described as a naturalistic director. He respects his script, but casts and directs with a particular eye for expressive action and the use of emblematic objects. On casting he has said that unless "the character is somewhere in the actor himself you shouldn't cast him" (Young 128). Kazan is best viewed as a director with a strong commitment to the social and social psychological – rather than the purely political – implications of drama.

The emphasis in *On the Waterfront* on the protagonist's testimony to the Crime Commission as a "way of fighting back" may reflect the labor conditions of the waterfront or a parallel with the friendly testimony of both Kazan and Schulberg, but it is also consistent with the absence of collective action as a Hollywood narrative option. Part of the film's "force of nature" impact was at the time ascribed to its documentary aspects, including the real waterfront locations, the local extras, and the obviously freezing temperature. Yet the depiction of the locality is relatively limited, beyond the tenement roofs, the shape-up scenes, and establishing and background shots of the harbor. The emphasis on closely framed shots of two or three central characters, designed to intensify the drama of these key relationships, often flattens the image in a way that reduces the sense of the immediate environment. Kazan and Arthur Miller, when they originally worked on their waterfront project, had apparently talked of neorealism as an influence, and the strongest indications of this are in the roof-top scenes, which do recall something of the untidy, derelict ambiance of the postwar Italian films (Miller 195).

The "look" of the film is most distinctive in these scenes on the roof. It is there that the dominant practice of tight two- and three-person framing is often relaxed, and the key characters, in particular Terry and Edie, are in shown in context, and in Terry's case on home territory. The view of this world, between Joey and Terry's pigeon coops, is of a mess of slopes, ducts, odd angles, skylights, aerials, and shacks. We see Terry casually accessing the roof from a window, climbing ladders, guiding Edie down a fire escape, and generally criss-crossing his private domain, often accompanied by the young boys in his "Golden Warriors" gang, and in particular Tommy. Our first view of this rather strange world, accompanied by one of Bernstein's more atonal scores, comes when Tommy steps above the horizon and slides down a roof; the camera swings round with the boy allowing spectators to spot Terry first, crouching down by his pigeon coop. Critics have drawn attention to the notion of entrapment that is suggested by the filming of Terry from the other side of the wire net enclosing the pigeons, but this is balanced by the sense of freedom associated with the deep background vistas of the waterfront. Objectively the fences may circle and confine this world, but subjectively it is a territory where Terry in particular, tending his birds and shadowboxing his way through life, lives on his own terms.[10]

Kazan has pronounced himself uncomfortable with the term "actor's director" when used to praise him, seeing it as pointing to a lack in his work. In his autobiography he cites (and argues with) Haskell Wexler's comment, as cinematographer on *America America*, that he lacked an "eye," while elsewhere he argues that the art of motion pictures is photographing looks not dialogue (*A Life* 640 and Ciment 37). Kazan's direction provides plenty of examples of meaning revealed through thought and reaction, rather than action or dialogue. He has also paid abundant tribute to Marlon Brando's abilities to reveal meaning not only through gestures and his use of symbolic objects but through the camera's detection of his thinking. Johnny Friendly refers mockingly to Terry as "Einstein," but in the drama as filmed it is Terry, rather than his older and better-educated brother Charley, who appears as the "deep thinker." The whole emphasis in Kazan's Production Notebook on the film concerns Terry's "inner conflict." For example, in a handwritten note to his script, relating to the moment when Terry finds his pigeons slaughtered, Kazan reminds himself that "You have to be close on Terry here to photograph his inner processes" (Director's script at Wesleyan).

A number of Kazan's strongest directorial qualities evolved from his theater experience, including his selection of actors. The care over relatively small parts is indicated by the choice of John Hamilton as Edie's beaten-down father and of Actors Studio member Pat Hingle in a bit appearance as a barman. There is an attempt, in the Group

Theatre tradition, to link the individual to the broader social conflict. Yet even where the emphasis is on two or three central characters, with limited depth of field, there are some striking scenes. In the bar where Terry takes Edie the screen is dominated by the two faces, and by the two philosophies, with Edie in the foreground. The framing suggests an unresolved dialectic. More often Terry is "favored," as when Edie brings her brother's jacket to him on the roof at night. Terry is stretched out on a ledge at the bottom of the frame so that the figure of Edie approaching at the top of the frame almost seems to be part of Terry's subconscious. In terms of gesture there are numerous examples, although many may have been the invention of Brando. When Terry discovers the slaughter of his pigeons, for example, he stands by his coop, waving one arm at Edie, to warn her, ward her off, protect his own anguish. Kazan remembers suggesting this, although he credits the effectiveness of the celebrated cab scene to writer and actors. It is a classic example of Kazan's concern with meaning generated outside of the script, by movement, gesture, and the use by actors of symbolic objects.

Another example of meaning through gesture comes in an early scene in which Terry asserts his solidarity with the waterfront code by giving "short shift" to the inquires of the Crime Commission investigators. Far from stressing oneness with his fellow workers, the staging and Brando's performance suggest the opposite. The conventional shot is given its value by Terry's exaggerated turn to his right to address the investigator's sidekick – his "girlfriend" – directly behind him. Perhaps the most discussed method scene is introduced by a tracking shot of Terry and Edie in the park, leading to the moment when Edie drops a glove and Terry, perched on a swing (another childhood thing to be cast off), plays with it and tries it on, suggesting both an intimacy and an awkward experimentation with a different view of life. Eva Marie Saint's fretting response to Brando's improvisation is arguably equally responsible for the effectiveness of the scene.[11]

Kazan had taken to heart the advice that John Ford had given him in Hollywood about deriving staging ideas from the set and environment. The sequence where Terry and Edie are chased down a dark alleyway by a truck also reflects the broadening of the director's range during his New Orleans work on *Panic on the Streets*, while the point-of-view shot that follows allows the audience to experience Terry's shock in discovering his brother's body hanging up on a wall. Drawings in Kazan's script suggest that both these sequences were devised and planned by the director on location; the hook suggested to Kazan the brutality of Charley, reduced to being "just meat" (Director's script at Wesleyan, Young 170–1, and *A Life* 255). The lyrical shot of the liner on the Hudson has been mentioned, while the use of dancing in Kazan's films is often expressive of important feelings. One thinks of Cal's dance over his rows of beans, grown to please his father, in *East of Eden* (1955), and in *America America* the manic dance of Stavros as his ship reaches New York harbor, indicating the intensity and madness of the journey. In *On the Waterfront* there are Johnny's playful fencing with Terry in the early poolroom scene, Edie's efforts to wrest her father's metal work tab from Terry at the shape-up ("it's been nice wrestling with you"), and a brief reverie between Terry and Edie at the wedding party they stray into. In this last scene, despite their philosophical differences, they connect through dance, with the camera briefly retreating with Edie "floating" in Terry's arms. The love story, both as a central motif and as interwoven with broader social dynamics, becomes a characteristic feature of Kazan films such as *A Face in the Crowd*, *Wild River* (1960) and *America America*.

The ending of the film has been much discussed (in this volume see especially the essay by Chown). An influential interpretation in Britain came from critic and director-to-be Lindsay Anderson, who saw Terry's walk as fascist, albeit unconsciously, in terms of the men's transfer of allegiance to the reluctant leader. There is certainly a straining for effect in Terry's final "walk," which contrasts with the unforced nature of previous scenes, although Robert Hughes, in a rebuttal to Anderson, provides a closer reading of the ending as a whole, while John M. Smith argues that when Terry recovers his respect he "is granted the awakening respect of the dockers, so that his personal victory becomes social" (20). Some sense of Kazan's thinking at the time is provided by his marginal note to his script: "The <u>Point</u> is that the men are ashamed of themselves for <u>not</u> helping . . . for just standing there while their comrade is slaughtered" (Director's script at Wesleyan). It is certainly interesting that some critics have read the ending as inconclusive, others as falsely triumphant. The weight of a medium close shot of Johnny Friendly, shouting that he will be back, does not quite counteract the sense of resolution that was false both to the spine of the film itself and to the documented history of challenges at the time to corrupt unionism. However the lowering of the iron door of the pier building, following the slightly cloying two-shot of a smiling Father Barry and Edie watching the men go in, casts its own doubt on what, if anything, has been achieved, outside of Terry's personal redemption. In terms of Kazan it is interesting that the last shot of his last film, made over twenty years later, seems to echo the ending of *On the Waterfront*. In that scene, in *The Last Tycoon* (1976), a method actor of a new generation – Robert De Niro as Monroe Stahr, looking much like a young Kazan – pauses before the large open door of a sound stage, before walking, viewed from behind, into the darkness. The ending, perhaps, is beyond ego.

PLACING *ON THE WATERFRONT*

The Communist Left was quick to respond with a hostile analysis of the film. John Howard Lawson wrote in 1954 of the film's "anti-democratic, anti-labour, anti-human propaganda," and saw it as emblematic of the "influence of McCarthyism on American film production." He contrasts the film with the portrayal of working class life in *Salt of the Earth* (1954), the film about a New Mexico strike which raised ethnic and feminist issues ahead of their time, and which was made by blacklisted artists, despite every kind of official hindrance (1). Peter Biskind, in a later, closely argued critique, saw the Terry Malloy figure as manipulated by church and state, although such a reading seems to underplay the power of Terry Malloy as written, acted, and directed (*Film Quarterly*). It is in some ways Father Barry who adopts Terry's discourse after Charley Malloy's murder, first landing a left hook on the longshoreman, and then suggesting testifying as the best means of private revenge.

One obvious American film tradition that *On the Waterfront* recalls is that of the "topicals," often with a gangster theme, made by Warners in the thirties. Examples include *Marked Women* (1937) and *Racket Busters* (1938), both turned out quickly and exploiting interest in working class stories that were making headline news.[12]

While the ideological context of *On the Waterfront* is different, there are some continuities, not least those implied by the crime angle; Schulberg's original script was called "Crime on the Waterfront," following the title of Malcolm Johnson's award-winning newspaper articles of the late forties. While *On the Waterfront* is sometimes seen as a specific response to the era of McCarthyism, promoting the informer as social hero, the film should also be seen in terms of a broad Popular Front tradition influenced in particular by left and liberal artists, especially writers. There are also residues of a tradition of using boxing as a vehicle for social analysis that includes Odets' Group Theatre production of *Golden Boy* in 1937, in which Kazan, Lee J. Cobb and Karl Malden appeared, and the fable of working class success and failure, *Body and Soul* (1947), written with a characteristic mix of analysis and lyricism by Abraham Polonsky and directed by Robert Rossen for the independent (and short-lived) Enterprise Studios. Michael Denning goes so far as to see *On the Waterfront* in terms of the continuing impact of the traditions of what he calls "ghetto pastorals and proletarian thrillers, a combination of the proletarian avant-garde of Kazan and the Hollywood Popular Front of Schulberg" (257).

The weight of script and direction is evident in *On the Waterfront*, but the evidence suggests that Kazan, working in particular with Brando, shifted the balance toward the central character's inner conflict and redemption, his struggle for dignity. Kazan's concern with underlying needs and wants, and in finding behavior and staging to express them, has rarely been better realized. The film has certainly been seen as constructing a powerful notion of working class individualism at and for a time when traditional working class and ethnic neighborhoods were in decline. Stanley Aronowitz saw two key independent films of the mid-fifties, *Marty* (1955) as well as *On the Waterfront*, as telling the working class spectators that "You're on your own, young man" (106–7). Yet Brando acts out a powerful and still resonant struggle for identity and respect. *On the Waterfront* is classically a collaborative film, but Kazan's own dramatic method, and the intensity of his involvement, helped realize its local specificity while pushing it out of this time and context toward myth.

NOTES

1 See also Kenneth Hey, "Ambivalence as a Theme in *On the Waterfront* (1954): An Interdisciplinary Approach to Film Study," in *Hollywood as Historian*, Peter C. Rollins, ed. (Lexington: Univ. of Kentucky Press, 1998), 159–89.

2 Kazan's letter to Brando, November 2, 1953, is part of Kazan's Production Notebook, *On the Waterfront* (marked "Golden Warrior") in the Kazan collection, Wesleyan University Cinema Archives, Middletown, CT. This Notebook will hereafter be cited as "PN" in the text where possible.

3 For a similar critique of Miller's play see Warshow. Molly Kazan's *The Egghead* also contains a questioning of the parallel of contemporary events with the Salem witch trials. For Schulberg's view on Molly Kazan's influence on her husband's testimony, see the Newfield and Jacobson interview.

4 See Bentley 434–57 for Schulberg's testimony and 482–95 for Kazan's. Also Navasky 246.

5 On "beats" see Kazan, "Dialogue on Film," *American Film*, 1.5 (March 1976), 40.

6 This is also true of the play, *On the Waterfront*, which Schulberg and Stan Silverman later wrote (see Rapf).

7 The script reference is to an undated 148-page version, titled "The Golden Warriors" and "On the Waterfront," and was obtained from Hollywood Scripts, London.

8 Kazan makes a number of references to Tony Mike in his Notebook and in marginal notes to his own script in the Wesleyan Cinema Archives.

9 *The Egghead*, undated typescript in the Theatre Collection, Library for the Performing Arts, New York Public Library, New York.

10 In his letter to Marlon Brando in the *Waterfront* Production Notebook Kazan writes: "I thought that his greatest solace in times of stress or pain or confusion might be shadowboxing. I thought of him shadowboxing, when he's confused, with tears in his eyes."

11 The point about Eva Marie Saint's reaction was made by the director Terence Davies at a BFI Seminar, July 23, 1993.

12 The Director's script at Wesleyan includes two pasted clippings, a double-page *Newsweek* report, "Death on the Docks," of May 18, 1953 and, opposite the script section depicting the reaction of "Mr. Upstairs" to Terry Malloy's testimony, an unidentified magazine picture which includes William J. McCormick, president of Penn Stevedoring Co.

2 Schulberg on the Waterfront

However often *Death of a Salesman* is produced for the stage or on film, the authorship of the work is never at issue. That the key creative vision belongs to Arthur Miller is not questioned. This judgment is routinely applied to the work of all playwrights. Such has never been the case for writers of screenplays. A film's artistic identity is often credited to the director, the producer, or the lead performer. Less often authorship is thought to reside in a creative team that is usually a combination of the director and the writer or of the director and the cinematographer. In regard to films of the studio era, one may even speak of the studio itself as author. Most rare is the film in which authorship clearly resides with a writer who does not also double as director. Paddy Chayevsky's *Marty* is one such example. *On The Waterfront* may be another.

The genesis of *On the Waterfront* was a visit by director Elia Kazan in the spring of 1952 to the Bucks County, Pennsylvania farm of author Budd Schulberg. Kazan, still smarting from the controversy of his House Un-American Activities Committee (HUAC) testimony, wanted to show that socially progressive films could be made by people not dominated by the Communist Party. In his autobiography he states "I was also determined to show my old 'comrades,' those who'd attacked me so viciously, that there was an anti-Communist left, and that we were the true progressives as they were not. I'd come back to fight" (*A Life* 488). He was proud of what he and John Steinbeck had accomplished with *Viva Zapata* (1952) and thought Schulberg would be an ideal partner for a similar venture, all the more so given

Schulberg's clash with the Communist Party over the publication of *What Makes Sammy Run?* and Schulberg's own appearance before HUAC.[1]

Schulberg, disgusted with the Hollywood film industry, had left California in 1941 and had been living in Bucks County for some seven years.[2] In an Afterword to the published shooting script of *On the Waterfront*, he writes that Kazan came to visit him at a time when "I was quite prepared to never write another screenplay for the rest of my life" (142). Chief among his complaints about Hollywood was that the screenwriter was low man on the totem pole: "Producers and directors used a writer's work but never seemed to respect him as the true source of production. Even famous writers, be they Dorothy Parker, Scott Fitzgerald, Aldous Huxley, or John Van Druten, were treated as dispensable and expendable hired hands. Screenwriting, it seemed to me, simply was not a self-respecting line of work" (141).

Early in their conversation Kazan made a pledge that would be the cornerstone of their working relationship. He promised that he would treat any screenplay written by Schulberg in the same manner he would treat a script for the theater written by Tennessee Williams or Arthur Miller. No changes whatsoever would be made without the consultation and approval of the author. Nearly half a century later, Schulberg remained deeply appreciative of that pledge which was faithfully observed.[3] Kazan's fidelity is all the more remarkable in that the road from the conception of *On the Waterfront* to the final cut was unusually grueling.

Kazan and Schulberg discussed two possible topics for their projected film: a sensational court case in Trenton involving six black teenagers caught in a miscarriage of justice reminiscent of the historic Scottsboro Case of the 1930s, and the turmoil on New York's waterfront involving the attempt to dislodge organized crime from its control of longshoremen through corrupt unions. Each man had considerable knowledge about the waterfront from projects that had failed to materialize and leaned toward that topic, but Schulberg, always interested in racial issues, agreed to look into the Trenton case. After a week or so of research, he determined that the events on the waterfront offered the better basis for a film. Kazan agreed.

Schulberg already had a waterfront script titled *The Bottom of the River* that was a dramatization of Malcolm Johnson's Pulitzer

Prize – winning newspaper series titled *Crime on the Waterfront.* The script had been commissioned by a nephew of Harry Cohn's for production by Columbia, but the project had not come to fruition. Kazan recalls reading the script at Schulberg's farm as he sprawled on the floor. The script opened with the dredging of the Hudson River for the body of a murdered rank-and-file longshoreman leader. Kazan thought that the script needed "lots of work" but that Schulberg had a solid grasp of the subject matter. Although that script was not the basis of *On the Waterfront*, it did contain a character similar to Terry Malloy.[4]

Kazan's knowledge of the problems on the waterfront was related to *The Hook,* a screenplay by Arthur Miller. The plot revolved around a dissident longshoreman in Brooklyn who has been murdered by the mob. Columbia had begun the preproduction process and Kazan was to direct. The film came to a halt when Columbia demanded significant changes in the film's orientation. Miller who had returned to New York first heard of the studio's demands through a phone call made by Kazan who was still in Hollywood dealing with studio head Harry Cohn. Miller was told that Roy Brewer, the conservative leader of the International Alliance of Theatrical and Stage Employees, had read the script and had been so disturbed by it that he had brought it to the attention of the FBI. Brewer had told Cohn that if *The Hook* was filmed as presently written, he would pull out on strike all the projectionists whenever a Columbia film was being exhibited anywhere in the United States. Brewer, who became notorious for his complicity in Hollywood blacklisting, insisted that the none of the practices and problems Miller had written about were true for the Brooklyn waterfront and to say so might impede the Korean War effort. In Brewer's view, this meant the film verged on being subversive. The real problem for longshoremen as far as Brewer was concerned were the activities of the Communist Party. On the West Coast, this meant the policies of Harry Bridges, the left-wing leader of the West Coast longshoremen, against whom Brewer had successfully struggled in a bitter battle for control of the Hollywood craft unions. What Miller had to do if he wanted to see *The Hook* made was substitute Communists for gangsters as villains of the piece. Cohn had capitulated to this demand. Miller describes Kazan's voice on the phone as being "even and hopeless" as he conveyed the ultimatum.

Miller rejected the suggestions as absurd and withdrew the script (308).[5]

After the initial meetings between Kazan and Schulberg culminated in an agreement once more to take on a waterfront project, Kazan went to work on the New York production of Tennessee Williams's *Camino Real* while Schulberg began to immerse himself in on-site research. For the next year Schulberg spent almost every day on the waterfront (*Waterfront* 142).[6] His left-wing social consciousness was stirred by seeing rank-and-file longshoremen struggling to rid the Manhattan, Brooklyn, and Hoboken waterfronts from a mob tyranny administered through corrupt unions. His safety was always at issue. Neither reporters nor social scientists were welcome on the docks and any unknown face was suspect. He was able to get around this problem due to his status as a boxing cognoscente who had even co-managed a fighter. Schulberg told strangers that he had drifted to waterfront watering holes after hanging out at the nearby Stillman's gym, the legendary haunt for New York boxers and their fans. Drawing on his insider's knowledge of the fight game to tell entertaining stories, Schulberg was able to interact relatively easily with longshoremen who tend to be avid fans of boxing. Nevertheless there were a number of times when he almost got a beating when saying the wrong thing in the vicinity of mobsters.

Schulberg quickly discovered that the rank-and-file insurgency on the docks owed much to the efforts of Father John Corridan of St. Xavier's, who eventually became the model for the Father Barry character (Karl Malden) in *On the Waterfront*. Schulberg describes him as a priest who spoke in a unique blend of Hell's Kitchen and baseball slang to convey the teachings of papal encyclicals on the need to reconstruct the social order (*Waterfront* 143–4). Father Corridan, an American counterpart of the worker priests who were then active in France and Italy, was furious with Cardinal Spellman who did not share his passion for reform and in many ways abetted the social forces that made life on the waterfront so grim.

Among the insurgents around Father Corridan whom Schulberg came to know was Arthur Browne or Brownie, who became the basis for the Kayo Dugan character (Pat Henning). In real life Brownie had survived many violent incidents with mob enforcers, including being thrown through a skylight and later being tossed unconscious into the Hudson River. Schulberg reveled in Brownie's company and for a time lived with Brownie and his wife in a cold-water flat on Manhattan's West Side. Schulberg listened to how Brownie and the others talked, and kept a notebook of "lines I could never make up: 'You know what we got to get rid of – the highocracy!'" (*Waterfront* 145). Moving around the docks with Brownie and others, Schulberg also concluded that filming on the New York side of the Hudson would be nearly impossible due to the congestion of the city, the available spaces involved, and the threat of violence. The Hoboken side was more practical in terms of sites, was far less noisy in the off-dock areas, was less congested, and somewhat better in terms of security.[7]

Kazan was aware of what Schulberg was doing on the waterfront but only came on the scene at a later point. He notes that Schulberg was personally transformed by the work he was doing:

> I will not forget Budd Schulberg on the streets of Hoboken and in its dockside bars. And I will never forget "Brownie." Budd was doing research, but not as I'd done research. He was immersing himself in the subject as he would a cause; he'd become a partisan of a rotten union's rebels. By the time I got to the waterfront, the longshoremen we encountered and to whom we talked had accepted Budd as a champion of their side.
>
> (*A Life* 492)

Kazan further notes that Schulberg had an enormous capacity for remembering details. He was able to repeat entire speeches spoken by the workers and could recall every article of clothing they wore. He had also begun to write about the waterfront revolt for the *Commonweal*, a liberal Catholic magazine. Later would come articles for *the New York Times* and the *Saturday Evening Post*. Increasingly the film began to be seen as more than a motion picture with a social edge. *On the Waterfront* was now part of the actual struggle that it was dramatizing. It would speak to a mass audience in hopes of bringing overwhelming public opinion to the cause of the embattled longshoremen.

Father Corridan and other advisors of the insurgents were convinced the rebels could win, but that they would need outside help, namely law enforcement agencies of the state and federal governments. To that end there were to be public hearings by the Waterfront Crime Commission about corruption on the docks. If the hearings produced enough evidence to generate public outrage, a genuine reform might take place. A major problem with that scenario was that the code of silence was a deeply rooted tradition of the docks. This tradition was reinforced by the national cultures of both the Italian and the Irish longshoremen, the two major ethnic groups involved. Italian consciousness included the concept of "omerta," which roughly means keeping silent about family or community problems in the presence of outsiders. "Informing," in turn, was taboo among the Irish and related to their long struggles with the British. In street language the workers were expected to be "deef 'n' dumb" and had to "take care of business" on their own. This reality offers a context for the criticism frequently voiced that *On the Waterfront* is simply a disguised apologia by Schulberg and Kazan for their HUAC testimony. Arthur Miller has put the charge most tactfully by stating, "At the time I felt it was a terrible misuse of the theme" (Kazan *A Life* 155).

What should be absolutely beyond question is that Schulberg did not artificially insert the testimony theme into a waterfront story; and he did not purposely seek out a story where testifying before a governmental committee was a natural element. At the time Schulberg became part of the anticorruption movement on the docks, the role of the crime investigators was paramount. Indeed, as subsequent history has aptly demonstrated, the mob's power began to wane *only* after the code of silence was breached. Schulberg saw the work of the Waterfront Crime Commission as essential to the cause of reform. Leaving that element of the story out would have been dishonest and perhaps even a betrayal of the insurgent cause. He has asserted time and again that he did not make a conscious connection between the HUAC experience and the scenes he wrote for Terry Malloy. Kazan has written of Schulberg's motivations that, "Budd had made himself more than a writer engaged to prepare a screenplay. He'd made himself a champion of the humanity on that strip of shore" (*A Life* 494).

Kazan has also drawn a difference between his views on this matter and Schulberg's. Years after the film had become a classic, but his involvement with HUAC continued to be controversial, Kazan stated that although he had always seen a parallel between the behavior of the Communist Party and the behavior of organized crime, that parallel was not what had motivated him to direct *On the Waterfront*. Furthermore, "I never meant any parallel between Terry and me..." (Young 179).[8] Nonetheless, he has noted that he was greatly affected by hearing the story of Tony Mike diVincenzo, a man who had once had his own pier but had testified against the mob and suffered various hardships as a result. At the time *On the Waterfront* was being researched diVincenzo was a supervisor of the Hoboken Sewer System. Kazan describes Schulberg's reaction to diVincenzo as far less emotional than his own:

> I doubt that Budd was affected as personally as I was by the parallel of Tony Mike's story. His reaction to the loss of certain friends was not as bitter as my own; he had not experienced their blackballing as frequently and intensely as I had in the neighborhood known as Broadway. I believe Budd regarded our waterfront story with greater objectivity, an objectivity I appreciated. But I did see Tony Mike's story as my own, and that connection did lend the tone of irrefutable anger to the scenes I photographed and to my work with actors. When Brando, at the end, yells at Lee Cobb, the mob boss, "I'm glad what I done – you hear me? – glad what I done!" that was me saying with identical heat, that I was glad I'd testified as I had. ... So when critics say that I put my story and my feelings on the screen, to justify my informing, they are right.
>
> (*A Life* 500)[9]

In spite of these and many similar comments, numerous critics routinely equate Schulberg's and Kazan's motivations. Nor is there much consideration that Kazan as director was like an actor who finds personal motivation in a scene not written with personal touchstones in mind (see Thomson's essay in this volume). Given the moment in waterfront history in which the film's script was written, the testimony is valid reporting. With the passage of time, any real or imagined parallels with HUAC have begun to fade. Viewers who are unaware of Schulberg and Kazan's personal histories are not likely to attach Malloy's testimony to the HUAC hearings any more than they attach them to the now-forgotten crime commission headed by Senator Estes Kefauver, an effort that brought him the Democrat nomination for vice president in 1956.[10] Indeed, most contemporary viewers did not see the HUAC parallel. Nora Sayre, author of an important book on the films of the cold war, has written "I should add that I didn't detect the social metaphor in the fifties: as an apolitical English major I was gripped by the film's fervor without realizing its relevance" (150–63). Nonetheless, writing some thirty years later she is certain that "Today, we can't help but regard the movie as an impassioned defense of the informer, and as a petition for sympathy for the pain inflicted by the wrath of former friends" (150–63).

Another way of looking at the testimony controversy is to consider the participation of Leonard Bernstein. The composer did not become involved with the film until the final cut was ready (see Burlingame's essay in this volume). He was asked to do the musical score and was more than pleased to participate. He obviously had no problem in associating his name and talents with the project. For that matter, Brando, who was opposed to HUAC and had been leery of working with Kazan again precisely because Kazan had been a friendly witness, also saw no connection between his actions in the film and that of Kazan or Schulberg in regard to HUAC. Ron Steiger, who brought considerable power to the role of Charley Malloy, was also a HUAC critic.

From the first, Schulberg has been adamant that the testifying theme was simply a factual element anyone writing about the waterfront would utilize. Nearly fifty years after the film's release, he was still fielding questions about the testimony theme. In early 2000, he responded to questions by Jack Newfield and Mark Jacobson by stating

> Can you imagine Kazan coming to me and saying, "Budd, I want to write a movie that justifies my testimony before the Un-American Activities Committee . . . " and me saying, "Jesus, I just can't wait to do that?" What happened was that as I researched, I was still working on the ending. I attended the hearings of the waterfront commission for forty days, just the way anybody writing for the *Herald Tribune* was doing. I told Kazan that I felt that life was writing the ending of our film.
>
> (Newfield and Jacobson 9)[11]

Regardless of how one judges the "informer" theme of the film, it is simply one element and it is never the kind of political act that marks the betrayal in John Ford's *The Informer.* What we see in *On the Waterfront* is that although Terry Malloy has been abused by Johnny Friendly and by his own brother, neither the mob boss nor the brother dislikes Terry or is disliked in turn. While exploiting Terry at one level, they also do him favors. Their paternalistic relationship to Terry is complex, making the changes that occur psychological rather than political in nature. Terry's behavior involves personal redemption, not political insurgency. Key to that redemption is the love of Edie Doyle (Eva Marie Saint) and the fervor of the crusading Father Barry.

Often neglected in analysis of Malloy's motivations is his identity as a boxer and how that identity reflects Schulberg's lifelong passion for boxing. Even as a child, Schulberg had been taken to see prize fights by his father, B. P. Schulberg, the long-time studio chief at Paramount. As an adult, he has not simply been a devoted fan, but a reporter who routinely has, even today, a ringside seat at various championship and nonchampionship bouts in various weight divisions whether staged in the United States or abroad. For years he habituated boxing gyms, training camps, weigh-ins, and other boxing venues. This aspect of his life involved personal and professional relationships with scores of fighters, managers, trainers, gamblers, promoters, and sports columnists. His novel *The Harder They Fall* became the basis of a film with the same title and he would write a book about Muhammad Ali. His writing on boxing has appeared in sports publications such as *Boxing Illustrated* and *Sports Illustrated,* newspapers such as *Newsday* and the *New York Post,* and general publications such as *Playboy, Saturday Review,* and *TV Guide.*[12]

To shape the psychology of Terry Malloy, Schulberg drew on all of his first-hand knowledge of fighters. No other author who has written about fighting for the screen has had such an intimate relationship with the world of prize fighting. All the details in the film related to prize fighting are authentic. Schulberg even arranged for middleweight Roger Donoghue to coach Brando on typical "fighter's moves" and for middleweight Billy Kilroy to serve as Brando's double. An indication of his enthusiasm for boxing is that when he and Kazan were still working on the script at his farm, Schulberg insisted they interrupt their work to return to New York to take in the Rocky Marciano–Archie Moore fight. This was not just a matter of spending a few hours at ringside, but involved the full panoply of prefight and afterfight activities.

Schulberg also reached into his own life while writing the pigeon scenes involving the more tender aspects of Malloy's character. He recounts in *Moving Pictures* that as a youngster living in Hollywood, he and Maurice Rapf had built rooftop lofts to breed and race pigeons (*Moving Pictures* 321–7). When he discovered that keeping pigeons was one of the hobbies of Hoboken longshoremen, he immediately understood how that activity could be used to develop further the complexity of Malloy's personality and social relationships. This does not signal that Malloy is an alter ego of Schulberg, but that what amounts to props or environments for Kazan and Brando had a deeper significance for Schulberg who understood the subtleties about the passion for pigeons just as he understood the frustrations of a fighter who could have been a contender.

Although *On the Waterfront* is often discussed as a labor film or in the context of anti-Communism, the film ultimately is a morality play. Schulberg has written that meeting Father Corridan revolutionized his views concerning religion and religious crusaders. *On the Waterfront* is replete with Christian imagery and philosophy. Religious themes are even stronger in *Waterfront,* Schulberg's novel dealing with the same events that came out some eight months after the film. The story in the novel is told primarily through the perspective of the crusading priest, tortured by the disparity he finds between his Catholic convictions and the practices of the Catholic hierarchy. The testimony aspect of the story is secondary.[13] The novel won The Christopher Award, given by the Catholic Church to books that advance Christian ideals. Schulberg has observed wryly that this may be the only occasion when that award was won by a Jew.[14]

The script for *On the Waterfront* was ready by early 1954. After a final reworking in which Kazan participated, the script was sent to Darryl Zanuck at Twentieth Century-Fox. Kazan, still under contract to Fox for one more film, was sure that Zanuck who had produced *Viva Zapata* and *The Grapes of Wrath* (1940) would see the merits of the script. Zanuck responded with guarded approval but asked that Kazan and Schulberg come to the studio to discuss the project. At those meetings, various suggestions were made regarding possible changes in the script. The director and writer returned to the

New York area. Kazan completed the staging of *Tea and Sympathy* while Schulberg worked on revising the script. The play went on the boards in early April and Kazan spent the balance of the month working with Schulberg on the final draft which was sent to Zanuck at the end of that month.

Four weeks passed with no response and a worried Kazan and Schulberg went west to see what the problem might be. They quickly learned that the studio was in a serious financial crisis and that Zanuck was sure that the way out was with Technicolor epics shot in Cinemascope. His pet project at the time was *Prince Valiant.* Their proposed black-and-white social problems flick set in the East was no longer on Zanuck's radar. At a script conference with the potential filmmakers, Zanuck was more than blunt. He said he had tried to imagine Terry working for or with the FBI, but nothing clicked. "I'm not going to make this picture. I don't like it. In fact, I don't like anything about it. It's exactly what audiences don't want to see now. Who gives a shit about longshoremen?" (Kazan 508).[15] Moreover, he pointed out that Kazan's last three films had lost money at the box office. The worst performer of the three was the just-released *Man on a Tightrope* (1953).

Although badly shaken by the turndown, Kazan sent the script to Warner Brothers, who found it of no interest and returned it within an extremely short period. This was followed by rejections at Paramount and MGM. *The Hollywood Reporter* added to the script's woes by publishing a story that a script about waterfront radicals that had Communistic elements was being given the cold shoulder by all the studios. Kazan was so frustrated that he pledged to make the film whatever the circumstances, even if he had to shoot it in 16 millimeter. This circumstance was avoided by an eleventh-hour intervention by maverick producer Sam Spiegel (then going by the pseudonym of S. P. Eagle).

One of the world's few truly independent film producers, Spiegel had scored big with *The African Queen* (1952), but *Melba* (1953), his latest, was a flop. After hearing about the problems Kazan and Schulberg were having during a chance meeting at the Beverly Hills Hotel where their rooms happened to be across the hall from one another, Spiegel agreed to consider producing their script. While Spiegel hosted a long night of partying, Kazan and Schulberg stayed in their room working on the script. The next morning Schulberg crossed the hallway to tell the story of *On the Waterfront* to Spiegel who lay in a bed with covers up to his nose. Finding merit in the story and relishing the idea of working with a big-name director dedicated to a script by a best selling novelist, Spiegel agreed to take on the project.[16]

Using the bargaining skills for which he was justly famous, Spiegel soon got United Artists to agree to put up $500,000 to do the film as a low-budget feature. The sweetener in the deal was Frank Sinatra, the kid from Hoboken, who agreed to do the part of Terry Malloy.[17] Kazan was sure that Sinatra would give an admirable performance, but he had always preferred Brando for the role. The quixotic Brando, however, wary of renewed association with Kazan, returned the script unread. Although Spiegel told Kazan to begin consultations with Sinatra about costuming, he continued to court Brando. Turning on his charm full blast, he reminded Brando of how instrumental Kazan had been in launching Brando's career by first casting him and then getting a name-creating performance in *Streetcar Named Desire*. Brando eventually agreed to read the script and then to take on the role of Terry Malloy. With Brando on board, Spiegel ungraciously forced unacceptable conditions on United Artists. When the studio withdrew from the project, he finalized a deal with Harry Cohn of Columbia to do the film on a budget of $800,000. This was Cohn's third consideration of a waterfront film, but this time it would materialize. Kazan has written eloquently of these events, including how poorly he felt about the way Sinatra was treated (*A Life* 17).

Hollywood producers are notorious for desiring changes in scripts. Sam Spiegel was no exception to this rule. Schulberg was soon infuriated by Spiegel's saying, "Let's open it up again." Nonetheless, Schulberg, as well as Kazan, has repeatedly credited Spiegel with greatly improving the script, making it faster, more economical, and more logical. What characterized Spiegel's input were not the usual requests for additions or alterations, but a passion for cuts. Schulberg puts it succinctly by saying that Spiegel "just squeezed and squeezed and squeezed."[18] Kazan credits Spiegel with a wonderful sense of story and sequence. The two scenes that caused the most acrimony involved the sermon in the hold (referred to by Schulberg as the Christ-in-the-shape-up scene) and the final fight at the pier.

4. Father Barry [Karl Malden], along with Pop Doyle [John Hamilton] in the sermon scene in the hold. Spiegel was worried that it would involve too much talk, but it was finally shot largely as written. (Copyright Columbia Pictures Corp., 1960. Courtesy of the Museum of Modern Art Film Stills Archive)

In the printed version of the script, the sermon scene is a full six pages. Most of it consists of a soliloquy by Father Barry. Spiegel thought this was far too much talk for any one scene. Such a speech might be suitable for the stage but not for a film. The producer, director, and scriptwriter wrangled over the scene for three full days. Schulberg recalls that each session would begin by Spiegel asking what cuts Schulberg had made overnight. Schulberg would say none had been made and then the discussion would commence. Feeling the scene was essential to the film, Schulberg finally demanded Kazan weigh in decisively. The director then stated that Spiegel did not fully appreciate how the scene would actually play on film. The camera would not remain fixed on Father Barry. Rather, as the priest spoke, the camera would roam around the ship to record the reaction of Malloy, the other workers, and the union goons. This explanation mollified Spiegel and the scene was shot pretty much as originally written.

The final pier scene has always been troubling to critics and labor historians. The implication seems to be that the toughest guy gets to lead the working class. Such a might-establishes-right solution is virtually indistinguishable from that of the gangsters. This was not Schulberg's concept. Carrying out the religious theme of the picture, he thought Malloy should die. Terry's martyrdom, not his survival, would rally the longshoreman to revolt, completing the Christian theme enunciated earlier by Father Barry. Spiegel, in true producer's spirit, wanted a happier ending, and Kazan was unsure of the most effective way to conclude. Schulberg reluctantly consented to Malloy's survival, but he gave the film's final words to Johnny Friendly, who shouts, "I'll be back. I'll be back." In Schulberg's mind, this threat was not the wishful thinking of the defeated, but the threat of a man very likely to return to power. Schulberg would have preferred to have the film end with a close-up on the snarling Johnny Friendly. He admits the film's apparently happy ending is misleading.[19] In his novelization of the film, Schulberg restores his original concept. Malloy is killed.

Despite the film, the Waterfront Crime Commission, and elections run by the National Labor Relations Board, in the real world of the docks that *On the Waterfront* had sought to change, the mob retained its power. The novel foresees this outcome. In an essay that deals with the different problems of writing for film and the printed page, Schulberg discusses why the novel has less of a focus on Malloy and is able to focus more strongly on the mob's historic control of the waterfront:

> ... the film's concentration on a single dominating character close to the camera-eye mode made it esthetically inconvenient – if not

> impossible – to set Terry's story in its social and historical perspective. What I have tried to do in the novel is to use Terry's story as a single strand in a rope of intervening fibres, in order to suggest the knotted complexities of the waterfront that loops around New York, a lawless frontier almost unknown to the metropolitan citizenry.
>
> ("Schulberg, Why Write It. . . ?" 26)

Spiegel was also not particularly enthusiastic about the love story, but Schulberg insisted it was critical. In this context it is important to note that one reason Kazan believes Brando was so effective was the tenderness he was able to develop in his scenes with Eva Marie Saint. Considerable critical comment has been directed to how masterfully Brando improvised in the scenes where Saint inadvertently dropped her white gloves or how Kazan has them interact in the bar where a wedding party is being held. What Kazan has pointed out is that this love story, which gives the film so much of its poignancy, is entirely Schulberg's creation. The love story is one of the few elements in the film not based on actual events or persons. Even more so than making Malloy a betrayed boxer or using pigeons as a plot element, the love story is the imposition by the writer of his sense of how the story must be told.

In terms of visual authenticity and practicality, Kazan had quickly seen the wisdom of shooting in Hoboken rather than New York. Schulberg took him on long walks around the waterfront where the two men roughly sketched out where the various scenes might be shot. Specific houses were later found by location people, but it is significant that in a film in which all but two scenes are shot on location, the writer was the person who discovered the basic locations for filming.[20] Later, Schulberg would also walk Brando through Hoboken to familiarize him with its ambiance. This involvement in location scouting by an author is unusual. Far more common is the practice of a set designer finding the locations without the involvement of the writer and then securing the approval of the director.

When the time came to cast, Kazan, as was his usual practice, turned to the Actors Studio which he had co-founded and where he still served as a director. All the major actors were drawn from the Studio and most were performers with whom Kazan had previously worked. Rehearsals for the film would also take place at the Actors

5. The Hoboken waterfront in the 1950s. (Courtesy of the Museum of Modern Art Film Stills Archive)

Studio. Kazan certainly played the main role in terms of casting, but Schulberg participated fully. This harmonious partnership is in sharp contrast to the usual Hollywood practice of casting which routinely excludes scriptwriters. The most daring casting decision was the selection of Eva Marie Saint to play Edie Doyle. Although she now seems an ideal choice, Saint had not previously appeared in a motion picture and had only come to Kazan's attention through the Actors Studio and in a play in which he thought she was miscast. Brando, among others, was not originally convinced she had the presence the role required. Kazan observes that eventually Brando began to find Saint's genuine innocence attractive and then felt guilty about his emotion, all serving to make Malloy an unforgettable portrait (Young 135).

Schulberg was instrumental in casting some of the minor characters. Kazan, aware that Schulberg had frequently expressed displeasure with the actors Hollywood selected to play tough guys, challenged him to do better. Schulberg responded by recruiting retired boxers to play Johnny Friendly's thugs. "Two-Ton" Tony Galento,

Abe Simon, Tami Mauriello, and Roger Donoghue, among others, added considerable verisimilitude to the look, sound, and ambiance of the waterfront scenes. They were all the more effective in that they were not familiar faces previously seen in a score of gangster films. Schulberg also insisted on casting an African-American in a speaking role as a dissident longshoreman. Union locals at that time practiced de facto segregation, but Schulberg believed that having a black character was more important than this minor breach of reality.

Another interesting casting decision involved extras. Because the weather was so cold during the actual filming, few professional actors showed up for the bit parts and Kazan was able to hire actual longshoremen. Again, the rapport Schulberg had built up along the docks was useful. Nonetheless, the longshoremen had to be guaranteed at least four hours work per day at the going hourly union rate for dock work. Their pay had to be in cash at noon the day following any scene in which they appeared. On one occasion when Spiegel was late coming with the money, there was a near riot.

One of the most unusual aspects of the shooting was Schulberg's nearly daily presence in Hoboken. He was rarely on the set itself, but he was at the hotel that served as production headquarters. This made him available to deal with any changes or adjustments that had to be made as the filming proceeded. Schulberg would meet in the evening with Kazan to map out the next day's shooting and anticipate any problems that might arise.[21]

Like any successful film, numerous unplanned elements added to its effectiveness. Rod Steiger thought of wearing the long camel hair coat that perfectly expressed the personality of his character. The air was so cold that mists often hung in the air when the actors spoke, silently conveying the chill of the waterfront. The shooting days happened to be particularly gray, which pleased cinematographer Boris Kaufman who wanted to have the specter of Manhattan hovering in the background but not overpowering the action. The sounds of working Hoboken heard throughout the film were often just lifted from the environment. And although Kazan hated to shoot actors smoking cigarettes, Karl Malden was often shot with a mauled cigarette dangling from his lips because that was the way Father Corridan smoked.

Thinking back on the film's extraordinary success many years later, Kazan has isolated the four elements he considers the most important. Giving no particular order of importance, he lists them as Schulberg's script, Spiegel's refinement of the script, his own direction of the script, and Brando's superb rendering of the script. He says of Brando, "If there is a better performance by a man in the history of film in America, I don't know what it is" (*A Life* 517). In that sense, Kazan, so often criticized for having an out-sized view of his talent, has always spoken of *On the Waterfront* as a collaborative effort. He has repeatedly referred to Schulberg's unique grasp of the film's themes and waterfront environment.

Schulberg also speaks of film as a collaborative art. He uses a sports analogy: "There is a great film only when the writer, the director, the performers, the cinematographer, and all the crew finish the race with their noses on the wire. Too often the victory is accorded to the director. I don't think we should deny credit to the director, but the director's contribution should not wipe out all other contributions."[22] He believes films would be of higher quality if the writer had to approve all script changes. In regard to the script of *On the Waterfront*, he says, "I don't know why they [people who put up money for films] don't think they can take a writer who is able to write a novel or play effectively, and give him his head, and believe he can do just as well on a screenplay. ... The only one who ever went every step of the way with me on this was Kazan, in the two films we did and a third one that never got to the screen [*In the Streets*, a film about Puerto Ricans]. He treated me and others – Inge, Williams, Bob Anderson – with the same artistic respect he accorded to writers in the theater. There are some pretty good writer – director relationships, but as far as I know, this may be the only instance where the director carried out the script and showed how the process I advocate could work" (Georgakas, *The Cineaste Interviews* 363).

In the latter half of the twentieth century, the proposition that the director is the author of films has gained considerable currency. More often than not, however, the idea that any one person determined the nature of any given film does not survive a rigorous analysis of how that film was actually conceived and realized. Nonetheless, if one wished to single out an individual as the person most responsible for the look, sound, and passion of *On the Waterfront*, its director would not be that person. With all due respect to the considerable input of Elia Kazan, we are speaking of Budd Schulberg's *On the Waterfront.*

NOTES

1   See Navasky, *Naming Names*, 239–43, for an account of the attempts of the Communist Party to dictate what members who were authors should write. Schulberg was virtually forbidden to write the novel *What Makes Sammy Run?* This became the basis of his leaving the party. More to the point, when the book came out Charles Glenn wrote a laudatory review in *The Daily Worker,* but after being called in for political counsel by Party leaders, he wrote a second review recanting the first and focusing on the novel's weaknesses. Schulberg comments on the incident and his evaluation of Navasky's account can be found in the 1981 interview by Dan Georgakas in *The Cineaste Interviews*, 369, 372–3.

2   In *Moving Pictures: Memories of a Hollywood Prince* he offers an account of his life in Hollywood. Of related interest is his discussion of writers and Hollywood in *The Four Seasons of Success.*

3   Interview with Dan Georgakas, Feb. 3, 2000.

4   In the interview of Feb. 3 Schulberg indicates that the original *The Bottom of the River* screenplay has been misplaced but believes it will turn up in collections of other stored material of projects that did not materialize. There is an early version of the script, "Crime on the Waterfront," dated April 1951, located on microfilm in the Dartmouth College Library, in which Terry Malloy is Edie's brother. He is murdered and she tries to find out who killed him. Her love interest is a waterfront reporter named Al Chase. This may well be the script or a version of the script Kazan read. The difference in title may indicate the continual playing with titles common to film projects or an error in Schulberg's memory.

5   A similar account based on interviews with Kazan can be found in Nora Sayre, *Running Time: Films of the Cold War*, 51–4. A more sanitized view of the film's demise in which Miller's withdrawal of the script is made somewhat mysterious is found in Kazan, *A Life*, 410–16.

6   Schulberg notes that 25,000 longshoremen worked on a waterfront consisting of 750 miles of shoreline with 1800 piers that served 10,000 ocean-going ships and a million passengers annually. This activity involved thirty-five million tons of cargo worth eight billion dollars. The mob take on this commerce was estimated as being at least 10%.

7   The Hoboken piers accounted for about 9% of the work in New York harbor and some 420,000 "hires" over the course of a year.

8   These interviews were made in 1970 under the agreement that Young would not even consider publishing them until after Kazan had published his autobiography. In that regard they are conversations between a seasoned director and a beginner held private for more than a quarter century, rather than

an exchange meant for immediate publication and whatever influence that might have on short-term public and critical opinion. These interviews are extremely strong in describing Kazan's interactions with actors. Elsewhere, however, Kazan has drawn a parallel between himself and Terry (see Rapf's Introduction and Neve's essay).

9   The same sentiments are found in Young 180.

10   This committee should not be confused with the New York Waterfront Crime Commission, which is a totally different entity.

11   This interview also discusses how scenes between Father Corridan and long-shoremen which Schulberg personally observed became scenes in the film. The interview, however, errs in identifying the priest as Father "Corrigan" rather than as Father *Corridan.*

12   Budd Schulberg, *Sparring With Hemingway,* offers a collection of boxing articles from the time of the writing of *On the Waterfront* through 1994. The collection also contains essays on *The Harder They Fall* in which Schulberg explains why he feels the film misrepresents his views and has an approach to boxing reform that he does not share.

13   Schulberg began the novel when it looked as if none of the studios would accept his script.

14   Interview with Dan Georgakas, Feb. 3, 2000. In *Running Time* Nora Sayre seems to question the sincerity of Schulberg's enthusiasm for Father Corridan by writing "One wonders if Kazan and Schulberg felt that they had been crucified for their testimony, and if – as very bitter anti-Communists – they had lauded the Catholic church in deference to its powers during the political investigations" (61). Schulberg wrote extensively about this enthusiasm for Corridan in magazines such as *The Saturday Evening Post* and *Commonweal.* The hierarchy, as he noted, was not particularly supportive of their attempts to reform the waterfront. On this point, the attitudes of Kazan are more problematic. Kazan had starred in and helped make the very anticleric *Preacher and Slave* in the late 1930s for Nykino, a left-wing independent film company. His experience in independent left-wing filmmaking is largely omitted from his autobiography. For background on such activities see Dan Georgakas, "Radical Filmmaking, 1930s" in *The Encyclopedia of the American Left.*

15   Schulberg, *On the Waterfront,* 147, reports on the meeting in similar fashion.

16   Among other Spiegel productions are *The Bridge on the River Kwai* (1957), *Suddenly Last Summer* (1959), *Lawrence of Arabia* (1962), and *Nicholas and Alexandra* (1971). He worked again with Kazan on the ill-fated *The Last Tycoon* (1976).

17   Schulberg had approached John Garfield about the role when he first began his research. Garfield was interested but was overwhelmed by his difficulties with the HUAC scene and died from a heart attack before the project got underway.

18   Interview with Dan Georgakas, Feb. 3, 2000.

19   Interview with Dan Georgakas, Feb. 3, 2000.

20   Kazan had always had a penchant for shooting on location, beginning with *Boomerang!* (1947) and *Panic in the Streets* (1950), films he felt had a direct

impact on how he went about organizing the scenes for *On the Waterfront*. Direct reference to this process can be found in Young, 39.

21   This is one of the few points on which the two men's accounts of the making of the film are different. In his Feb. 3, 2000 interview with Dan Georgakas, Schulberg was insistent that he was in Hoboken nearly every day as noted above. In *A Life* 521, Kazan says Schulberg came to Hoboken rarely, but it is not clear if he is speaking only of a period when it was extremely cold or for all the shooting. In any case, he agrees that when Schulberg was in town, he was usually at the hotel. Both agree that no changes were made without Schulberg's permission. Kazan states that he used the phone to speak with Schulberg about such changes. His account in no way attempts to diminish Schulberg's importance. Schulberg's memory seems more accurate in this regard, as Kazan's memory may have conflated Schulberg's not being on the set with not being in Hoboken. In Ciment, Kazan writes that Shulberg was "standing by during much of the shooting" (48). This piece was originally written in 1956, which makes it much closer to the actual time period than the autobiography and other writings Kazan wrote many years later.

22   Georgakas, *The Cineaste Interviews*, 364. See also Schulberg's foreword to this *Handbook*. Schulberg also discusses *Citizen Kane* as a collaborative effort rather than the singular vision of Orson Welles. He cites the critical contributions of cinematographer Gregg Toland, scriptwriter Herman Mankiewicz, and editor Robert Wise.

3 *On The Waterfront:* Script Analysis Conventional and Unconventional

The real nature of dramatic action is never just the overt, immediate story being told, but a union of past and present from which conflict is finally purged. That action falls into a fundamental story pattern typical of all drama and exemplified by *On The Waterfront* in a way that goes far in explaining its grip on our imagination (Lee 1–7, 50–9). Structure and meaning are transparent parts of the same experience, brought home to us through our identification with the key characters who are the agents through which a screenplay's action is experienced. The following looks at the usual structural (plot) elements, character description and analysis, and thematic material through this perspective to give a firmer grip on Schulberg's storytelling and to avoid the usual fragmentation of script analysis.

THE FUNDAMENTAL STORY PATTERN
AND *ON THE WATERFRONT*

Most of us are familiar with the idea that dramas have Beginnings, Middles, and Ends; commonly this is what we mean by Acts 1–3. But even among professional screenwriters there is a certain fuzziness about the elements that come before and after the immediate story, however they wrestle with some of those issues in preparation, particularly if they first have to present a treatment to a potential producer, or even if they do no more than think a story through and then "pitch" it to a friendly director.

Dramas actually fall into five parts, and across the board, with inevitable variations and exceptions, individualize a pattern in which a significant event(s) has been mishandled in the past, resulting in a skewed life (lives) in the dramatic present.[1] Usually the main character is in ignorance of this event, or of its significance, or has worked out a false modus vivendi as did Terry in *On The Waterfront*. Into this modus vivendi intrudes one day an immediate problem, like the death of Joey and Edie's request that Terry help her find her brother's murderer – an immediate problem whose resolution is necessary but which the hero discovers he cannot solve without recognizing and also solving the mishandled problem from his past. Although all dramatic action takes place in the immediate conflict organized in Acts 1–3, *part(s) of the past which is troubled is relived in those acts, too:* in *On The Waterfront* past betrayal and the lost fight at the center of Terry's present condition are symbolically reenacted so they can come to different conclusions. A fifth element is added to the troubled past and Acts 1–3 when the conflict is resolved: a new future, one not explored but clearly in sight, in which a truer life has become possible (in tragedy it is the life for the community, although the hero dies).

Terry's story shows this pattern at work. Years ago he took a dive in the fight against Wilson that Glover draws him out on in Act 2 with the result that ever since he has been perceived as a bum by those around him, his conscience bought off by Johnny Friendly's favors. Johnny Friendly, his mentor and corrupter, and his brother Charley are the duo that forced Terry to betray himself then. The aspect of *On The Waterfront* that grips us today is the gradual revelation of these events and relationships as Terry struggles blindly at first to reinvent himself as a full human being in response to Edie's challenge, that is, as a person governed by the dictates of his conscience, not of convenience, which can only make him a slave to events, "an animal" in Edie's words (Schulberg, *Screenplay* 64).

This struggle is further complicated because Terry plays a role in causing Joey Doyle's death at the start of the drama. His subsequent falling in love with Joey's sister, Edie, becomes an event at once romantically anguished and conscience-testing. "Shouldn't we care about everybody?" Edie asks Terry in their long sequence together in Act 1: "Isn't everybody a part of everybody else?" (Schulberg 62).

She can get away with lines like that, a girl being educated by the nuns upstate, yet for a man suffering from a past betrayal by Johnny Friendly and his brother, those words cut to the bone. When Terry rejoins with his amoral "every man for himself" conception, she is revolted. When he adds a few moments later, "Keep your neck in and your nose clean and you'll never have no trouble down here," Edie's immediate comeback is "But that's living like an animal –" (Schulberg 64). Then she turns to him with "Help me, if you can – for God's sakes help me!" (Schulberg 65). That is as unforgettable as the guilty Oedipus in Sophocles' *Oedipus Rex* being implored for help. Edie's final expectation from Terry is of "Much more Terry. Much, much more!" as she runs off and Johnny Friendly shows up. (Schulberg 71).

Terry can help her only if he undoes the false modus vivendi by which he lives, and to do that he must somehow undo that past on which that modus vivendi is based. The importance of that undoing becomes increasingly urgent and immediately decisive as the drama unfolds. In Act 2 Charley lets Terry out of the taxi instead of taking him to Gerry G. after his anguished, famous reminder to his brother that "I could've been a contender. I could've had class and been somebody" (Schulberg 104). In the Climax Terry and Johnny Friendly argue directly over what to make of the past, with all riding on the outcome of whose version prevails. Terry's success clearly lays old conflicts to rest and opens the prospect of a new beginning.

ON THE WATERFRONT: ACT I

A first act, then, typically dramatizes this false life at the start of a drama while it locates us in the time and place and characters of the action – a false life first perceived as the "norm," the base from which the drama lifts, not wholly seen as false at first. An event intrudes into this life that cannot be evaded without the drama ending and a living death ensuing, which makes resolving an underlying problem from the past necessary for the resolution of the immediate, unavoidable conflict. But what to do is not immediately clear to the characters, any more than the full implications of change: the dramatic problem propels the main characters on a search for a solution they find and understand only gradually. False starts precede finding a direction worth pursuing.

We start with Joey's murder and Terry's unhappy reaction: he thought Johnny Friendly was only going to have Joey roughed up. This is not wholly convincing on Terry's part; he knows Johnny Friendly is bluntly ruthless and determined to maintain his stake on the docks. Terry, at least subconsciously, knew what was going to happen, but didn't want to admit it or face the consequences. That dramatizes exactly the false modus vivendi Terry has been living: he knew he compromised himself years ago yet hasn't wanted to face the consequences. That is why he is so sensitive to being called a bum. Developing a conscience, which he finds so painful, will force him to think and feel things through.

At the same time, Terry's unhappiness establishes that he isn't just a thug. He couldn't develop his conscience if it wasn't already there waiting for the opportunity to surface. But we do not live in isolation – we need help. Swiftly, thereafter, Edie and Father Barry meet over Joey's dead body, where Edie reproaches Father Barry for holding himself aloof in the Church. "'In the church when you need me?' Was there ever a saint who hid in the Church?" (Schulberg 12). Father Barry, in other words, is standing on false ground, too. Terry's conscience is bought off with a cushy job by Johnny Friendly, and then we see Terry with his pigeons (i.e., he is sensitive, while he keeps what he will become, a pigeon) and Jimmy, for whom he is something of a hero. The next day in the fight on the docks Terry, from guilt when he discovers who she is, gives Edie the marker that lets Pop work. At the same time Terry gives Glover and the request to testify before the Crime Commission, to rat, in effect, short shrift, while Father Barry invites Dugan and other dissidents to meet at the Church. Terry is sent to watch them – and guides Edie away from the violence. Before they talk we know what she wants, what Terry has done, and that he is already guilty and unhappy. Moreover, he is approaching thirty, a symbolically important date, for it's time Terry grew up and put childish things (illusions) behind him, as Charley in part points out to him later, little dreaming what direction Terry will take. Edie refuses to go away, as Pop asks her, determined to find who is responsible for Joey's murder, and instead seeks out Terry on the roof, where he is taking care of Joey's pigeons. (Joey became a pigeon: Terry is in process of taking his place.) Terry and Edie go to get a drink, in the scene we looked at where she makes her crucial demand for help. They fall in love hard, but as Terry tries to calm Edie she is outraged by his attitude and guesses he's part of the problem. "No wonder everybody calls you a bum" she lashes out at him (Schulberg 71). Johnny Friendly is not happy with Terry either, takes away his cushy job, pinches him harshly, tells him not to see the girl he has fallen in love with again, and leaves Terry torn in different directions. He doesn't know what to do. But he is working in the hold when Dugan (Nolan in the script) is killed and Father Barry tries to speak, pelted with refuse and a beer can. When one of Johnny Friendly's thugs reaches for something else to throw, Terry flattens him. Johnny Friendly and Truck (with Charley watching in the film) see and react to that action against Friendly's interest. Father Barry ends his famous peroration:

> **FATHER BARRY**
> But remember fellows, Christ is always with you – Christ is in the shape-up, He's in the hatch – He's in the union hall – He's kneeling here beside Dugan [Nolan in the script] – and He's saying with all of you –
>
> CLOSE ON FATHER BARRY
>
> **FATHER BARRY**
> If you do it to the least of mine, you do it to me! What they did to Joey, what they did to Dugan, they're doing to you. And you. And YOU. And only you, with God's help, have the power to knock 'em off for good.
>
> (Schulberg 83)

Edie is there and sees Terry's action, too. She pursues him back to the rooftop and his pigeons and gives him Joey's jacket. He's not ready to wear that: it is the reformer's mantle. Yet he does embrace Edie, which he cannot do without defying Johnny Friendly. That sets him on the path to wearing that jacket, little as he thinks about that with Edie in his arms. The die is cast: Act 1 has ended. Terry doesn't know how yet, but he is set on a course to honor his conscience, and find his own way – to find a new modus vivendi that will mean leaving the life and (false) commitments he has been following. The end of the Beginning, or Act 1, brings a character to this point, meaning, through him, we realize that a decisive shift has occurred in the underlying drama of self-transformation and a new direction been chosen, or stumbled into. It is to Schulberg's credit that both instinct and conscious choice have led him to find such a sharply defined moment. The next thing we see, at the start of the Middle, or Act 2, is Terry trying to confess to Father Barry, the man determined to bring down Johnny Friendly . . . .

NECESSARY AND PROBABLE, AND OTHER MATTERS

This is a good place to reflect. The most trying element for contemporary student writers that Aristotle reviews in his *Poetics* is the joint notion of necessary and probable (Aristotle 66, 82). We easily grasp that a dramatic action should have a cause-and-effect sequence, but less easily that the action should be necessary, and what is necessary should also be probable. We tend to observe this in the breach, in the sense that we will grant a particular premise (a technologically advanced civilization in another galaxy long ago, as in *Star Wars*) that may have no real probability or credibility at all, and then weigh necessity and probability within that premise. We even expect some genres, like horror movies, or farce, to move from the marginally credible to the wholly implausible, and will accept that if each step looks causative or at least follows conventional expectation within a given genre. But the stories we most highly praise hit us as necessary and probable without qualification.

On The Waterfront upholds an uncompromised version of necessary and probable, resulting in a powerful sense of verisimilitude. That is an illusion, of course, for in life much is unnecessary and improbable, yet probability and necessity give imagined stories this sense of ultrareality. From the summary of Act 1 above we see those standards being maintained from the start. Terry quite probably is sent to call out Joey. He is Joey's friend, a fellow pigeon keeper, and although a hanger-on of the Friendly crowd, not one of its prime active thugs, like Sonny. It's also necessary: Johnny Friendly can't have somebody rat on him. Similar justifications hold when Charley is sent to discipline Terry in Act 2. Charley is Terry's brother, and it is long established they have close feelings for each other: who better to deal with Terry? Charley is horrified at having to cause Terry's death if he doesn't comply, as we would be, and in fact can't bring himself to do so, which is also quite probable. He lets Terry go and pays the price, both probable and necessary, as Johnny Friendly can't let disloyalty go unpunished.

The same verisimilitude applies in Act 3 as Terry testifies. Father Barry gives us the underpinnings that make probable Terry's choice to testify against Johnny Friendly instead of shooting him: it is obviously necessary that Terry act after Charley's murder. It is equally probable that Terry is ostracized after he testifies, so he discovers testifying isn't the way to bring Johnny Friendly down. Johnny Friendly must be directly confronted, not shot but out-countenanced, as happens climactically.

Similarly it is clearly reasonable for Edie to be around: she's not in school just now and she obviously wants vengeance for her brother. Pop naturally wants to send her back to the nuns. That she and Terry connect is inevitable the moment we see the two of them together, he full of inchoate wants, she pure as only the inexperienced can be, with the promise of a renewed life implicit in their attraction. Love itself we understand to be a force, and will believe its outcome if we see it act passionately, and their hunger for each other is amply dramatized. Terry's breaking the door down to see her in Act 2 is a screen classic.

We can go through the same arc with all the characters and events: Father Barry, Johnny Friendly, Charley, Pop, and the longshoremen waiting on the outcome of Terry's final confrontation with Johnny Friendly. The fact that the screenplay so powerfully supports our perception of its actions as necessary and probable goes a long way toward persuading us, first through feeling, then through reflection, that it is true and real, as we come to feel *Hamlet* is true and real, or *The Godfather*, however much a product of the imagination, however far removed from a precise historical/biographical existence. Truth is not just a quality of fact, but of imagination. Schulberg imagines truly.

STRUCTURE IS MEANING IS STRUCTURE

We need now to attend to the relation between structure and meaning touched on earlier. We have been examining them simultaneously all along. Yet we are too used to separating these elements analytically. A story has a theme, we say, and a structure (Acts 1–3, and so on). Nothing could be farther from the truth. Just as dramatic action really only exists when it exists in us through our immediate identification with the characters, structure and meaning are labels we use analytically to speak of our experience. But structure is the expression of meaning: meaning is what is communicated by structure. In good writing everything tends to bear, we say, but in great writing everything bears absolutely – or as much as that is possible where human effort is involved! By Act 3, in effective drama, this relationship between structure and meaning becomes transparent.

Look again at Act 1. Joey is called out and killed. That is not just vivid action, but communicates to us immediately before Joey falls through the use of the pigeon motif that a betrayer is going to be killed. We no sooner see who is doing the killing than we know the bad guys are out to maintain an evil status quo. Before we leave that piece of action, we see Terry's unhappiness differentiate him from the bad guys whose company he keeps. From that moment any appearance of conscience is acceptable, if not inevitable, in Terry.

In other words, the events are organized to communicate swiftly a set of meanings, just as less conventionally we could say the meanings are swiftly communicated in a sequence of events chosen for their thematic nature. Edie demands help from Father Barry (the good guys show up), then Johnny Friendly demonstrates his ruthlessness and fobs off Terry with the cushy job (the hero can be bought, or isn't himself yet). Glover shows up for the Crime Commission on the docks to make the investigation underway manifest, while we see Terry, touched by conscience over Edie's identity, give the marker to her that lets Pop work. Father Barry appeals to the longshoremen to stand up to Johnny Friendly, which Terry is dismissive of, but hears nonetheless while in the Church (there's an alternative for the courageous and honest). He rescues Edie from Johnny Friendly's ambush of the longshoremen – the start of a long sequence in which they fall in love and directly clash over moral systems: whether to help one another or to look out for oneself. Even their romance is thematic.

By the time Johnny Friendly demands Terry stop seeing Edie we know that means: don't think of looking out for anyone but yourself.

For Terry then to intervene on Father Barry's behalf in the hold after Dugan is killed, or to see Edie after, is not just action motivated by spur-of-the-moment events, but thematically communicative, cumulative, and decisive behavior. We know Terry will defy Johnny Friendly when the first Act thus ends, and that this means accepting and acting on his conscience, for we must, after all, look out for each other if we are to look out for ourselves. Otherwise, as Edie says, we are just animals. Terry can no longer go on being a bum, while being a bum is a result of his past. That, too, then, will have to be undone.

We don't know how: we're in suspense. Suspense in writing of this quality means suspense over meaning. Whatever is done we know will have different meanings, some good (desirable), some bad (undesirable). Urgent writing creates its own moral universe, and when that writing seems necessary and probable we identify with that universe. The meanings that emerge and are defined from the conflict are defining for *us* through our identification with the hero/heroine.

Structure, when effective, is simultaneously this combination of events following a cause-and-effect chain we experience as more or less necessary and probable, and a set of ever-more defined meanings. All action in good writing carries this kind of symbolic weight. The choices looming so much more strongly at the end of Act 1 were merely incipient at its beginning, and what marks the transition from Act 1 to 2 is this simultaneous sense of the action shifting decisively, and the meaning of the action moving toward a new sense of definition at odds with the "norm," the false modus vivendi, we experience at a story's start.

ON THE WATERFRONT: ACT 2

Now we can understand Act 2. Development is traditionally harder than Beginnings and Ends; the colloquial history of stage and film productions is full of stories of writers harassed by actors, directors, and producers to get the middle of the story right, or else. "Or else" in film usually means bringing in another writer: in theatre, an out-of-town hotel window may simply be opened as an option for a playwright to drive home the necessity of going back to his or her room and trying yet again. It never does good to get too reverential about these matters, to forget, if you will, that Shakespeare had inky hands. We may end thinking a genius has been at work, but we shouldn't forget the way the mundane and inspired must work together.

This makes Schulberg's achievement in Act 2 one of those remarkable feats that sometimes survive every obstacle and find their way permanently into our imagination. The groundwork laid so carefully in the first act now flowers with memorable concision and definition. Immediately Terry confesses his role in Joey Doyle's death to Father Barry, who in turn immediately makes him confess the same to Edie in the imaginatively written and filmed scene of Terry gesticulating to Edie while his words are largely drowned out by a liner's whistle, followed by Edie running from him in horror. We have moved into the realm in a story where action alone in some decisive moments can now carry meaning more powerfully than words: nothing is more expressive of the overwhelming nature of Terry's confession on Edie than this obliterating blast of sound and her flight.

Terry retreats to his rooftop, where Jimmy is horrified at the thought he might talk. In the script, when Glover shows up he offers to lie for Terry that he is out. That's no longer possible.

TERRY
But I ain't out. I'm in. I'm in. Who's lying to who?

(Schulberg 93)

We don't need the line in the film, where it is omitted: its sense is already implicit in Terry's behavior. He has confessed to Father Barry and Edie, and now he talks with Glover instead of dismissing him with a sneer again. Terry is already unable to escape his conscience, or responsibility, or the demands of the full self: he can't kid himself that these can be avoided and have anything resembling a full life. This is the truth the imagination brings us to *in drama*. Glover continues the same deft, casual approach to Terry he has shown on the docks and in the bar in Act 1, and elicits from him the overt recitation of the fight with Wilson years ago that turned him down the path to being a bum, now understood as a man wholly false to himself: a "mutt," if you will, like the character Mutt. It is anguishing for Terry to remember this. In the script he says:

TERRY

Yeah. My own blood – and they sell me out for a lousy bet – I had it
in me to hit the top and –
> (sighs)

Boy, if I wanted to, the things I could tell you about them guys –
> (then catches himself and pauses)

(Schulberg 94–95)

In the film he just indicates some friends had a bet on. The full revelation of Charley's role in betraying him is left to the scene between
Terry and Charley in the taxi for maximum dramatic effect. Glover,
however, understands Terry took a dive. Terry is in an impossible
situation, caught up in his brother and Johnny Friendly's net and
affection, but at the cost of maintaining self-betrayal. No wonder he
doesn't know what to do. But we now know the importance of what
went wrong in the past, and the way it is intimately bound up with
Terry's present state.

This has a deep pull on us through our intuition of the importance
of what has happened to ourselves, and the equal intuition of the
extreme difficulty of undoing what must be undone even if we see
our life is based on a bad choice.

Immediately the action turns to Johnny Friendly, alarmed over
Terry's behavior, who makes it clear to Charley he must deal with his
brother, or Terry will have to die – be delivered to Gerry G. for that
purpose by Charley himself. No sooner has the connection of past
and present come into critical view, with the price of Terry's choice,
than he is to be given no time to sort things out. Unlike the first act,
things are moving at an electric pace. This is no reflection on the
first act: all first acts have the burden of building and populating a
particular world with characters we must first meet, then see in difficulties from which the hero can only slowly stumble clear. Second
acts are always beneficiaries of the groundwork laid, although not every writer can see fully what has to be achieved in the development
that follows.

Agonized, Charley and Terry meet in one of the most famous scenes
in cinema. The issues are drawn sharply: Terry can have a bigger
stake in the future in Johnny Friendly's organization, but at the price
of keeping his mouth shut. Conscience has to be quelled. Johnny

6. One of the most famous scenes in cinema. Charley [Rod Steiger] breaks with the past and lets Terry go. (Copyright Columbia Pictures Corp., 1959. Courtesy of the Museum of Modern Art Film Stills Archive)

Friendly has taken on quasi-mythical overtones, the ogre or giant or dragon who guards the treasure a hero has to find, here the mature mind governed by morality and fidelity to self. Terry can't accept: what he wants is a space to think these issues out for himself. Why does Charley let him go? As Charley sits back in defeat over his attempt to bribe Terry, memory turns inevitably to Terry's lost moment of greatness in the fight he was forced to lose in the past. That is *the* open wound, and can never be ignored for long: the past in the fundamental story pattern is alive and unresolved. That memory provokes Terry's great outburst, quoted earlier, and the anguished reminder to Charley of who was the real betrayer: "It was you, Charley" (Schulberg 104). Just as right now it is Charley betraying him again by taking him to Gerry G. So Charley breaks with the past from guilt and lets Terry go, in the film giving him the gun that in the script he takes from a pawnshop.

The past, in short, while unresolved is never "past." We keep reliving it in one guise or another, and renewing our self-betrayal. Until resolved, this past remains all there is, past, present, and future. That is the full, terrible burden of the false modus vivendi the hero lives at a drama's start.

In desperation, Terry breaks in to see Edie: she has been the avenue to his conscience from the beginning like a Jungian anima figure, or in a Campbellian sense the inevitable bride, union with whom will represent a making whole of the psyche (Jung 188–211 and Campbell 109–120).[2] This scene, too, lives on in the imagination as he grabs her, insists on her love, and kisses her into submission. Because of these larger associations, not thought but felt, as is the way at first, always, in drama, the scene is not melodrama, or an absurd, outdated exercise in machismo that our feminist-colored perceptions reject. We sense instead the presence of a larger meaning, the guilty man loved by the sister of the man he helped kill, who with her help is seeking the path of self-assertion that is also one of atonement.

They are allowed no more than this desperate embrace before Terry is called out, as was Joey, and finds Charley dangling from a long-shoreman's hook (in the film) or propped against a lamp post (script). What can he do? He has to take on Johnny Friendly. Now the end is in sight that was implicit from the start. Terry cannot become whole unless Johnny Friendly is broken: Johnny Friendly can only remain on top if Terry is kept down. When Terry sees this, *we* see it, and feel the inevitability of what the action has been building toward. But the path won't be straight: Father Barry intervenes, and persuades Terry to testify to the Crime Commission as the real way of undoing Johnny Friendly. He's wrong, which, among other things, is why this story isn't topically dated. His being wrong, however, is all-important.

THE HANDLING OF THE CRISIS

This is another good place to pause. We are at the end of Act 2, in the Crisis.[3] What is the Crisis? Why is this one so unusual?

Typically Act 2 ends with the failure of the hero's resolve (chosen or stumbled into) at the end of the first act: there is always a direct link between the Act 1 turning point and the Crisis. Here, Terry's effort to take responsibility for himself, to exercise his conscience, clearly stares failure in the face. His life is in danger; his brother has been killed; even Edie wilts under the pressure: "Terry, let's go away" she pleads when he finds Charley (Schulberg 112).

> EDIE
> (hysterically)
> I mean it, let's get away from here, first Joey then Nolan, now Charley – and any minute....
> (stares at him, almost saying "you.")
> ...I'm frightened – I'm frightened.

Terry seems not to hear. There are tears in his eyes but fury in his voice as he mutters to himself.

> TERRY
> I'll take it out of their skulls.

> EDIE
> I don't want to see you killed. I want to live with you. Live with you. Any place it's safe to walk the streets without...

> TERRY
> (in a terrible mutter to himself)
> I'll take it out of their skulls.

He rises, in a dangerous, animal rage.

> (Schulberg 113)

There is the problem: for the transformation by conscience to be made, Terry has to do it as a human being: how manage that in an "animal rage"? Instead of ending with him in that state, Schulberg runs the Act 2 Crisis into the missed confrontation with Johnny Friendly where Father Barry intervenes and persuades Terry to testify instead as the really effective way to bring him down. No one knows, of course, that Father Barry is wrong: he seems right, and introduces in the midst of the profundity of despair typical of the Crisis a hope that the way to resolve the Crisis positively and without bloodshed is at hand.

Contrast the handling of the Crisis in Kieslowski and Piesiewicz's *Blue* as Julie confronts Olivier and is forced to realize that her intention of not being involved at all with life, announced at the start of Act 2, cannot be maintained. In *High Noon* Kane must watch his wife and mistress ride past him out of town, and then begin the long walk toward the final shootout in total isolation, all efforts to find help having come to nothing. Princess Leia makes Luke and Han Solo in Lucas' *Star Wars* realize they have not escaped the Death Star but have been allowed to leave so they can be tracked, while Luke is distraught over Obi Won's death: he had joined forces decisively with him at the turning point of Act 1. Book and Rachel in *Witness* are found by the corrupt police, which puts an end to their safety and Book's attempt to find a solution of his own for his problems which he initiated by his flight at the end of Act 1. This is typical: the Act 2 Crisis ends in apparent or actual failure of the resolve undertaken at the start of the first act, whatever its nature.

But as we look back over the second act in *On The Waterfront* we can see how tightly written it is, how clearly the past has connected with the present, and how powerfully the need for a human, not animal, solution is underscored by this tilting of the Crisis toward hope through Father Barry's intervention. It is easy to imagine a more violent resolution, a gunfight, an action sequence all too common in films, even some good ones. By the same token we can imagine how easy it would have been to reach a less profound insight into what is needed here. However current events may have weighed on Schulberg's mind, in the Crisis he is in the grip of the action, answering to its inner life, and plotting a profounder victory for Terry through the hope Father Barry introduces than simply killing the ogre.

ON THE WATERFRONT: ACT 3

That hope is instantly disposed of at the start of Act 3. Terry testifies, but at the cost of becoming what he tends, a pigeon. He is ostracized: even the police think of him as a betrayer.

TERRY
Trailing me like that, you make me feel like a canary.
FIRST COP
(grinning)

Well?

(Schulberg 124)

Though we have seen a quick scene where a mobster declines to take further calls from Johnny Friendly, Friendly is still in control on the docks, his thugs are still in power. Testifying has not been enough. Even Jimmy has turned against Terry, killing all his pigeons – the inevitable fate for a pigeon like Terry, too. There can be no easy fix, no simple topical solution. A deeper solution is needed. Yet, through the same action, Terry no longer has a gun. In fact, he has moved past that level of action by testifying.

What is he to do? Form and content are here entirely transparent, as they become in serious and successful writing in Act 3, in the Climax. *What is he to do*? Terry puts on Joey's jacket *now* and goes down to the docks with his longshoreman's hook simply to get his rights. He is going to claim all that is his, by right: all we have discussed hangs on that simple demand.

Inevitably, he is not chosen for work. But the longshoremen are uncertain, and wait – Terry may have testified against Johnny Friendly, which is good, but that was also ratting – and he's still one of *them*. *What is he to do*? If we were to tell someone who has never seen the film that the Climax turns on an argument about the past, he or she might not think that particularly inviting or dramatic. But from what has followed before, we now see how it is everything. Terry does the only thing he can: he takes the past, and the meaning given the past, from Johnny Friendly. That is the treasure Johnny Friendly has been hoarding. Terry gives the past *his* meaning by taking it for his own. His meaning affirms the rightness of his actions against Johnny Friendly, the exercise of conscience, the primacy of truth in our relations with one another if we are to be more than animals. As he confronts Johnny Friendly, he says

TERRY
(voice rising defiantly)

I'm glad what I done today, see? You give it to Joey, you give it to Dugan, you give it to Charley who was one of your own. You thought you was God Almighty instead of a cheap – conniving – good-for-nothing bum! So I'm glad what I done – you hear me? – glad what I done!

JOHNNY
(coldly)

You ratted on us, Terry.

7. Johnny Friendly [Lee J. Cobb] and Terry in their final confrontation. "You ratted on us, Terry." (Courtesy of the Museum of Modern Art Film Stills Archive)

> TERRY
> (aware of fellow longshoremen anxiously watching the duel)
> From where you stand, maybe. But I'm standing over here now. I was rattin' on myself all them years and didn't know it, helpin' punks like you against people like Pop and Dugan an'...
>
> (Schulberg 132)

When he flings himself on Johnny Friendly when challenged, Luke observes, "That kid fights like he useta!," that is, before he took the all-important dive and still hoped to be somebody (Schulberg 133). He has recaptured his unfallen self: the "fight" with Johnny Friendly is a replay of the fight with Wilson, and carries the burden of Terry's becoming "somebody" again, as the scene with Charley in the taxi was a replay of Charley's past betrayal. This fight has become the physical symbol of the screenplay's meaning, boiled down to one exchange of blows. When Terry is overwhelmed by the thugs, the longshoremen, who sense what is riding on the contest, wait. Father Barry gets Terry on his feet again by again calling on the past: "Johnny Friendly is layin' odds you won't get up" (Schulberg 137). In the final, famous image of the film Terry leads the men to work, and to everything he now represents, something far more than simply a clean union. Johnny Friendly has become the bum, the punk, the "good-for-nothing" (Schulberg 132). There has been a complete transvaluation of meaning and stature, a profound assertion of the connection between selfhood, conscience, and truth. Terry is a hero on a high level: the wisdom he has learned and imposed is ethical, not violent; metaphysical, not of the streets, although paradoxically this wisdom must live in the streets in our mundane lives if it is to live anywhere at all.

CHARACTER, SUFFERING, AND EXPIATION

Terry isn't the only character transformed by this convergence of past and present: all are dragged along in Terry's wake or important for helping him to the next stage in his transformation.

The simplest to see this in is Pop. He's let Johnny Friendly push him around all his life, to the extent his only reaction to his son's death is to try and make Edie leave when he sees her with Terry. The Terry he sees is the Terry of the false modus vivendi; of course he wants Edie to go. But he doesn't tell even Edie Terry's role in Joey's death – the falseness of all their lives has Pop deaf and dumb within his own family. We see little of him as a figure of any consequence after the early scenes, although he is the recipient of Terry's charity after the fight on the docks. Yet Pop has a one big act reserved for him in the Climax: it is he who after witnessing Terry's beating by Johnny Friendly's thugs pushes Johnny Friendly into the water.

POP
(sounding more sad than angry)

All my life you pushed me around.
Suddenly he shoves Johnny off the ramp into the water scummy with oil slick and riverbank debris.

JOHNNY IN WATER

Cursing.

POP AND LONGSHOREMEN

Cheering Johnny Friendly's humiliation.

(Schulberg 137)

The weakest of the longshoremen has acted. The others jeer. Johnny Friendly is finished before Terry is on his feet, because Terry has gone down to his stronghold and paid the price for his past association. As Johnny Friendly says as he heads toward Pop and the longshoremen,

JOHNNY FRIENDLY

You want 'im? (as he goes) You can have 'im. The little rat's Yours.

(Schulberg 135)

Now the longshoremen can accept Terry. *Now* Father Barry and Edie get Terry on his feet to lead them.

Edie is changed just as profoundly by Terry's transformation, as we have seen, although in her case her love turns her into a blind supporter of Terry once he turns on Johnny Friendly, one willing to flee before Terry's work is done for fear of its consequences to him. Her baton, so to speak, is passed on to Father Barry, who continues crucial throughout. Father Barry misguides Terry, in several senses. It is also entirely probable and necessary that Father Barry act in the way he does, as a churchman. He understands the political and topical stakes in play. He also realizes that Terry's transformation has to be carried through on his own, and so stops Edie from helping Terry walk up the ramp to lead the longshoremen to work. By the End Father Barry understands the profound connection between past and present – he uses the dive against Wilson after Terry is beaten to get him up again.

FATHER BARRY

Johnny Friendly is layin' odds that you won't get up.

JOHNNY

(in background)

Come on, you guys.

Friendly's voice acts as a prod on Terry.

TERRY

(dazed)

Get me on my feet.

(Schulberg 137–8)

8. At the End, with prodding from Father Barry, Terry walks up the ramp alone to lead the longshoremen to work. "Terry won't go down again." (Courtesy of the Museum of Modern Art Film Stills Archive)

Terry won't go down again. Father Barry has discovered too that his work can't be completed unless Terry completes his transformation from bum to hero.

This is the implication of drama's fundamental story pattern. The false modus vivendi that exists at the start of the drama for the hero extends to all the characters. No one can be on true ground until the hero is. Character development turns out to be expressive of the identity between structure and meaning. As we have seen with Pop and Father Barry, they can neither act in the former case, nor carry through their own intentions in the latter, except as these are subsumed into and made possible by the hero's development.

We have already seen how Johnny Friendly and Charley have been touched and transformed in this process, but a few more words are due Schulberg's handling of Terry. Schulberg moves Terry onto an archetypal plane by making him such a weak, if troubled character at the beginning, and one so changed in a personal, existential sense at the end, written with the great sensitivity and force to which

Brando gave such a memorable screen embodiment. Literature and film are full of examples of men either thought of poorly or without proper respect who are stripped to their own resources and then triumph against almost impossible odds. Terry is a powerful example of such a character. A writer doesn't have to know he is writing archetypally: more often, that power is gained through force of writing. Self-conscious attempts to write archetypally are suspect; Lucas' involvement with Joseph Campbell in the first three *Star Wars* films is a rare exception.

The emergence of such a character touches a profound chord in ourselves, who are not heroes, but dream of the possibility. Such a character also lends a luster not otherwise available to all those around him. But we shouldn't forget the need for the hero to suffer. A terrible price has to be expiated for having accommodated a false modus vivendi and participated in evil. It is because they sense this price hasn't been paid that the longshoremen won't follow Terry at first in the End. Horrified, they watch Johnny Friendly's thugs overwhelm Terry, but won't intervene. Terry has to pay by suffering, and takes a savage beating. He can't even tell if he's on his feet when Father Barry helps him up.

TERRY
(continued)

Am I on my feet?

(Schulberg 138)

The longshoremen can only follow Terry if he survives the punishment that frees him from Johnny Friendly – who is literally "all wet." Johnny Friendly has become the rat, the bum, a man with no place in the new order only Terry could create through realizing his own promise.

The private conflicts of the greatest characters, in the greatest dramas, always become public and defining in their resolution for all around them.

END THOUGHTS AND THE NEW BEGINNING

I wanted to bring out this essential identity between structure and meaning and their relation to character in *On The Waterfront* because

Schulberg's success is rooted in that fusion and the vision he has used to communicate that fusion irrespective of topical or biographical references. The story of past and present conflict and their transformation in a particular story is the dramatic action. This is as it should be. We may remember those individuals photographing license plates at the start of *The Godfather*, with the obvious reference to the efforts to keep the mob under surveillance, but our focus is wholly on the personal dimensions of the story. Whatever topical biographical or political references there may be in *Hamlet* are not apparent to us, while the unhappiness of the Athenians with *The Trojan War* of Euripides with what they took to be criticism of their own behavior in the Peloponnesian War is lost on us, who see only the greatness of that drama's antiwar stance.

Contemporary viewers or even those with specialized interests, like graduate screenwriting students, find that this personal story of Terry's struggle to follow the dictates of his conscience and set right the wrongs of his past far outweighs whether Schulberg and Kazan "ratted" on their friends before the House Un-American Committee, or whether the film can be seen in that light as a justification of "ratting." Neither knowledge nor ignorance of this aspect influences the impact and memorability of the film for the contemporary viewer. The same is true of the possible biographical bases for some of the characters or the topicality of the Crime Commission.

This is not dismissive of these elements. Topical and biographical elements are relevant to the study of any drama when we want to understand how a dramatist's experience is transformed in a given text. We can never know too much if we want to understand the genesis of a story in its own time or place, or understand the workings of creativity. Yet vanity has its moment of ultimate deflation when we realize that a good drama would still be experienced as a good drama if we knew nothing of the writer or his times. The endless efforts to understand Shakespeare's life, to affirm his authorship, to deny his authorship, to prove this philosophical position or that, should keep any critic or dramatist humble about the importance of his views or private life. It is the work that counts, however we hunger to know all we can about a writer able to create something that survives the erosion of time and bodily death.

Dramas become great in our minds because they speak deeply to our hearts. Dramas are able to speak deeply to our hearts because of the power of the writer's imagination in handling the *action* – the simultaneous transformation of immediate conflict and past trauma into the new beginning we have traced here. The final element of *On The Waterfront's* success is how strongly it implies the nature of that new beginning, part five of the fundamental story pattern. It is a part we almost never investigate (and which sequels almost never live up to), but which we need to see open before us at the end of a drama because this new beginning is at once the true end of a story and the beginning of a new one, at once hopeful and bringing a sense of the community and continuity of our lives which the main action of the drama so long seemed to threaten. We live in hope, and *On The Waterfront* propels us there through its world, however Johnny Friendly screams "I'll be back" (Schulberg 140). The dangers we and Terry must confront and overcome are always there, always waiting, again, for their moment.

NOTES

1   See Aristotle 47, 79–80, 106 and Brustein 35–84. Aristotle talks of a tragic deed that is usually in the past, whether the murder of his father by Oedipus or the sacrifice of a daughter by Agamemnon. His remarks on Homer and Sophocles make clear his awareness that while a dramatic action had to be contained immediately within the Beginning, Middle, and End, it did indeed exist within the context of a larger story, as Homer's *Iliad* exists within the framework of the nine-year siege of Troy and evokes that story while concentrating on the anger of Achilles, and Sophocles' *Oedipus Rex* is comprehensible only within the context of the larger story of Oedipus' attempt to escape the prophecy he would marry his mother and murder his father and the lifetime of actions accordingly taken.

    Ibsen, who founded our contemporary style of dramatic writing that film absorbed once it learned to speak, and in drama, spoke of a typical structure however varied where there is some significant event in the past with which the hero/heroine must eventually deal. Nora has lied about how she obtained a loan to save her husband's life in the past in *A Doll's House*, and, in fact, counterfeited her father's signature, which makes her vulnerable to Krogstad's blackmail attempts when Nora's husband fires him.

    The same pattern appears, for example, in *Star Wars* where all that Luke has to learn about his father, the emperor, and just about everything else is already in the past. Even in the initial segment of the saga, the corruption of the Senator who will become the emperor, and his training of an opponent to the Jedi knights, are left to the past. This pattern is omnipresent whether we are dealing with popular drama or drama with greater ambition.

2   Jung's remarks on the anima are spread throughout his works: this reference gives a good overview of his views. The anima, in general, being the male opposite, compensates for male one-sidedness, as Edie does almost programmatically with the opposition of her altruism to Terry's cynicism. As naturally she is the guide toward the wholeness referenced below in Campbell. This is not to imply a deliberate knowledge or use of Jungian concepts by Schulberg: the fact that his conception so unself-consciously falls into this pattern shows instead the power of his writing and indicates something of its grip on us.

3   When "Crisis" is capitalized, *the* crisis at the end of the Middle, or Act 2, is referred to; the "Climax" refers to the Act 3 climax.

4 An Actor Prepares

Harold Clurman met Lee Strasberg in New York in 1925. They were the same age, 24, and young actors attached to the Theatre Guild. Elia Kazan was only 16, still at New Rochelle High School. Movies then were silent, and acting in America was whatever actors chose to do and could make work. There was little sense of doctrine or aesthetic necessity – of what actors should do, for truth's sake. But among young Americans, anxious to win respect for their field of work, acting and theatre were being talked about as never before. So that meeting in 1925 began an argument – never settled – but vital to any consideration of *On the Waterfront*. And for the purposes of this essay we start with three basic propositions about that film – not necessarily reconcilable: 1) that it is the passionate expression of the man who conceived it, writer Budd Schulberg; 2) that it is an outstanding example of American ensemble acting; and 3) that it is also the passionate expression of its director, who may have been the most needy actor in the company. For the essential actor or protagonist on *Waterfront* was less Marlon Brando than Elia Kazan.

This is how Clurman recalled his developing relationship with Strasberg:

> We were drawn together by our common dissatisfactions, our still unshaped ideals. Strasberg talked mostly about acting, upon which he seemed as concentrated as a jeweler over the inner mechanism of a watch. I never dreamed that there was that much to it. I had a broad background in the arts generally, and my complaint was against

the nature of most plays: their thinness, lack of depth, eloquence, substantial theme. It didn't matter so much that a play was "well done"; what mattered was what was being done.

No, no, Strasberg argued with astonishing heat and pedagogic finesse, the manner in which a play is done is in itself a content. What I was talking about was literature, what he was interested in was theatre. How much acting is of great quality? I countered. Are we to wait around seeing agreeable mumming in the hope that every once in a while a performance will turn up that will justify so many stupid or negligible plays? I didn't understand, Strasberg retorted when I thought I had him stopped – and the debate continued for hours, afternoons, weeks (11).

In 1925, the best recent American plays were O'Neill's *Desire Under the Elms* (in which Walter Huston had played the father), and Sidney Howard's *They Knew What They Wanted* (with Richard Bennett and Glenn Anders as the male leads). Alfred Lunt and Lynn Fontanne had just had their first hit in *The Guardsman*. Only two years before, John Barrymore's *Hamlet* – done when he was 41 – had been a Broadway sensation. Jed Harris had recently started to work as a director – he would have hit after hit in the late twenties with *Broadway*, *Coquette*, *The Royal Family* and *The Front Page*. No play had yet opened by Sidney Kingsley, Clifford Odets, or Lillian Hellman. Orson Welles was 10. Eva Le Gallienne had begun a revival of Ibsen plays. Noel Coward's *The Vortex* had just opened, with Coward playing the lead. Elia Kazan was sneaking into the movies, his passion, without paying. The kid born in Constantinople wanted "to be an American" – to be Kazan instead of Kazanjioglou; and to do "Just the most ordinary, the most common, and the most precious things" (Kazan, *A Life* 29).

Strasberg's obsession with "the manner in which a play was done" was a rejection of English attitudes to production. Instead, he sought a new realism and a psychological authenticity in (and within) acting. It was as if people behaving naturally on stage might raise the level of accuracy or truthfulness in a play. That naturalness was not just individual; it affected the ensemble – the way people were together and the ideas they held in common. Born in Austria, Strasberg had come to America at the age of nine, and had later joined the American Laboratory Theatre. That had been the creation of Richard Boleslawsky, a Pole who had studied under Konstantin Stanislavsky with the Moscow Arts Theatre, returned to Poland in 1919 (to fight against the Bolsheviks), and had then gone to Germany and America to act and direct. His partner was Maria Ouspenskaya, Russian, an actress, who had toured America with the Moscow Arts Theatre in 1922–3, and had elected to stay on.

Strasberg knew Stanislavsky very well – the Russian's book, *My Life in Art*, had been translated into English in 1924, and the recent tour had excited admiration for the Moscow Arts' level of ensemble naturalism – the feeling that one was witnessing not just one play, but a time and a place and a world from which the play was emerging like a new plant. Stanislavsky was at war with the tradition of stylish, or stylized, impersonation based upon sound stagecraft more than inner inquiry. He was interested in a deeper exploration of motivation, need, desire, and fear in a character – the subtext – and in the kind of ensemble process in which all the players were asking the same kind of questions, bound by similar rules. Strasberg brought something else to this "method" – a psychoanalytic probing in which the personality of the actor himself might be mined for a character's inscape. Thus, casting was all the more reliable if a company director knew his players well enough to have unearthed their own personal problems. If he could then harness those traumas to certain roles, not only was a play enriched, but the director began to assume the role of personal teacher or analyst to the actors. They came to depend on him – and thus, his inner need for authority was catered to.

In the late twenties and early thirties, as a group of actors began to gather around Clurman and Strasberg, so Clurman observed the way Strasberg would employ "sense or affective memory" as a training technique – not so much in rehearsal for a specific play, but as part of the overall fitness required in an actor: indeed, it was a way of gaining access to one's own emotions and summing them up for a character:

> Strasberg was a fanatic on the subject of true emotion. Everything was secondary to it. He sought it with the patience of an inquisitor, he was outraged by trick substitutes, and when he had succeeded in stimulating it, he husbanded it, and protected it. Here was something new to most of the actors, something basic, or something almost holy. It was revelation in the theatre; and Strasberg was its prophet.
>
> (Clurman 44–5)

But it's intriguing to note that Strasberg was seldom himself very effective as either actor or director. When Clurman saw him in Pirandello's *Right You Are If You Think You Are*, he was impressed by Strasberg's intelligence. But reckoned he was not an actor. Kazan found him remote, but noted the religious authority he had with actors as a teacher, an analyst, a rehearser and a co-preparer. Strasberg reached actors in their own lives, but he was not as successful in turning that advantage into stage magic. There was always some feeling that as a director Strasberg was more devoted to the principles of his method than to the play at hand.

Nevertheless, when the Group Theatre was formed in 1931 by Clurman, Strasberg, and Cheryl Crawford, there was little doubt about Strasberg's ideological and pedagogic eminence. A year later, having graduated from Williams College, Elia Kazan joined the Group, at first as an apprentice, and felt the way in which fear as well as respect was at work in Strasberg's manner.

> He carried with him the aura of a prophet, a magician, a witch doctor, a psychoanalyst, and a feared father of a Jewish home. He was the center of the camp's activities that summer, the core of the vortex. Everything in camp revolved around him. Preparing to direct the play that was to open the coming season, as he had the three plays of the season before, he would also give the basic instruction in acting, laying down the principles of the art by which the Group worked, the guide to their artistic training. He was the force that held the thirty-odd members of the theatre together, made them "permanent." He did this not only by his superior knowledge but by the threat of his anger.
>
> (Kazan, *A Life* 61)

The first works by the Group Theatre were hailed for their novel truth in acting – and this was sometimes taken as a model for America. But it's worth observing several other forces in the culture that encouraged it, and which made fertile ground for Strasberg's teaching.

In prose fiction, Ernest Hemingway had signaled a more naturalistic way of writing and delivering dialogue. It was, allegedly, closer to the way ordinary, hard people thought and felt – it was a deliberate departure from literariness, with a nearly political undertone.

Such talk, and such "common" characters could be seen in the stories of *In Our Time* (1924), *The Sun Also Rises* (1926) and *A Farewell to Arms* (1929). Closer and later inspection suggested that Hemingway's terseness could be as mannered as much more flowery writing. But the immediate attention to common speech was enormous.

It was in the same period, and thanks in large part to Louis Armstrong's recordings with the Hot Seven, that jazz became a serious influence on the artistic classes in America. And jazz had a very striking lesson for anyone interested in Strasberg's location of inner emotion. For within the framework of a set tune, a "classic" song, the musicians were encouraged to play solos that might be elaborate, improvisational departures from the melody (while keeping its chord progression). Over the last seventy years or so, there have been many examples of actors who loved jazz, and who found lessons and inspiration in it. And at the very same time, Strasberg was encouraging actors in rehearsal so to know the text that they could embark on improvs derived from it, and to be faithful to it, in which their sense memories unfolded.

There's another lesson that may have been picked up from Armstrong. He was a singer as well as a trumpet player, and in his "scat" vocal improvisations, he would turn lyrics into pure sound. This is not far from the actor's discovery of an array of sounds – sighs, groans, exclamations – that may be added to the strict text of a play, or used as replacement. And Strasberg was by no means a scrupulous textualist. He did not mind changes or departures. "Words are decorations on the hem of the skirt of action," he would say, quoting Meyerhold (Kazan, *A Life* 66). In other words, the actor might legitimately adapt the text, or break it up with hesitations, sighs, or scat – all the passing noises of something less than coherence – so that his or her emotion came out more faithfully.

Writers have not always appreciated this. Audiences have been equally puzzled if they could not hear or understand, or if the pace of a scene became as slow and self-concerned as the actor's neurosis. Those are real dangers in living theatre; they risk being mannerism in the movies. But the advantages are also clear – that an actor might seem to be thinking of what to say (like a real person), instead of reciting a learned text.

All of these things were enhanced by a far greater novelty, one that had an especially exciting allure for actors – talking pictures. The medium began to talk, in 1927, with *The Jazz Singer*. The talk was crude, as maudlin as Al Jolson. For a few years, the arrival of talk had the further effect of hobbling the camera. Still, by 1930, it was plain that there could only be talking pictures. That ensured a new type of movie writing, just as it drew a generation of Broadway actors to Hollywood – including Cagney, Bogart, Spencer Tracy, Paul Muni, Edward G. Robinson, Cary Grant, and Franchot Tone (who was persuaded to give up the Group Theatre for pictures).

Within a few years it was evident that talkies had promoted a new naturalism. The close-ups of the talking, and above all of the listening face, were revealed as key shots. Actors could be silent in a way not possible in silent films. Silence in silent films required titles. But in talkies you could see the inward acting that preferred to say nothing. You could believe you were thinking the character's thoughts. It was an astonishing and unexpected manifesto of what Strasberg had been seeking. And actors went to the movies – and dreamed of doing pictures.

So the Group Theater began its work in 1931, with Paul Green's *The House of Connelly*, an attempt to examine how slavery had debased the great southern families. It was directed by Strasberg and Cheryl Crawford (with Strasberg seeming to be in charge), and its leading players were Franchot Tone, Ruth Nelson, Stella Adler, Mary Morris, and Morris Carnovsky. Clurman was deeply impressed by what Strasberg achieved:

> He is the director of introverted feeling, of strong emotion curbed by ascetic control, sentiment of great intensity muted by delicacy, pride, fear, shame. The effect he produced is a classic hush, tense and tragic, a constant conflict so held in check that a kind of beautiful spareness results.
>
> (Clurman 60–1)

That "classic hush" was all very well – it was not unlike the response to the Moscow Arts Theatre. But the Group was working against economic crisis and Depression. American urgency called for a fiercer voice. Just as the Group had difficulty staying solvent, so an increasingly radical attitude shaped their choice of material. They found their natural playwright in Clifford Odets who would give them *Waiting for Lefty* (1935), *Awake and Sing* (1935), *Golden Boy* (1937), and *Rocket to the Moon* (1938). *Waiting for Lefty* was especially crucial in that its action was built around a meeting of the taxi drivers' union and their eventual decision to strike.

It was more melodramatic than Strasberg's "hush," but Harold Clurman noticed a "hot assent" in the audience (148). At one point, an actor (pretending to be an ordinary member of the audience) leaped up on the stage, encouraged to cry "Strike!" It was a trick, of course, more manipulation than method, but it worked. As Clurman felt, "It was something more than a tribute to the play's effectiveness, more even than a testimony of the audience's hunger for constructive social action. It was the birth cry of the thirties" (148).

For the actor who played that modest role, a spark of energy jumped up at him from the audience:

> My appearance was a complete surprise to the audience. I was not a familiar figure in the theatre. I would not have been noticed or remembered from any of the Group productions. I looked like a man off the street outside, and a cabbie for sure. Oh, the balcony, the people in the cheap seats, how they cheered! Their approval came down on me like Niagara. Falls. I'd never heard anything like it in the theatre, and I've never heard anything like it since. History had been made.
>
> (Kazan *A Life* 114)

That actor was Elia Kazan. In his Production Notebook for *On the Waterfront* at the Wesleyan University Cinema Archives, Kazan remembered that glory as he tried to define his sense, his understanding, of Schulberg's character, Terry Malloy: "Likely he has a swagger. It's as though he's still walking down the street, being smiled at by everybody, pointed out by everybody (cf Yourself during *Waiting for Lefty* – or when you were the white-haired boy-director. With what pride you used to walk around! – with what confidence!)."[1]

The Group was an inspiring but very competitive gathering. There was a tendency for the company to knot together, even when they might have been relaxing. There were famous summer camps where Clurman and Strasberg gave lengthy talks and lectures on their ideas. Politics crept in increasingly, so that sometimes the Group resembled a series of cells. Several of the members would join the Communist Party – if only for a short period. As time passed, so the list of names in the Group grew – Luther Adler, Robert Lewis, Irwin Shaw, Sanford Meisner, Kermit Bloomgarden, Lee J. Cobb, John Garfield, Sam Jaffe, Martin Ritt, Eleanor Lynn, Art Smith, Phoebe Brand, Frances Farmer, Leif Erickson. And Elia Kazan.

One of the fascinating things in Kazan's *A Life* – and a revelation of how much Strasberg's search for the inner self had affected him – is that his ambition, his drive, and his paranoid feelings about being a smothered outcast are so palpable. Kazan had grown up with an un-shakable sense of being an outsider, "the Greek." At Willams College he had regarded himself as the very horny, ugly guy looked down on by the beautiful, classy, "American" girls. So he saw himself as an insurgent. At Williams, to make money, he worked as a servant at fraternity parties. He'd watch the girls, the sex, and burn with envy:

> My face, serving breakfast, was the face Puerto Ricans call the face of stone. No one could have guessed what I was thinking and feeling. It wasn't friendly. I was quickly developing the mask that I was to wear the rest of my life.
>
> (Kazan 43)

Things were not a lot better for Kazan within the Group – if only be-cause he was so dependent on feeling aggrieved, or wronged. When he auditioned, he felt boredom or disdain in both Clurman and Stras-berg, and he was angered enough to grab their attention, when they asked what did he want, by saying their jobs. He became an appren-tice, assistant and stage manager, as well as a player of small roles. He was dedicated, industrious, ever-present, a Jack-of-all-trades, an invaluable solver of physical problems – that's how he got the nick-name, "Gadget," the guy who could get the stage machinery to work when others had failed.

So Kazan observed the Group with mixed feelings. And he studied Clurman and Strasberg with the predatory instinct of someone eager to steal their girl – their opportunity to direct, and their access to the secret of acting. If that seems harsh, consider all the evidence of driven careerist in Kazan. For that is the energy that made him such a potent director. Still, it helps us see the opportunist ready to run off with other men's methods.

Clurman was at his best introducing a play to its cast. He spoke like a professor of dramatic literature or a critic (he would later fill that role at *The New Republic* and *The Nation*). He could convey a fine, overall grasp of a play that inspired everyone. Then reality set in:

> After a glorious start came the second and third weeks. It quickly became evident that Harold had little stage facility. He had trouble turning the psychology he had so brilliantly detailed in behavior ¬at the same level of penetration and originality. There was often something inept about his staging; he had trouble getting people in and out of doors. He relied on the actors to work them out, and occasionally, when he had a clumsy piece of stage movement to deal with, he'd ask me to work it out for him. I'd do what he asked, feeling not that Harold was incapable but only that he was above what he considered to be the mechanics of directing. An architect need not be carpenter, mason, electrician and plumber.
>
> (Kazan 122)

Strasberg was a tougher rival. He loved detail, and he had a casuist's intricate mind that was hard to challenge. He was quiet, yet intimidating – think ahead, three decades plus, to his Hyman Roth in *The Godfather Part II*. He had a way of routing opponents and turning enemies into slaves. But he had an unmatched insight into how actors functioned; and he collected real knowledge about them that he could exploit. In time, Kazan would be famous for the same leverage. Strasberg found scant professional success, yet he became the man famous for having Marilyn Monroe as his unquestioning disciple (though this came after Kazan's physical affair with the actress). Strasberg was not a womanizer in Kazan's sensual way. He was so austere, or so shy, he preferred his own authority to be intellectual. He was married to Paula, a part of the Group, and a fellow Communist with Kazan.

As he had with Clurman, Kazan sometimes served as Strasberg's stage manager. They clashed, yet Kazan refused to yield. As he wrote:

> I am a normal man, which is to say I do not forget slight or injury: I am not forgiving. Although there were to be times in the years to come when I admired Lee and was impressed with his insights and observations, from then on I was always on guard with him.... I

felt – and often felt again – that in order to be close to this tight knot of a man, one had to knuckle under. Others did; I did not.

(Kazan 111)

Not knuckling under is very much the theme of *On the Waterfront*, where a humble and inarticulate ex-boxer, Terry Malloy, stands up against the code in which he has lived most of his life, and reclaims his own dignity or pride. For taking action is a moral imperative by the film's standards, the opposite of so much compromise and knuckling under to drab reality and practice. Indeed, Marlon Brando's Terry is in search of a way of acting that will transcend the massive, bravura intimidation of Lee J. Cobb as a character called Johnny Friendly. If that seems not entirely laudatory of *On the Waterfront*, it is because I am trying to see Kazan's direction of this film as a climax in his long-pending emotional need to take action, to be actor and protagonist, himself. Schulberg's script, although based on real-life waterfront situations and on real-life waterfront people, also allowed Elia Kazan to act out some of his own inner demons.

The Group Theatre did not last long. It gave way to its own tensions and to the ambitions of its members. Strasberg withdrew in 1937 because of differences over theory and disparities in felt power. There was a conspiratorial energy within the Group that always had to be resisted. And there were constant money problems, allayed by the financial aid Franchot Tone sent back from Hollywood. Other figures were invited west, too: Frances Farmer, 1936, to make *Come and Get It*, where she experienced the "method" according to Howard Hawks; John Garfield, 1938, for *Four Daughters*; Morris Carnovsky in 1937 for *The Life of Emile Zola* and *Tovarich*. Lee J. Cobb was busy with film from 1937 onwards; Clifford Odets had begun to write for Hollywood in the mid-thirties. As the Group finally dissolved in 1941, even Harold Clurman was receiving offers. Lee Strasberg was one of the few who had nothing to do with Hollywood. Kazan acted in a couple of films in 1940–1, *City for Conquest* and *Blues in the Night*. They were his last acting credits.

But giving up on the job of acting only freed Kazan's inner yearning. For he became, within the space of seven years, the most notable new director in America, working simultaneously on stage and screen. This was careerism, but without trickery or deceit. Nobody wanted success more. Nobody had as fresh, practical, and detailed an eye for bringing out the human truths of a play; nobody else could make himself so indispensable to the actors that they believed their breakthrough in a role depended on Kazan's presence and steady attention.

He had the insight of a Strasberg, the sheer spot-on effectiveness of a "Gadget," and the supreme emotional need of someone who had enlarged the role of director to match his own desires. When asked whether he still applied the collaborative notions of the Group, he answered with devastating frankness: "There's a fundamental difference: I think there should be collaboration, but under my thumb! I think people should collaborate with me. I think any art is, finally, the experience of one maniac. That's me" (Ciment 37). So many people have testified to Kazan's zest in the next few years, his appetite for wooing more conventional actors (like Tallulah Bankhead and Fredric March) or young playwrights (like Tennessee Williams and Arthur Miller). On Broadway, he rose fast, directing a series of more mainstream plays than the Group would have mounted. There was Thornton Wilder's *The Skin of Our Teeth* (1942), with a cast that included Bankhead, March, and the young Montgomery Clift; *One Touch of Venus* (1943), by S. J. Perelman and Ogden Nash, starring Mary Martin, with music by Kurt Weill; *Jakobowsky and the Colonel* (1944), by S. N. Behrman, starring Louis Calhern, Oscar Karlweis, and J. Edward Bromberg.

It was then that Kazan accepted offers to switch over to Hollywood: *A Tree Grows in Brooklyn* (1945), *Sea of Grass* (1947), with Tracy and Hepburn; and *Boomerang!* (1947), a fairly conventional police procedural thriller that starred Ed Begley, Arthur Kennedy, Karl Malden, and Lee J. Cobb – Group-type actors falling into the mold of Hollywood supporting players, without undue strain. These films were not remarkable, promising, or especially personal. Kazan was learning the new medium haltingly – as yet, he could see no role for the director, except to manage the show. He was not expressing himself, just shooting the pages.

But on the New York stage, in 1947, he directed Arthur Miller's *All My Sons* (with Clurman as his producer), and with Begley, Kennedy, and Malden acting. Then, at the end of the same year, he directed the first production of Tennessee Williams' *A Streetcar Named Desire*.

This was a landmark event, and a key demonstration of the new acting. Above all, the Broadway audience was stunned by the animal-
like presence and realism of Marlon Brando as Stanley Kowalski.
Brando was very much Kazan's discovery: they had worked together already in an experimental production of *Truckline Café*, and
it was Kazan who urged Williams to go with Brando in the lead
(other considerations had been Garfield, Burt Lancaster, and Jack
Palance).

More than that, Kazan built Stanley's role, if only to ensure that
he himself had a character to identify with. The Williams play as
written was more centrally a study of Blanche. But Kazan is the kind
of director who requires a strong heterosexual surrogate, and in that
first production through a mixture of stagecraft and urging he made
Stanley dominant and glamorous. The production carried a real tension between Williams' half-smothered gay stance and Kazan's bold
male thrust. You could argue that the text was manipulated, but it
worked – there were ovations that lasted nearly thirty minutes on
opening night, and there was a new figure on stage: the modern
beautiful beast, a strange crossbreed of Williams' poetry, Strasberg's
precision, and Kazan's bursting fantasy life. And Stanley is, in some
ways, the father to Terry Malloy, the inarticulate savage. In his Production Notebook on the film, Kazan often compared Stanley and
Terry, while stressing the boxer's lost confidence.

The work on *Streetcar* fell tidily between the shooting and the release of *Gentleman's Agreement* – a very obvious, if not trite, exposé of
anti-Semitism, written by Moss Hart, starring Gregory Peck, Dorothy
McGuire, and John Garfield. In an age when Hollywood was too
ready to flatter its own liberalism, the film won Best Picture and
Best Direction Oscars. Thus, on stage and screen, within a matter of
months, Kazan had won most of the desirable prizes. Nevertheless,
he had not yet come close to making a good or striking movie.

In the following years, Kazan's films were *Pinky* (1949), a grotesque
mishmash on race, taken over from John Ford in which the alleged
master of dramatic realism was trying to mine the depths of half-caste
torment in Jeanne Crain; *Panic in the Streets* (1950), a good, routine
documentary thriller; the film of *Streetcar* (1951), with Vivien Leigh
replacing Tandy in the original cast (out of box-office aspirations that
were undercut by the inescapable censorship imposed on the text);

and Brando and Anthony Quinn as brothers in *Viva Zapata!* (1952). On stage, meanwhile, and with considerably more artistic success, he introduced another classic – Miller's *Death of a Salesman* – with Lee J. Cobb, Mildred Dunnock, and Arthur Kennedy. But *Zapata* was an advance for Kazan – it was his most deeply felt movie, even if the acting came dangerously close to the impersonation of Mexican-ness. Still, Kazan felt unfulfilled or unreleased in film, and there was no question in his own mind but that film was the more important and pressing of the two media. He had done good work on stage: he had made two great new plays feel electric in their rooms. But he preferred to be great on film for its infinite audience.

There was one more thing to prove his status. Doctrinal approval, and the very character of the priesthood of American acting, were seen to belong to Kazan through the formation of the Actors Studio in 1947. The co-founders were Kazan and Robert Lewis. Both men had been taught and shaped by Strasberg, yet he was not invited to be part of the enterprise that owed more to him than to anyone else alive. Of course, in 1947, the Studio rode the bandwagon of method fashionability, and Kazan was its clear star and attraction. The first clutch of students included Brando, Clift, Julie Harris, Eli Wallach, Karl Malden, Patricia Neal, Mildred Dunnock, James Whitmore, and Maureen Stapleton. Within a short period of time, everyone wanted to be at the Studio – not least because of the chance of being in a Kazan production in one medium or another.

But there was a crisis looming. In 1947, the House Un-American Activities Committee made its first moves against Hollywood people – against screenwriters. Kazan felt that the search for witnesses would eventually reach him, because he had been a member of the Communist party for a little over a year in 1934–5. He asked others whether they were going to testify; and he searched his inner being for what he should do. As Strasberg might have said: a man does not necessarily know when he is going to need to be an actor – and only then does he grasp the nature of his own life.

He could tell himself that the Party had been one more source of humiliation, for he had been scolded for indiscipline and "independence" in the 1930s, for not knuckling under to the secret systems of command. That is why he had resigned – because that kind of repression was anathema to him.

By the early fifties he could tell himself that that clandestine mood was akin to the spirit of Soviet Communism, the disasters of which were now so much better known. He could grow angry at the insidious ways in which Communism sought to undermine America. He wondered if all reds didn't deserve to be exposed. And he wanted to work – no, he needed to work. Whereas the threat of unemployment – in Hollywood, if not on Broadway – was what faced every person refusing to testify.

But there were others who might have predicted the simple superiority of need – and there is an analogy here with acting: no matter how elaborate the actor's motivation, he needs to do what the text says. Walter Bernstein, the writer, saw even then a strange tug of charm and brutishness in Kazan. It was like a warning. "Once he talked eloquently to me of wanting to play Richard the Third, knowing the evil uses of charm. He would have made a fascinating Iago. Both women and men responded to him and his ability to seduce was one of the qualities that made him such a good director. He was able to get performances from actors that they themselves did not think they were capable of" (16).

Or from himself. To read everything available from Kazan is to note how long he agonized over the decision to testify – and how steadily it has preoccupied him ever since, even up to the moment of his hotly contested honorary Oscar in 1999. It is the defining crisis in his drama, the one so grave and damaging (to him and others) that it lifts his life above the ordinary. Surely he has had his critics, and detesters. Yet has anyone matched his self-loathing, or caught the pitch of self-dramatization? For the testimony is the moment of ultimate discovery in Kazan's life, where he becomes character, actor, and director. And where he finds the nobility in wickedness.

A couple of years before this decision, and after the Broadway opening of *Death of a Salesman*, Kazan and Arthur Miller had talked of a film project together – called *The Hook*, it was a waterfront story about the role of organized crime in the corruption that existed there. Miller had pursued and researched *The Hook* personally. He had no doubts about the role of gangsterism in the waterfront unions. Kazan accepted that research. But the project was not easily launched. Warners passed. So Kazan and Miller went to Columbia where the boss, Harry Cohn, seemed ready to proceed. Then Cohn said he needed to consult with the FBI first. He came back with this stipulation: that the crooks in the story be changed to Communists. Roy Brewer, the union chief in Hollywood, had lent his backing to the order. This was 1951, and Miller finishes the story:

> Nearly speechless, I said that I knew for a fact that there were next to no Communists on the Brooklyn waterfront, so to depict the rank and file in revolt against Communists rather than racketeers was simply idiotic, and I would be ashamed to go near the waterfront again. His voice even and hopeless, Kazan repeated that idiotic or not, it was what Cohn-Brewer-FBI insisted on. In an hour or two I wired Harry Cohn that I was withdrawing my script as I was unable to meet his demands. Next morning a boy delivered a telegram to my Brooklyn Heights door: "IT'S INTERESTING HOW THE MINUTE WE TRY TO MAKE THE SCRIPT PRO-AMERICAN YOU PULL OUT. HARRY COHN"
>
> (Miller 308)

So much of that is a rehearsal for Kazan of the battle between career expediency and truth to material, and so much of the actor is in the voice "even and hopeless."

Kazan had been warned already by Twentieth Century-Fox, his main employer in Hollywood, that without his testimony he was in danger of being barred from work. Equally, as Victor Navasky has suggested, Kazan was the biggest and most prominent of targets, one of the few who had a chance of defying the Committee [and the various studios that had agreed to be intimidated by it] (20). In January, 1952, Kazan talked to agents of the House Un-American Activities Committee, but did not name names. Then, on April 10 he went back and gave names from the period of his Party membership.

Kazan asked Arthur Miller to come see him. They walked in the Connecticut woods, and Kazan sought advice, or confirmation, from the writer. Miller was moved:

> To be barred from his metier, kicked into the street, would be for him like a nightmarish overturning of the Earth itself. He had always said he came from survivors and that the job was to survive. He spoke as factually as he could, and it was a quiet calamity opening before me in the woods, because I felt my sympathies going toward him and

at the same time I was afraid of him. Had I been of his generation, he would have had to sacrifice me as well.

(Miller 333)

As Miller withdrew from Kazan's life, so the director sought out Budd Schulberg (a novelist who had also testified before HUAC). When the topic of *The Hook* came up, Schulberg said that he owned the rights to a journalistic series, "Crime on the Waterfront," and that he had even done a script for it. Thus, *On the Waterfront* was born, or reborn.

Schulberg has subsequently denied that his piece was meant as a vindication for informing – he had written the first draft before HUAC's pressure had come to bear. In addition, Schulberg's script reiterated Miller's plain fact, that the problem on the waterfront was that of criminal organization, and Schulberg himself had been covering the Waterfront Crime Commission hearings every day.

But Kazan has never been shy about what *On the Waterfront* meant to him. Rather, he exults in the degree of self-identification with Terry Malloy, and with Brando, the actor who played the part – in what Kazan feels may be the finest performance ever in an Amenican film. From a critical point of view, I think one can be even more positive. *On the Waterfront* and *East of Eden* – the two films that followed the ordeal of testifying – are Kazan's most passionate and impressive works as a director, the films in which he finally was able to explore aspects of himself, notably the reviled stoolie, and the dark, furtive Cain-like "ugly" brother who has been misunderstood and whose need and capacity for "love" have gone unrequited. At last, his Iago had come into the open.

Yet notice how beautiful Brando's Malloy is. I am thinking not just of make-up and the way he is photographed, but the manner in which the script and the direction wait for him to speak, and act. In both *On the Waterfront* and *East of Eden* we see extraordinary examples of acting that deliberately delays or slows a film. Everything waits for the actor's hesitation, and that is the first sign of the character's fineness – or of the degree of narcissism in the concept. There is also a difference between seeing the film in 1954 and 2003. In nearly fifty years standards of authenticity change. We have lived with De Niro's Jake La Motta, and with the living portrait of lost wits in Muhammad Ali.

9. Marlon Brando as Terry Malloy. Everything waits for the actor's hesitation
. . . a revelation of realism. (Courtesy of the Museum of Modern Art Film Stills
Archive)

We know more about the brutalization of boxing and the humiliation of being punchdrunk. Whereas in 1954 Brando's Terry was a
revelation of realism sitting rather oddly beside the presence of two
real ex-boxers, Tony Galento and Tami Mauriello, as Friendly hoods.
Those boxers "look thick" and they are presented as mindless enforcers of Friendly's rule. There was even a moment when Kazan had
to hit Mauriello hard in the face to get the right look of hostility.

Seen today, Brando's Terry is less a real boxer than an appeal for
pathos. Of course, what we really love is Marc Antony's noble head
with Brando's own broken nose and a good deal of tasteful scar tissue
make-up over his eyes. Famously, he mumbles and comes close to
incoherence – but, as Schulberg has written, "as he moves out from
under Friendly's thought control, and as his conscience takes over,
his mind begins to clear and he begins to find the words for the
feelings he had been suppressing. The turning point is in the taxi
scene."[2]

But it brings up maybe the most worrying thing about the film, and the most serious question for the Strasberg method.*On the Waterfront* was emotionally overwhelming in 1954: its violence was more terrible then; the grittiness of its location felt harsher; and the acting was more surprising, even if one could see how Malden's priest and Cobb's mobster hardly departed from conventions established in the 1930s. But melodrama has pushed its way through the truthfulness, and thus we watch not just Terry but the enormous skills of Brando in the role. There is something here of the rapidity with which most films go stale. But it is also a sign of failings in the script and sentimentalities in the attitude that are harder to ignore.

The ending is so badly fractured, it's hard to know what the very blunt approach wants to say. Terry has been badly beaten by Johnny Friendly and his thugs. And now the ordinary stevedores are so disturbed they are prepared not to go into work – this is the new version of the old "Strike" call, and the first sign of organization or involuntary defiance against the Mob. It might be a fine ending if, in beating and even killing Terry, the Mob lost its power, but Friendly is defeated only for the moment.

Instead, there is a sequence of masochistic hysteria in which Terry is urged to get back on his feet and go staggering into the pier building, past the impassive boss figure. What can this conclusion mean? That the show goes on, no matter that it is the brutal, exploitative way of the docks that has been saved? Surely going back to work sustains the crooked system and Friendly's rule – plus even the tender feelings of those like Harry Cohn and Roy Brewer. It may be rousing at the moment (though even in 1954 there were those offended or bewildered by the ending), but today it looks like incoherence.[3]

Let me go further. There is a critical flaw earlier in the story, a slackening of plot logic that explains the untied end. Terry's brother, Charley (Rod Steiger), is Johnny Friendly's right-hand man. It is clear that he is as smart as Terry is vulnerable. It is Charley who counts the cash at Mob headquarters. It is Charley, in his dress, who most resembles Friendly. So, when Terry becomes a questionable element – so soft on Edie he might betray the Mob – why is Charley in danger?

Friendly may tell Charley that Terry has to be eliminated – and there is potential here for making Charley the central character of a more interesting story. Terry is the threat to the Mob. He and he alone could testify to the Crime Commission. In all logic, he needs to be removed (after the film, in a novelization, Schulberg finally killed Terry off). But why sacrifice Charley along the way? Or implicate him? A subtle Friendly would give the job to someone else on the waterfront where people regularly fall off roofs.

Granted the Terry we come to know, it's inevitable that he talks when he finds Charley dead. Whereas, a Charley confronted with Terry's death would likely submit – a born careerist, one who speaks in "even and hopeless tones," utterly aware of how far his own weakness has trapped him. It seems to me now that that is a more poignant redirecting of the story – the portrait of an organization man, too timid not to knuckle under. But this is another script.

I remain impressed by Brando's performance – but I am more moved by his flights and rhythms than by Terry's character. Whereas in Steiger's Charley there is still no such rift. Uncommonly for him, Steiger underplays everything so that there remains something mysterious or touching about the corrupt brother, something that understands or concedes Terry's rhetorical charges, and his very romantic acting (with all that talk of what might have been), and is crushed by them and by what is.

In the famous taxicab scene, when Charley cannot bring himself to kill Terry, when Brando's sad, sweet smile waves away the gun (as if it were the toy of their childhood) Steiger is impressive still, nearly silent but mesmerizing. The actors sit in a rocking cab set (agitated by stage hands), as a flashing sidelight suggests passing traffic. Brando had Steiger to feed him in his close-ups. But then Brando begged time to see his analyst (that early!), and Kazan was left to read the lines for Steiger's close-ups. Kazan has admitted how unfair that was, but he was a chronic needler with actors and he could have packed Brando off just to make Steiger insecure. (He deliberately created mistrust between Brando and Quinn on *Viva Zapata!*, and that feeling lasted over a decade!) Even so, I find now that, despite Brando's brilliance in the scene – the lovely musical emanation of inner being (or an ideal view of it) – it is Steiger who is the real human being, torn, reduced, increasingly tragic, hushed, and crushed.

On the Waterfront was an immediate success – it won Kazan new freedom and unquestioned position as a film director. Although the movie came a little after the great impact of the Actors Studio, it established the Method in popular idiom. The Academy gave the film twelve nominations and eight Oscars. Five of these nominations were for acting. Eva Marie Saint won as best supporting actress. Brando won as best actor. And Steiger, Malden, and Cobb were all nominated as supporting actor. Apparently, the voters were reluctant to pick any one over the others, and so the Oscar went to Edmond O'Brien in *The Barefoot Contessa*. But *On the Waterfront* won for best picture and best director, and for best story and screenplay.

Since then, the Actors Studio has become an orthodoxy in the land – and much less influential. There is a Bravo series on the Studio but it takes in actors who hardly know the place. And while we revere some of its masters – like De Niro and Pacino – we allow that they sometimes get away with murder, shameless, show-off performances, as large and pleasurable, or as silly, as those of Laughton or Muni. Equally, we are readier now to see the play, the fun, the pretense in acting in an age of *The Truman Show*, *Being John Malkovich*, and the permanently curled lip of Kevin Spacey. Acting is what actors do to make the thing work. Sometimes they are solemn and doing it from the doctrine of Russian masters. Sometimes they are having fun.

In creating Terry Malloy, Schulberg was writing about men he met and knew in the basement of St. Xavier's Church in the dangerous Dunn-McGrath waterfront neighborhood. But what I have tried to show in this essay is how far the film was also vital in the selfdramatizing progress of one unconventional actor, Elia Kazan, who happened to be the director. Actors do what they have to do – and they have to work. Lee J. Cobb was maybe the greatest Willie Loman, and the only Johnny Friendly. But he was in countless pieces of trash to make a living. And he named names, too, and cowered from meeting those he had wronged. In his nearly abject autobiography, Brando says he thought of refusing the role of Terry because of Kazan's treachery to others. But didn't. Decades later, as the Kazan controversy refused to die, Rod Steiger said he had never known about the testimony, an impossible claim since he accepted the role of Charley two years after Kazan's testimony which had set off a furor in the Actors Studio, of which Steiger was a member. James Dean was heard to say that he would not work for Kazan – but then he did in *East of Eden*, because he guessed it might make him. Even Arthur Miller worked with Kazan again. Seduction – actors do it to us; and the business does it to them. Though they move us, so that we sometimes love them, it is not the most dignified performance.

I remain fond of *On the Waterfront* – I first saw it when I was 13, the right age for responding to its intense if rather shallow romanticism. But when *Waterfront* won best picture, it beat out *The Caine Mutiny, The Country Girl, Seven Brides for Seven Brothers,* and *Three Coins in the Fountain.* In other words, *Rear Window* was not even nominated. Yet, today, I find James Stewart's performance in Hitchcock's film more profound and intriguing. I think it has lasted better, which suggests that sometimes there may be more complexity in methods innocent of the Method.

As for *On the Waterfront* as a whole, it has survived most vividly as a crucial act in the Kazan melodrama as well as a riveting cinematic exposé of a social problem and the deeply felt social concerns of the men who made it. The Jersey waterfront may be corrupt still, but we don't hear much about it, not even in *The Sopranos,* the grandest celebration of the New Jersey undergrowth we have ever seen. And you can recognize the family ties of some of the minor figures in both – if only in that inherently American confusion in tough guys, as to whether they are acting mean or really are mean. But even as a piece of history, *On the Waterfront* is a fascinating demonstration of how the actor in America has gone from being a servant to our pleasure to a cultural hero. And surely young actors everywhere know the back-of-the-cab routine by heart, and serve it up for auditions.

NOTES

1   Reprinted with permission of the Wesleyan University Cinema Archives and the Kazan family.
2   Letter to Joanna Rapf, September 7, 2000.
3   For a contemporary perspective on the problem of the ending, see especially John Howard Lawson, "Hollywood on the Waterfront: Union Leaders Are Gangsters, Workers Are Helpless," in *Hollywood Review,* 1.6 (Nov./Dec. 1954): 3–4.

5 Visual Coding and Social Class in *On the Waterfront*

Let us begin with the end. A joke's success hangs on the appropriateness of its punch line. A love story depends on the revelation of whether boy and girl achieve union. Mysteries are made not mysterious by the last frame. Whodunits tell us who did it. Quests end in success or failure. Tensions in a narrative generally demand resolution. However, in the case of narratives about social problems – such as labor injustice, corporate greed, racism, sexism – the question of closure is necessarily more complicated. Social problem films depend upon arousing concerns in the audience that go beyond the resolution of the immediate story. Our concern about the problem posed in the narrative has a dual function in that the concern exists both in the space of the story enacted on the screen as well as in a perceived real world that exists beyond the fictional screen. The ending of the story foregrounds the incompatibility of the two worlds. Are we supposed to walk out of the theater feeling that the problem in the screen story was satisfactorily resolved even though the "real world" concern aroused by the observation of a social problem should not be sated, less we become apathetic? The audience generally expects either explicit calls to action against the putative injustice or implicit inspirational solutions based upon heroic models of action. Social problem films should advance our ethical and empathic spirits. We want to feel ennobled by our concern about the issue; that in itself is a form of closure.

If the above has any truth, then the ending of *On the Waterfront* does not clearly fit generic expectations. The ending is disquieting,

even as the film itself is certainly entertaining and artistically satis-
fying. The ending's ambiguity has been notorious and extensively
discussed, especially in a 1954 polemic by Lindsay Anderson in *Sight
and Sound* titled "The Last Sequence of *On the Waterfront*," wherein
Anderson argued that the film's ending demonstrated fascist sym-
pathies in its emphasis on leaders rather than collective solutions.
Anderson's perspective is of course couched in the political concerns
of a 1954 British leftist. The concern in the present essay will be
to examine how the ending, as well as the rest of the film, functions for a contemporary audience. This would be an audience far
removed from Anderson's concerns, an audience viewing the film as
a "classic." However, even within the perspective of history, political
concerns do play a part in the experience of the film.

It will be my contention that *On the Waterfront*'s ending functions
as something of a cinematic Rohrschach test. In 1954 the ending revealed much about the class politics of the creators of the film and
the sensitivities of the original post-World War II audience. However, in contemporary showings, and this would be predominantly
either university film courses or art house historical retrospectives,
the now-venerated classic often arouses perplexed and even antag-
onistic responses, particularly from neophyte film students. *On the
Waterfront* tells us a good deal about the difference between films
then and now, both in terms of the changing aesthetics of film reception as well as the political landscape in which a film is received.
As with the Rohrschach test, our response may tell much about ourselves, particularly in our sensitivity to the social problems and class
politics the original film addressed.

So again, let us begin with the end. The forward thrust of the last
half of the narrative of *On the Waterfront* is toward the question of
whether Terry Malloy will cooperate with the Crime Commission and
testify about Waterfront racketeering. On the one hand, he is threatened physically by mobsters associated with his brother Charley,
while love interest Edie, as well as the Irish-American priest, Father
Barry, attempts to persuade him to act upon a conscience based on
helping his fellow workers. After his brother is murdered, in an act of
vengeance mixed with morality, Terry does decide to testify. However,
On the Waterfront deals elliptically with the effect of his testimony on
the actual Crime Commission's hearings. In a veiled shot just after

the hearings, we see a "Mr. Big" watching the hearings on television and then instructing his servant not to take any more calls from Johnny Friendly, the corrupt union boss. For all the anguish over whether Terry should testify, we never actually see much result of his testimony. There is a shot of a tabloid-style newspaper with news that Johnny Friendly will be indicted for murder. Then in a quick scene before the final confrontation, Johnny Friendly takes the guns from his thugs and says, "I'm on the hot seat. We're a law-abiding union." Without further explanation, this seems inconclusive and temporary. We don't really believe him. More compelling remains the Hollywood dictate that a film end with a dramatic action. Consequently, Terry must face Johnny Friendly outside the courtroom, where conflict and resolution can be expressed in terms of physical action. Despite Edie's pleas to move somewhere else, Terry returns to the docks and demands his right to work. The union's refusal to allow him to work precipitates a confrontation between Terry and Friendly. Terry rediscovers his boxing prowess and physically attacks the labor boss. As he begins to win the fight, the mob of gangsters intervenes and delivers a brutal beating that leaves Terry dazed. Then in an act of stamina and willpower, Terry staggers to his feet and leads the workers back into the loading zone, against the wishes of Friendly. In the best interpretation, Terry's courage and leadership inspire his co-workers to act in their own collective interests by ignoring the directives of the corrupt union boss.

However, the iconography and visual composition of the last scene contribute to an effect I call "disquieting." Kazan cuts to high-angle shots of Terry leading a throng of workers into the pier building. As an aggregate, they move by the blustering Johnny Friendly, who stands in counterpoint to their forward motion. A medium closeup, low-angle shot of the well-dressed shipyard owner is punctuated with his "Let's go back to work." He is not too worried about fighting on the dock. Then in a long shot, a gigantic door shuts as the workers march *en masse* into the pier, as if a gigantic capitalist maw has devoured them. Perhaps my reading of the iconic symbolism of the final image is itself class-based, but to me, this image suggests consumption or erasure. Had Kazan shot a low-angle close-up of workers with determined visages marching into the loading area, we would have had something completely false to the situation, that is workers who seem fulfilled or empowered in their work. Far from it, these men are merely interested in survival. Schulberg has put it this way: "All they could think about was getting a few bucks together to try to feed their wives and kids."[1]

In an interview, Elia Kazan described his interpretation of the workers' plight at this point in the film as follows: "The workers gather around Terry, as if they were going to continue their struggle. But after all they have to work for a living, they're not going into some intellectual state of withdrawal from it. It was as close as I could get to what actually happened on the waterfront" (Baer 176). In fact, the film reflects quite accurately that corruption and brutality toward the longshoremen did not end either with the actual Crime Commission hearings nor with the publicity afforded by the success of the film. Johnny Friendly shouts "I'll be back!" which was the case in reality even after the film was picking up Oscars.[2] Still, Kazan's frequent defense of the film on grounds that it reflected actual circumstances that he and Schulberg experienced is not the final word on how modern audiences will apprehend the film. Audiences mostly judge films by what is on the screen, and that judgment may be affected by class-based sensitivities they bring to the viewing.

André Bazin once marveled at American movies' ability to show visually the vitality of how Americans work. Yet all the dialogue about work in On the Waterfront is negative and alienated, as is most of its visual rendition. Pop Doyle talks about how one of his arms is longer than the other because of years of swinging a hook. Sarcastic remarks about the status of being a longshoreman abound. The workers seem hardened and stoical. When one of the longshoremen steals a bottle of Irish whiskey during an unloading, it seems a typical response to the exploitation these workers feel.

This presents a problem with a modern audience. Imagine college students half a century after the film's premiere watching this film for a general education class. The negative dialogue about blue-collar work reconfirms students' own aspirations toward white-collar careers. Chances are they relate more to the well-dressed shipyard owner who probably lives in the suburbs than to the now united longshoremen marching in solidarity toward another day of alienated labor. In today's political economy, manufacturing jobs are shipped to the third world and robots replace manual laborers, at least in the eyes of the forward-thinking business major. Students may recognize that *On the Waterfront* argues for the decency and humanity of the working man, but the film will never suggest to them that these jobs are essential, fulfilling, or worth dying for. College students in 1954 probably reacted the same way, but they would have been a small subset of the mass audience the film was intended for. The original 1954 audience would have included many people capable of fully empathizing with characters who depended on a labor union to protect their basic rights. Again, the ambiguous and disquieting effect of the final image may be entirely appropriate as a statement of both the prospects of the main character beyond the immediate narrative, and a modern audience's difficulty with empathy toward the historical situation of work in a manufacturing-based economy.

Kenneth Hey, in his analysis of Leonard Bernstein's score for the film, makes a similar argument regarding the sound track. On the climatic image of Terry reporting for work, a tone of indeterminacy is established by not resolving the final chords, as if the waterfront conflict is far from over, or that Terry working is not necessarily the final expression of his dreams and aspirations (147). Modern audiences share the ambivalence about Terry's return to manual labor. We would prefer to be with Edie and Father Barry on the shore, looking forward to lives where workmen's compensation is not an issue. Triumphant music would have been ill advised. Terry has no guaranteed contract.

On the Waterfront proceeds from an era when social realist filmmakers felt that if they put the mirror up to society and showed its injustice, a viewing public would demand needed change. This view was expressed in Italian neorealism of the late 1940s, the 1950s Angry Young Men in Britain, as well as in the technological advances that led to Direct Cinema and Cinema Verité in the late 1950s. The social positivism of these movements seems an concept alien to cynical, post-Vietnam, post-Watergate audiences. Contemporary student audiences are inclined to see the mirror held up to society as not asking for any response on their part. Students to whom I show Barbara Kopple's *Harlan County U.S.A.* wonder why the striking miners don't leave the economically deprived area and get a job at Wal-Mart. When they see *Roger and Me* they agree that General Motors is mercenary and exploitative, but they are very comfortable making fun of the working class characters whom they see as too stupid to leave Flint. Most college students do not pursue education out of love of learning; they pursue education to get the job that ensures that they are never as vulnerable as the working class characters on display in these films. Further, the concept of being geographically and relationally bound is foreign to students today. They take geographic mobility as an inalienable right.

There is not a strong legacy of 1950's social realism in the contemporary films that make it to suburban malls. Film audiences today demand feel-good endings with affirmative characters who by the end transcend their social class, e.g. *Erin Brockovitch*. If the audience is made aware of a class-based inequity, then they want to know what the positive resolution is before they leave the theater. The 1950s social realist notion that an audience should leave uncomfortable or even angry is a bygone notion attached to the concept of self-sacrifice for a greater common good. Some of the success of *Hoop Dreams* is attributable to the fact that even though we see a cinema verité depiction of a family dealing with poverty and drug abuse, by the end we know those two teenagers have gotten into colleges, a gauge for their success as athletes, for better or worse.

Indeed modern students are perplexed when they discover that labor injustice with the longshoremen in *On the Waterfront* did not stop when either the original Crime Commission hearings depicted in the film occurred, or public attention focused on the issue via the popular culture sensation of an eight-Oscar box office hit film. Schulberg has stated the results of the film rather modestly: "One of the things I'm proudest about this picture is something Father Corridan (real life model for Father Barry) said: Once the public saw what a shape-up was really like, the mob and the stevedore companies could never hire men like that again'."[3]

In a college film class setting, we often ask too much in the assumption that a social realist film can present analysis and prescriptions for social problems such as labor injustice, presumably leading to redress. An essay by Karl Marx might do that, but as Siegfried Kracauer suggested, film clings to the surface of things. *On the Waterfront* is a popular culture vehicle and as such may necessarily be rather muddy in the recipe it does provide for combating the corruption it exposes so vividly. Terry Malloy is angry about his brother's murder. So this one man stands up, takes a beating, and in his symbolic crucifixion, workers are inspired to throw off a corrupt union leader?

Put that baldly, the surface logic is never really satisfactory; now that the workers have abandoned Johnny Friendly and marched into the maw, with what do they replace him? Earlier it was mentioned that British film director Lindsay Anderson was incensed with the politics of the final images. He felt the film's ending presented a model where workers bent and swayed with the whims of powerful leaders, the workers unable to make up their minds about anything beyond their immediate well-being. Kazan has responded that he and Schulberg were being true to what they saw: "What we intended to show at the end was that the workers there had found, or thought they'd found, a new potential leader. He had almost been killed, remember? And very often, in the labor movement, a new movement starts with the death of a person, through the memory of a martyr" (Baer 176).

But the film is cautious about offering prescriptive political solutions to the exploitation of labor. In fact, the most vivid exploitation seems to be coming from the working class itself, as Johnny Friendly has come up through the ranks. One of the leftist objections to the film over the years has been that by foregrounding a corrupt labor union infested by racketeers at a time when few Hollywood films took organized labor as a subject, that the film in effect condemns labor unions as a solution to the working man's exploitation. Indeed, the resolution of the film turns on Terry Malloy's ability to take a beating and go on working, rather than any demonstration that effective alternative leadership will replace Johnny Friendly.

Even *Harlan County U.S.A.*, which gives a thoroughly realistic background and context to a labor struggle, still depends on footage of individual leaders who seek to motivate the apathetic collective. However, in that Academy Award-winning documentary, we don't find out about the leaders' romantic lives, nor are they represented as romantic and charismatic. This discussion should remind us once again that we are dealing with a Hollywood film and a distinguished one at that.

On the Waterfront won an impressive eight Academy Awards, was lucrative at the box office, and did much to solidify the stardom of

Marlon Brando. Historically, the film was an early example of independent filmmaking, by which I mean feature filmmaking outside the confines of Hollywood studios that gained a measure of artistic success in the process. Method acting and a new approach to masculinity were also advanced in Brando's performance. In most historical accounts of Hollywood in the 1950s, *On the Waterfront* stands as one of the most important films of the decade because of its innovation, influence, and daring.

Yet for all this same artistic brilliance and historical importance, as I have been trying to suggest, it can be a difficult film to screen for a modern audience of college students. Any film from the 1950s will demonstrate visual codes and ideological assumptions differing from our vantage point of present retrospection. However, Hollywood genre pieces such as Hitchcock thrillers, historical epics, big budget musicals, or even John Wayne westerns somehow feel more familiar to contemporary audiences because they fit easily into a generic lineage of our current popular entertainment that constantly recycles the myths of the past. Every year sees a new batch of Hitchcock stylistic imitations, and the codes of the fifties Western are easily traced to modern science fiction and action films. *On the Waterfront*, however, is more of an anomaly. It purports to be a "message" film, relying on journalistic research aimed at exposing corruption and extolling the workingman. Arguably, its own lineage goes back to the 1930s Warner Brothers social problem films, such as *Marked Woman, Angels with Dirty Faces, Dead End, I Cover the Waterfront*. Yet for all its stylistic accomplishment and seriousness of social purpose, its moment of political and social insight may now be somewhat dated.

For example, as with the Warner Brothers films, contemporary audiences have difficulty taking seriously stories that expose urban problems but are devoid of characters who are not white. Only one Afro-American character in *On the Waterfront* has a couple of lines. However, it turns out that the one character was in fact a distortion of the historical situation. Schulberg, who organized an important writers' workshop in Watts during the turbulence in the 1960s, has written "This is a movie of the fifties, reflecting a time when Blacks were not in the work gangs except in the lowest pissant jobs. I took a slight liberty in putting my friend, ex-fighter Don Blackman, in it. Incidentally, today's Jersey waterfront, under the Genovese family,

10. Schulberg's friend, ex-fighter Don Blackman as Luke, along with three other longshoremen, gives Terry the cold shoulder after he has testified before the Crime Commission. (Copyright Columbia Pictures Corp., 1960. Courtesy of the Museum of Modern Art Film Stills Archive)

has a white local and a black local, both run by racketeers, dangerous men."[4] It is, of course, difficult for college students watching the film today to understand the class/racial aspects of what is going on in the film; they simply see what appear to be a few token Afro-American characters. Further, they have difficulties with the ethnicity of the white longshoremen, who have accents and the class perspectives of recent European immigrants. Noel Ignatiev wrote *How the Irish Became White*, describing Irish competition with Afro-Americans in the nineteenth century for the lowest paying jobs prior to Irish assimilation into the mainstream "white" culture. *On the Waterfront* and the social conditions it describes suggest that assimilation was not necessarily finished in the nineteenth century. Students need to think about why Pop Doyle is sending his daughter to a convent.

On the Waterfront presents an unusually detailed depiction of labor struggles for 1950s Hollywood (or any other period for that matter). Over a period of three years, Schulberg did his best to conceal his Dartmouth education and upbringing as a son of a Paramount studio executive so that he could hang out in waterfront bars and absorb the idioms and perspectives of New York's longshoremen. During this time he wrote a number of exposés for New York publications detailing what was going on with the murder and intimidation of the longshoremen. One of his pieces is credited with convincing Tony diVincenzo, on whom Terry Malloy is partly modeled, to join the "insurgents."

Schulberg used his lifelong affinity for boxing as a way to get people to warm up to him even as he was an outsider to their community. His effort and a highly sensitive ear paid off in entirely convincing dialogue. When Karl Malden's Father Barry delivers a eulogy in the hold of a freighter following Kayo Dugan's murder, Schulberg used actual phrases from sermons delivered by the real life model, Father John Corridan. When Terry Malloy finds his murdered brother hanging by a hook in an alley, he says "I'll take it out of their skulls!" again from a line Schulberg heard from a waterfront acquaintance. The considerable power of *On the Waterfront's* dialogue is dependent on Schulberg's ear for capturing the color and use of idiom of the longshoremen. He was also active in the recruiting of extras, even to the point of getting a longshoreman to coach Brando on the proper accent for Terry Malloy.

Appreciating the artistry of this film, therefore, depends in part on sensitivity and curiosity about cross-cultural or class differences as expressed in language. Students today see movies with working class dialogue derived from B-movies, such as Quentin Tarantino's *Pulp Fiction*, or rap idiom based drugs-in-ghetto films such as *Boyz in the Hood*. Further, television's omnipresence may be diluting regional and class-based accents and vernacular to the point that the dialogue in *On the Waterfront* sounds foreign to modern ears. Contemporary students need to be prepared to listen to the dialogue as a valuable tool for understanding an earlier America where language was used in a highly expressive fashion.

Another barrier contemporary audiences feel in the reception of *On the Waterfront* today is its depiction of gender. Initially, Eva Marie Saint's Edie Doyle seems a strong female role model character. She's gone to college. She demands action when her father and neighbors react passively to her brother's murder, as if her education has given her the power to speak out. She seems forceful and brave in confronting Terry's moral ambivalence and in asking him to respond. However the depiction soon takes a detour toward a more traditional rendition of females in violent, action sagas. Once Terry's brother is murdered, Edie begins to argue that the situation is hopeless, that she and Terry can only run away from the problem. The groans in the college auditorium are particularly loud during the scene where she locks the door attempting to keep Terry away. Brando plays the scene with raging testosterone and breaks down the symbolic door. To contemporary audiences sensitive about issues such as date rape, Terry kissing Edie, initially against her will, makes many uncomfortable, regardless of whether Brando previously seemed tender and gentle when he was trying on her white glove. Edie's final disempowering is that she stands ineffectively on the sidelines during the climatic dockside confrontations. Brando's sexuality is used to recuperate her from her social activist position to a traditional, docile female role. Not only does Terry affirm macho physical violence as a solution to the problems of the longshoremen, but Pop Doyle, Edie's father, regains his earlier compromised potency by being the worker who shoves Johnny Friendly into the water. Terry and Pop Doyle trudge into work while Edie smiles, standing next to the priest; there is nothing ambiguous about the resolution of this gender dilemma, as students are quick to point out.

Thus *On the Waterfront* flirts with having a feminist character, but ultimately ends up reinforcing the church, the family, and traditional gender roles. Not surprisingly, some cultural studies critics have posed the film as a fantasy vehicle for conformity-conscious 1950s America. Peter Biskind has argued that the film is about fantasies of breaking free of social control, but that it presents Brando, as many other films do, as a rebel in need of a beating. Once the antihero's impulses are tamed by the symbolic beating, then "The hero who betrayed his friends, as Terry Malloy does in *On the Waterfront* ... could sit down at the table with Ozzie and Harriet and be assured a piece of the pie" (Biskind, *Seeing is Believing* 165–6).

Biskind approaches *On the Waterfront* as a piece of popular culture. One can understand Schulberg's objection that this trivializes a narrative that emerged from real life heroes who risked their lives for a higher standard of living. It is important to recognize, however, that in post – World War II America, *On the Waterfront* spoke to many people for many reasons. But no general audience in 1954 or in the present would see a connection between Terry Malloy and the HUAC testifiers, as Biskind also asserts, unless coached by an over-zealous film professor (170). Kazan has fostered this reading over the years by talking about how he empathized with Terry Malloy, in his Production Notebook at the Wesleyan University Cinema Archives as well as in his autobiography.[5] But reading the film as an allegory of Kazan's HUAC testimony is a great example of the perils of the auteur theory, when artists, particularly those embroiled in political controversy, are allowed to dictate the interpretation of their work.

Still, the spectacle of a divided Hollywood at the 1999 Oscar ceremony when Elia Kazan was presented a Lifetime Achievement Award must have confused many viewers not familiar with the blacklist period of history. The past can be a foreign country, and many students wanted an explanation of why certain Hollywood luminaries were applauding while others sat on their hands. But any film teacher who would privilege the allegory of McCarthyism in the interpretation of *On the Waterfront* would be doing a disservice to the power of the film. If anything, Kazan and Schulberg's preoccupation with informing, or "ratting," in the narrative of *On the Waterfront* may be overdone to a contemporary audience whose first response to Terry's final actions is that he is a whistle blower rather than a stool pigeon. Biskind is insightful here in reminding us how 1950s audiences had more knowledge of European ethnicity than audiences today. Irish traditions about informing during the British colonial period or the Sicilian/Italian code of "omerta" would figure into the 1954 reception, yet seem baseless today (170). We live in a society where European ethnicity is progressively being erased, and students have difficulty identifying the traditions to which *On the Waterfront* alludes.

It should be apparent from the discussion so far that to recover the innovative brilliance of *On the Waterfront* one has to attend to it as a 1954 film. It cannot be fully appreciated and understood without a context, which of course is one of the purposes of reviving classic films in an educational setting. In the remainder of this essay, I want to concentrate on another aspect of the film's original context: its visual codes. These codes are different from what young people are used to with their post-MTV sensibilities.

One of the most negative aspects of the film for today's general education student is its black-and-white photography. At my Midwestern public university, a groan goes over the auditorium when any black-and-white title image appears. Students see black and white as a mark of technological inferiority, as if any director who would choose this technology is not really in the big leagues yet. They would see Ted Turner's colorization efforts as a sensible solution to a technological failing. The instructor's path is fairly clear here. You explain how composition and lighting are enhanced by black-and-white photography with many easy-to-locate illustrations in the film, such as the Christian allegory compositions of crucifixion, or the *film noir* lighting schemes when Terry Malloy is attacked in the alley. Then you illustrate further advancements in use of black and white with clips from Scorsese's *Raging Bull* (particularly the scene which quotes from *On the Waterfront*) or an even newer film such as John Boorman's *The General*. Finally, you remind them how often MTV and television advertising resort to black and white as a way to break through the clutter of television and capture their attention.

More difficult to explain to modern students is that Kazan and Schulberg's decision to tell their story in black and white had more to do with generic codes of realism and social class than purely budgetary considerations. The now legendary story of Schulberg and Kazan's trip to Hollywood to pitch the script to movie executives speaks directly to these aims. (See Georgakas's essay and Schulberg's foreword in this volume for a fuller account.) Kazan convinced Schulberg to go west with him to pitch the script to Darryl F. Zanuck, chief of Twentieth Century-Fox, based on the notion that Zanuck would see the project as another social problem film similar to the big success he had produced in 1939, *The Grapes of Wrath*.

In the aesthetic codes of pre-Vietnam Hollywood, color was associated with big-budget fantasy films such as the MGM Freed-Unit musicals or the lavish Bible epics. Black and white was associated with social realism for several reasons. It was cheaper, and with a wider exposure latitude, it allowed documentary photographers to enter unprepared locations and receive an acceptable image. Also an accumulation of films made in this manner, such as those of post – World War II Italian neorealism, began to dictate an expectation that black

11. Boris Kaufman's black-and-white cinematography, noted for its rich blacks, emphasizes *film noir* lighting schemes as Terry and Edie are attacked in the alley. (Courtesy of the Museum of Modern Art Film Stills Archive)

and white was somehow more appropriate for social realism than color. Thus, not surprisingly, Kazan and Schulberg specified in their meeting with Zanuck that the story, based on labor union corruption, was to be told in black and white.

This presented immediate problems. Despite Zanuck's 1939 success with the black-and-white *Grapes of Wrath*, he was now excited by the possibilities of Cinemascope and had apparently made a commitment to make Fox's entire slate of pictures in the wide-screen color process. This decision is of course in the context of Hollywood studios feeling the competition of television and feeling the need to differentiate their product from the still mostly black-and-white medium of broadcast television. Zanuck felt *On the Waterfront* would not work in the Cinemascope process, and as Schulberg recalls the conversation in his "Afterword" to the published script:

> (Kazan) recited his lexicon of the script's virtues: "It's unique – something different – it catches the whole spirit of the harbor – the way

you caught the Okies in *Grapes*." (Zanuck replied) "But the Okies came across like American pioneers." The mark of a tycoon is to have answers ready for any challenge. "Who's going to care about a lot of sweaty longshoremen?" (147)

Eight Oscars later, of course, the egg was upon Zanuck's face, as it was apparent that if the story were told well, many people *would* care about "sweaty longshoremen," even if it was in flat black-and-white images. One can only speculate what would have happened if a whim had struck Zanuck to the effect that he would finance Kazan and Schulberg's film only if it were done in color Cinemascope. The speculative question is whether a 1954 audience would have embraced the film's social realism as readily in color as they did in black and white. I think not. Visual codes and expectations have changed, however, and today's audience has no problem with social realism in color, although maybe muted colors are more appropriate than vivid hues. Until they become more familiar with film history, students today tend to see black and white as "unrealistic."

Perhaps examining the cinematography of the film is the ideal playing field for deconstructing these notions of "realism." Boris Kaufman frequently uses long-shot, deep-focus photography that situates the workmen versus the harbor. Students need to be encouraged to examine the relationship of the symbolic compositional schemes that Kaufman uses versus the conventions of social realism. For example, in the first introduction of Johnny Friendly and his gang, the mobsters come from low in the frame toward the camera, dominated by the large freighter in the background and the harbor. The compositional patterns suggest that the evil in the harbor is containable by the larger system and social structures. The drama of the narrative works out the same dynamics of the spatial representations only through temporal relationships. An easy example is the use of low-angle versus high-angle shots of the various characters. Terry Malloy is never shot against an open sky until he makes the decision to challenge Johnny Friendly. He is then effectively joined to the earlier compositions that arrange Father Barry against the sky whenever he attempts to inspire workers to make spiritual choices.

The world of the mobsters in the film is depicted with high-contrast, low-key photography quite reminiscent of *film noir* and gangster films. The dramatic lighting in the back alley when Terry discovers his murdered brother effectively expresses the good/evil polarity of Terry's situation at that point in the narrative. The more low-contrast, high-key lighting of the dockside confrontations suggests the complexity and ambiguity of the workers' situation with regard to work and organized labor.

Kaufman worked extensively in documentary photography and his brother was Dziga Vertov. If students have seen Eisenstein's *Potemkin*, they should be encouraged to look at some of the harbor action compositions for how Kaufman arranges vectors and compositions to enhance the dynamics of the conflict inherent in the story. It is strikingly reminiscent of the scene in *Potemkin* when the local population mourns the death of the sailor Vakulinchuk.

This issue of what is realistic and what is unrealistic is, of course, central for students coming to *On the Waterfront* for the first time. On the one hand the film presents realistic dialogue, a well-researched depiction of working class life, authentic location photography, and drama taken from newspaper articles. But then the film also presents the larger-than-life star mythology of Marlon Brando, a manipulative romantic plot, Leonard Bernstein's imposing musical score, and even what might be seen as violent melodrama. An argument can easily be made that the film succeeds not so much on its depiction of "sweaty longshoremen," but rather on Marlon Brando's sexual charisma, his chemistry with Eva Marie Saint, or even on the violent, melodramatic aspects of the drama.

Still, the film originated as a Pulitzer Prize-winning expose of union corruption by Malcolm Johnson. What attracted Kazan and Schulberg was not just the opportunity to do a documentary-style exposition of the longshoreman's plight, but also the chance to focus dramatically on the theme of individuals willing to risk their lives to tell the truth about corruption and exploitation. In interviews Kazan talks about an individual named Anthony diVincenzo; Schulberg says there were numerous individuals upon which Terry Malloy was modeled. However, Schulberg and Kazan were in enough agreement on the need for entertainment value, that the biggest fabrication they made to the mostly true story of the insurgents and the real life priest, Father John Corridan, was the extensive love story between Edie Doyle and Terry. This attraction is effectively the catalyst in Terry's decision to rat on the mob (Terry's brother is murdered mostly for his inability to keep Terry away from "the Doyle girl").

On the Waterfront does employ techniques and visual codes largely unfamiliar to contemporary viewers. However, interrogating these aesthetic choices should be rewarding and valuable. Their difference from today's codes should help us better understand contemporary film and have more appreciation for the artistry of the past.

An anecdote may quickly illustrate the reception problems I have been trying to outline. Recently at the very progressive, private Oberlin College, the student film society announced that it was "bringing *On the Waterfront* in honor of Parents' Weekend, as this is a film that spoke to our parents' generation, and also tends to be shown in religion classes at all-girls' Catholic high schools."[6] The student paper review is replete with inaccuracies about how the film was controversial in its day because of Kazan's testimony at HUAC and how Terry Malloy's standing up for justice in the film was "a trait not entirely valued by 1950s materialistic society – whose members, for the most part, had been swept away by commercial culture and in the process, tended to push aside issues of social welfare." However, Brando's performance as "the beefy boy with a heart of gold" is lauded, as are "beautiful shots of Hoboken when the waterfront still existed." I am sure the review was written quickly and haphazardly, but it still illustrates a condescending, postmodern attitude that history has collapsed and is not much worth looking into with any depth.

Such cultural amnesia, however, is precisely why we use 50-year-old films as vehicles for understanding the culture and class politics of the American past. *On the Waterfront* reflects both a different set of social codes as well as a different set of visual codes when a modern audience encounters this classic. Yet it is difficult to think of a more essential text for opening up the aesthetic and social considerations important to 1950s America, both in its failings and in its strengths. Ultimately, we understand more about our own codes by understanding those of the past, which is why *On the Waterfront* will continue to remain on my film syllabus. If I continue to feel disquieted and uncomfortable about Terry's trudge into the maw at the end, well, that is a pleasure of the text. I like movies that make me think and feel.

NOTES

1   Letter to Joanna Rapf, September 7, 2000.
2   In an interview with Michel Ciment, Kazan commented: "I knew the water-front in Hoboken intimately. I spent months there. Schulberg spent a year there. There was an election, after the film was made, in which the 'good' side, our side, lost by something like a hundred votes, out of two thousand– a very small margin. The waterfront has never got any better, it's the same now, just the same" (Baer 161).
3   Letter to Joanna Rapf, September 7, 2000.
4   September 7, 2000 letter to Rapf.
5   In an interview with Jeff Young, Kazan said "When people said there are some parallels to what I had done, I couldn't and wouldn't deny it. It does have some parallels. But I wasn't concerned with them nor did I play on them. They were not my reason for making the film. I had wanted to do a picture about the waterfront long before any of the HUAC business came up" (118).
6   Sabrina Rahman. "Once Controversial *On the Waterfront* Screens Saturday." *The Oberlin Review* (November 3, 2000): 12.

6 Leonard Bernstein and *On the Waterfront*

Tragic Nobility, A Lyrical Song, and Music of Violence

Leonard Bernstein, the wunderkind whose multifaceted career as a conductor, composer, pianist, and television personality made him unique even among the giants of twentieth-century music, wrote just one original score for films: *On the Waterfront.*

That fact alone would make his music significant. But the circumstances surrounding the assignment, how the score was created and recorded, and what happened afterwards, make the *Waterfront* score an unusual case study in the history of Hollywood movie music.

Unlike any other film score of its era, Bernstein's *On the Waterfront* broke rules. It opened quietly, with a solo instrument, instead of the sweeping orchestral overture that was then routine in Hollywood films. Instead of the "musical wallpaper" that was commonplace, particularly in independently produced films, *On the Waterfront* dared to speak with a bold and identifiable musical voice. And with its memorably stated, creatively developed, and carefully interwoven themes,

For their assistance, my thanks go to Georgett Studnicka and Susan Slamer of Sony Pictures Music Department; Stacey Behlmer and Warren Sherk, Margaret Herrick Library, Academy of Motion Picture Arts and Sciences; Ned Comstock of the USC Cinema-Television Library; Stephen Fry of the UCLA Music Library; Kathryn Danielik, archivist, Local 47, American Federation of Musicians; Clifford McCarty, author of *Film Composers in America: A Filmography, 1910–1970*; Mark Eden Horowitz, music specialist, Library of Congress; Marie Carter of Amberson, Inc.; Rudy Behlmer, author of *Behind the Scenes: The Making Of . . .* ; composers David Bell, David Raksin, Bruce Babcock, and Earle Hagen; Ron Mandelbaum of Photofest; interviewees Budd Schulberg, Charlie Harmon, Herschel Burke Gilbert, George Duning, James Decker, George Greeley, Elmer Bernstein, and Sid Ramin; and David Mitchell, Anne Marie North, and Marilee Bradford.

it provided a solid musical framework that became a major factor in the picture's impact – an undeniable surprise considering that its composer had never before penned a dramatic underscore.

The combination of Budd Schulberg's screenplay, Elia Kazan's direction, and an especially gifted ensemble of actors has been written about at length over the years. Often unfairly omitted from these discussions is the extraordinary contribution of Bernstein's music – even though producer Sam Spiegel hired him more for publicity purposes than for his composing abilities, and Bernstein himself was less than entirely pleased with how his music was treated in the final film.

The composer immersed himself in the film for three months, ultimately designing a score that magnifies the emotion at key moments, infuses the most volatile sequences with intensity, and creates a momentum that propels the viewer into a stunningly powerful climax.

Kazan later said of Bernstein: "He was the most highly regarded man in the field of American music. I don't know if I even said much of anything to him because I was so glad to have him" (Young 183).

PRELUDE

In early 1954, 35-year-old Leonard Bernstein was already famous. He had studied music theory with Walter Piston and conducting with Fritz Reiner before becoming a protégé of the Boston Symphony's renowned Serge Koussevitzky, who brought Bernstein to Tanglewood for conducting studies in 1940. The story of Bernstein's triumph as a last-minute substitute for an ailing Bruno Walter on the podium of the New York Philharmonic on November 14, 1943, was legendary within, and even outside, classical music circles.

Bernstein, then assistant conductor of the Philharmonic, gained a major international reputation as a conductor and as a pianist (often conducting from the keyboard). Hardly lost amid all this activity was his burgeoning career as a composer, winning equal respect in the concert hall and the legitimate theater. He had already gained acclaim for a ballet (*Fancy Free*, 1944), two symphonies (*Jeremiah*, 1944, and *The Age of Anxiety*, 1949), and an opera (*Trouble in Tahiti*,

1952). On Broadway, his musical *On the Town* (1944) had been a smash hit; five years later it became an Oscar-winning movie starring Gene Kelly and Frank Sinatra. *Wonderful Town* (1953), written with his *On the Town* collaborators Betty Comden and Adolph Green, was still running on the Great White Way. He had already begun work with writer Lillian Hellman to adapt Voltaire's *Candide* into a hybrid of opera and theater.[1]

The musicals demonstrated that Bernstein could write a tune. The concert work showed that Bernstein knew his way around the orchestra. In all probability, neither of those things mattered to producer Sam Spiegel. What was important was that Leonard Bernstein was a *name* – an internationally famous composer who straddled the worlds of classical and popular music.

"Quite honestly," says writer Budd Schulberg, "I don't think Sam was that enthusiastic when we got the film done. He told Kazan that he was worried that people might not go to see it. That's really what motivated his thinking – it would get an extra 'utz' if he could get Lenny to do something he'd never done before, which was to write a film score. He thought it might help to sell the movie."[2]

Kazan, in his autobiography, concurs, noting that Spiegel was "anxious to get another prominent name on the advertising copy" and as a result invited Bernstein to see a rough cut of the film (*A Life* 526–7). Schulberg points out: "There was great concern that [Columbia] would just sort of bury the film, especially since they had what they thought was their Academy winner the same year in *The Caine Mutiny*, and they didn't really welcome any competition."

Bernstein was, in all likelihood, not Kazan's first choice as composer. That would probably have been Alex North, the New York composer whom Kazan had brought to Hollywood and who had won Oscar nominations for his brilliant music for Kazan's two previous films, *A Streetcar Named Desire* (1951) and *Viva Zapata!* (1952). Unfortunately, Kazan's 1952 testimony before the House Un-American Activities Committee destroyed his relationship with North, and the two never spoke again.[3]

Two other composers were on Kazan's short list, both from the New York theater: Bernardo Segáll, the Brazilian-born pianist who had recently collaborated with Kazan on the 1953 Broadway production of Tennessee Williams' *Camino Real*; and Frank Fields, who would later compose the score for the Sacco – Vanzetti musical *The Shoemaker and the Peddler*.[4] But Spiegel pressed for Bernstein.

Bernstein had been approached to score films before and had, he said, always resisted "on the grounds that it is a musically unsatisfactory experience for a composer to write a score whose chief merit ought to be its unobtrusiveness" (*The Joy of Music* 65–9). In fact, Spiegel's initial offer, which came early in 1954, was reportedly rejected (Burton 236).[5]

Ever the shrewd producer, Spiegel finally persuaded Bernstein to look at a rough cut of the film. In Kazan's view, Spiegel's "apologetic tone" and "mealy-mouthed pandering to Bernstein" were factors in Bernstein's decision; ultimately, however, the sheer power of the film convinced the composer (*A Life* 527). Thoughts of his music being buried as background accompaniment disappeared, he said, "in the surge of excitement I felt upon first seeing this film. I heard music as I watched: That was enough."

Bernstein recalled being "swept by my enthusiasm into accepting the commission to write the score." Indeed, Schulberg notes, "Sam was worried he might not even want to do this. But then he saw the movie. He loved the movie. He responded to it." Bernstein later wrote that he thought that, even in rough cut, the film was "a masterpiece of direction, and Marlon Brando seemed to me to be giving the greatest performance I had ever seen him give (*New York Times*)."

So Bernstein committed to writing his first original score for a motion picture. His contract was unusual for the time, and possibly unique: He would be paid $15,000 for his services; he could, if he chose to, conduct the score; and, most surprisingly, he was granted rights to arrange the music into "an orchestral suite . . . based in whole or in part upon" the material written for the film.[6]

The contract was not with Columbia Pictures (the studio that would release *On the Waterfront*) but rather with Spiegel's company, Horizon-American Corporation, which produced the film. Fifteen thousand dollars was the going rate for top-flight composers in Hollywood, and most of them did conduct their own scores. The right to create an orchestral suite – and, more significantly, that the composer would own those rights and be the sole financial beneficiary of the suite – was a favor rarely granted to a composer of a movie score.

Music in films fulfills a variety of functions. Depending on the skill of the individual composer, music can suggest the time and place, provide mood or atmosphere, and most importantly conjure up an emotional response in the listener (joy, sadness, amusement, tension, fright) that the visual element alone often cannot achieve. Because the composer typically collaborates with the director to accomplish this end, they usually run the film together, making decisions about where music should start and stop, what style of music is necessary, and what the music should be helping the viewer to feel.

Equipped with a Moviola – a viewing Machine that enabled Bernstein to run the film over and over, reel by reel, forwards and backwards, at his leisure – he began to compose in February 1954. Nearly all of the score, he later told a *Los Angeles Times* reporter, was written in New York.

> Me and a Moviola and a print of the picture alone in a dark room," Bernstein said. "Nobody told me I was supposed to be supplied with cue sheets, a cutter, and a converter table. I just did it all by myself, and this is a difficult picture to score. There are long stretches of dialogue with few breaks suitable for music alone."[7]

Later, in the *The New York Times* article, Bernstein amplified his comments. "I have seen the picture some 50 times, in sections or in toto, and I have never changed in my reaction. Day after day I sat at a Moviola, running the print back and forth, measuring in feet the sequences I had chosen for music, converting feet into seconds by mathematical formula, making homemade cue sheets; and every time I wept at the same speeches, chuckled at the same gestures."

On the Waterfront was always a Sam Spiegel production. But Columbia, which financed the film and was to distribute it, became more deeply involved in the postproduction phase. With music recording to take place on the Columbia lot in late April, the studio's music director, Morris Stoloff, entered the process by hiring orchestrators.

As a classically trained composer, Bernstein was accustomed to orchestrating his own scores. Orchestration involves assigning specific instruments to the music being performed, taking the initial "sketch" – the essential melody, harmony and rhythm, often written on two, three, or four staves – and expanding it into an entire

12. Leonard Bernstein at the time he did the score for *On the Waterfront*. (Courtesy of Photofest)

page, with each line assigned to an instrument of the orchestra (violins, trumpets, clarinets, timpani, and so forth). Based on Bernstein's sketches, now housed at the Library of Congress, it is clear that the composer made those decisions in shorthand form and committed them to paper.

The detail work of fully orchestrating every cue (i.e., individual piece of music) fell to two veterans of Hollywood movie music: Marlin Skiles and Gil Grau. Bernstein never mentioned either individual in any interview or published notes on *On the Waterfront*, thus minimizing their contributions. Most observers today believe their work was more secretarial than creative.

Charlie Harmon, who was Bernstein's personal assistant, later his archivist and music editor in the 1980s, believes that the composer probably intended to orchestrate the score himself and then, fond as he was of last-minute tinkering, "realized that it was just more than he could do. I would also bet that, just as with all the times that Hershy Kay and Sid Ramin [other orchestrators on Bernstein projects] helped out, L.B. reviewed every single note of the orchestration so that it really would bear his own stamp. The sketches are basically short scores."[8]

There are differences of opinion about exactly what Skiles and Grau were expected to do. According to one leading composer of the time, Stoloff confessed to him that Bernstein, unfamiliar with the proper use of the Moviola, made serious errors in timing, requiring that many cues be reconfigured. A musician claims the orchestra was rife with rumors that "they had to keep borrowing and making changes and doing all kinds of stuff to make it work."[9] The *Los Angeles Times*, on the other hand, stated that "he had made only a few miscalculations in timing, despite his inexperience and lack of the usual aids" (Goldberg).

Nonetheless, the names of Skiles and Grau appear on every cue (either as "arranger" or "orchestrator"), making them at least partially responsible for the final version of the score. Skiles appears to have begun work on the project in early April 1954, writing more than a third of the 238 pages of orchestral score that *On the Waterfront* would ultimately demand. Grau apparently joined the project later in the month, orchestrating the other two-thirds of Bernstein's music.[10]

Recording took place over three days on the Columbia Pictures studio lot on Gower Street in Hollywood: on Saturday, April 24; Tuesday, April 27; and Wednesday, April 28, 1954. Bernstein, per his contract, could have conducted, but as he told the *Los Angeles Times*, "I didn't conduct myself because there are so many mechanical complications. Morris Stoloff did a better job than I ever could, and what an orchestra! Maybe next time" (Goldberg).

In fact, a few days before the *Times* story, the show-biz trade paper *Daily Variety* erroneously reported: "Leonard Bernstein conducting the Columbia studio orchestra for the recording of the *Waterfront* score he composed."[11] Studio publicity people either misunderstood, or intentionally misrepresented, the facts.

The ensemble consisted of 36 professional musicians who formed the studio's contract orchestra, augmented by several freelance players required by the specifics of Bernstein's score: 11 additional musicians on Saturday and Tuesday, eight extra on Wednesday. On Saturday, after the rest of the orchestra had departed for the day, Bernstein himself played jazz piano for a scene in which Marlon Brando and Eva Marie Saint are having their first drink together in a saloon. He was paid all of $48.21, union scale, for his efforts.[12]

Conducting was 55-year-old Morris Stoloff, the head of Columbia's music department, a post he had held since 1936. Former concertmaster for the Paramount studio orchestra, he already had 15 Academy Award nominations and two Oscars (for the forties, musicals *Cover Girl* and *The Jolson Story*) by the time of *On the Waterfront*.[13]

"It was a big event in town," recalls composer Herschel Burke Gilbert, who attended the recording sessions. "Everybody talked about it. Lenny Bernstein was coming to do a score in Hollywood! What would he do?" Gilbert, then a two-time Oscar nominee (*The Thief, The Moon Is Blue*), would eventually become famous for his television scores (*The Rifleman, Burke's Law*). For *On the Waterfront*, however, he was merely an interested spectator. Bernstein and Gilbert had met once before, when the latter was a gifted viola player on scholarship at Massachusetts' Tanglewood in the summer of 1941.

"Morris conducted everything," Gilbert recalls. "Lenny stood mostly by Morris' side, as many of us did when our work – either as orchestrator or composer – was being conducted [in case] there were any questions. Or, if there were mistakes, we could correct them."[14]

MGM composer – arranger André Previn also visited and later spoke of Bernstein being on edge over issues of sound balance, but veteran Columbia composer George Duning (*From Here to Eternity, Picnic*) recalls that "Morris and Leonard got along fine. Once or twice, Leonard did not agree, but that happens on every score. A lot of times I disagreed with Morris when he was conducting things of my own." [15]

French horn player James Decker, who played the instrumental solo that opens the score, says "It really was a terrific score. We [the players] were all reading it for the first time. And, of course, the opening being what it was, it allowed me to do a little phrasing, which was nice. I was all alone; nobody had to blend in with me. I was able to milk it a little bit. You don't get that chance much in the studios."[16]

George Greeley, pianist in the contract orchestra, and a composer in his own right, was one of few musicians who chatted with Bernstein during breaks. "When he liked something done a little differently," Greeley remembers, "he'd come over to the piano and say, 'George, let me show you what I mean,' and he'd play something. He had tremendous technique." During one break, Greeley recalls, Bernstein sat down and played some of the music from his *Age of Anxiety*.[17]

Stoloff conducted the orchestra in each cue while the appropriate sequence of film was projected on the giant screen in front of him. The print was marked up with "streamers" and "punches," movie parlance for the moving white lines and round flashes of light that were routinely used by Hollywood conductors to ensure proper synchronization of music and image.

With union musicians, sound engineers, music copyists, and various other personnel working at high hourly rates of pay, Columbia (like every movie studio) had music recording down to a science. Stoloff averaged the recording of three to four usable minutes of music per hour, Greeley estimates, with musicians working an average of six to eight hours per day. The entire score, totaling approximately 48 minutes, was recorded in three no-nonsense days.

With recording completed, Bernstein might have been expected to return to New York. Instead, however, he remained in Los Angeles to oversee the dubbing of his score into the picture. Dubbing – the process of mixing together dialogue, sound effects and music – took place on the third floor of the Sound Department building on the Columbia lot. Bernstein called it Upper Dubbing and described its activities for an article that appeared in *The New York Times* on Sunday, May 30, 1954.

The headline read: "Notes Struck at Upper Dubbing, California; Tyro Film Composer Leonard Bernstein Lauds Sound Technicians' Marvels." As published in considerably expanded form in his 1959 book *The Joy of Music*, it was retitled simply, "Upper Dubbing, California."

The essay described Bernstein's frustrations with the mixing process, mostly over reduced-volume, truncated, and even lost musical moments. "By this time," he wrote, "I had become so involved in each detail of the score that it seemed to me perhaps the most important part of the picture.... I found myself pleading for a beloved G-flat."

Occasionally, he reported, a single musical cue would be "turned off completely... and then be turned on again" in order to avoid competing with dialogue. "Sometimes the music, which had been planned as a composition with a beginning, middle, and end, would be silenced seven bars before the end. This is, of course, frustrating and maddening for the composer."

It was also business as usual in Hollywood, something with which Bernstein was unfamiliar. It is instructive to compare the two versions of the same essay. The *Times* piece concludes with the upbeat, pre-release statement that "It was a glorious experience: I wouldn't have missed it for anything." The book version, although nearly 700 words longer, omits that sentiment, clearly reflecting Bernstein's less-than-rosy view of the process.

Dubbing can be painful for any composer, regardless of reputation. It is the first time that the director has heard all of the aural elements of a film together, and it entails a series of last-minute, theoretically creative, and usually practical decisions about how to intertwine dialogue, natural sound, artificial sound effects, and music in the most dramatically potent combinations. Sometimes, particularly with more insecure or less artistically inclined directors, music loses the battle and is "dialed down" or dropped altogether.

In retrospect, Bernstein was quite fortunate. Despite his public protestations, most of what he wrote wound up in the film. And the one instance about which he was most upset – the cue called "Pigeons and Beer," as Edie visits Terry on the rooftop and he asks her for a date – is not only mostly retained in the film, it's much more effective as played than as initially envisioned.

Bernstein's original plan (as described in the unexpurgated version of "Upper Dubbing") was to score this underwritten, pause-filled sequence with "love music that was shy at first," then build "with growing, *Tristan*-ish intensity" to a climax that "swamps the scene and screen, even drowning out the last prosaic bits of dialogue." He claimed that Kazan had agreed to this but reneged during the dubbing, citing what Bernstein referred to as an "ineffably sacred grunt which Brando emits at the end."

In the finished film, there is no such grunt. And nearly three-fourths of Bernstein's cue survives, albeit divided into the intense strings-and-piano opening and the touching, broadening love theme that concludes the scene. Not incidentally, the film's official cue sheet (the document that specifies, to the second, all music in the movie, by which composers and publishers are paid royalties) misstates the amount of music actually heard in the final print, according Bernstein payment for the full piece as written and recorded.

Two cues that were written and recorded appear to have been dropped entirely, each nearly two minutes in length. "The Accident" was to have underscored Kayo Dugan's murder in the cargo hold. As critic William Hamilton (who discussed the score with Bernstein for *Film Music* magazine) reported, "the soundtrack was already too full of dialogue and ambient noise to accomodate any music at all." "The Challenge," which should have accompanied Terry's verbal attack on Johnny Friendly prior to their climactic fight, was also omitted.

Regardless of the difficulties he experienced in the writing, recording, and dubbing of his music, Bernstein enjoyed his weeks in Southern California. "I've made millions of good new friends," he wrote his teacher Helen Coates, "and I find I actually like it here for the very reasons Hollywood is usually attacked: namely, that there is nothing to do but see people" (Burton 237).

When *On the Waterfront* opened on Wednesday, July 28, 1954, at the Astor Theatre in New York City, patrons read four names on the movie poster as the behind-the-scenes talent: producer Sam Spiegel, writer Budd Schulberg, director Elia Kazan, and composer Leonard Bernstein. The composer's name in the same size type as that of the director was highly unusual. It hadn't even been specified in the contract, but Bernstein's contribution had been deemed so significant – or his name so exploitable – as to merit equal billing with the film's other leading creators.

THE SCORE

Bernstein's score contains three primary themes. To use traditional movie-music terms, there is a main theme, a love theme, and a third theme, one that recurs with the greatest frequency, which represents the violence on the docks.

The main theme, stated in the French horn solo of the main title (the opening credit sequence), "is a quiet representation of the element of tragic nobility that underlies the surface crudity and violence of the main character," the composer wrote in his program notes for the symphonic suite he later prepared.[18] This is the theme for Terry Malloy (Brando), although it is rarely heard in the film: After the main title, it doesn't reappear until an hour and a half later as he firmly and finally decides to act against the union chiefs.

The love theme, or as it might also be viewed, the theme for Edie (Saint), is, in Bernstein's words, "a lyrical song." Initially shy and tentative, mirroring Edie's curiosity about the brutish Terry, it is first heard a half-hour into the film, as Terry and Edie take a walk after the incident at the church. It reoccurs throughout.

The violence theme – more accurately, two motifs initially heard back-to-back – pervades the film, in several forms. Heard in its most complete form at the opening of the film, it consists of a three-voice fugato for percussion, over which "an alto saxophone bleats out a tugging, almost spastic, motive of pain," the composer explained in his commentary. "These two germinal entities are responsible for much of the following music," he added.

The score, cue by cue, with Bernstein's original titles and approximate timings (given in minutes and seconds):

1. "Main Title" (1:24). The Columbia Pictures logo is accompanied by the first notes of the main title, played by a lone French horn, solemn and dignified. Bernstein's assistant, Charlie Harmon, recalls the composer saying he "really had to fight for that solo horn; they wanted big, sweeping music over the opening credits." The music

broadens into a duet, then a small ensemble, firmly establishing the theme.

2. "Opening Shot to Scream" (1:58). An energetic burst of timpani and drums introduces the first scenes of the waterfront and its giant ships in the harbor; the marking on the original score is "presto barbaramente," an instruction to the percussionists to play fast and fiercely. Our first glimpse of Johnny Friendly and his entourage is met by an alto saxophone (playing with a "dirty" sound, as the composer noted on the score). The music takes on a dangerous quality, with particular urgency in the lower strings, as Terry Malloy makes his nighttime visit to Joey Doyle's apartment. As the camera moves up the side of the building to reveal Friendly's waiting goons, Bernstein escalates the tension; it comes to a crashing halt when Doyle is thrown off the roof.

3. "Roof Morning" (1:00). Bernstein invokes a quiet, peaceful mood with an oboe solo over strings, woodwinds, and harp for Terry's early-morning visit to his pigeon coop on the roof.

4. "Scramble" (0:52). Bernstein's "fight" music, an explosion of staccato brass and percussion based on the saxophone motif in the violence theme, underscores the mad scramble for working tabs among longshoremen on the docks, and Edie's brief struggle with Terry for her brother Joey's tab.

5. "Riot in Church" (1:56). A brick through the church window starts the cue: Swirling strings, sharp brass, and percussion reprising the "fight" motif as workers run out of the church into the hands of Friendly's men. The excitement calms a bit as Father Barry talks to Kayo Dugan about testifying, and as Terry escorts Edie safely into a nearby park.

6. "Glove Scene" (1:42). Bernstein's love theme is heard for the first time, with a flute carrying the melody, as the chilly relationship between Edie and Terry begins to thaw. Strings take over as he asks to see her again; the cue ends on a questioning note as the flute and clarinet reflect her changing feelings toward Terry.

7. "Pigeons and Beer" (0:51; 2:13). Piercing strings and piano notes suggest Edie's continued anger over Joey's death; the mood calms a bit as she visits Terry on the roof. No music is heard for the next minute or so; then, as Terry and Edie talk about pigeons, Bernstein

launches into a full, rich version of the love theme that continues while Terry asks Edie out for a date.

8. "Piano Juke Box" (0:20). Bernstein himself played the jazz piano emanating from an unseen source as Terry and Edie sit down for a drink in a neighborhood bar.

9. "Saloon Love" (1:14). Edie and Terry have a heart-to-heart talk in the bar to another version of the love theme, interrupted by Gil Grau's intentionally awful bar-band arrangement of Wagner's wedding march from *Lohengrin*.

10. "Waterfront Love Theme" (0:56). Terry comes to Edie's rescue by taking her to a quiet side room, where they dance to another tune played by the band. It's a popular-song rendition of Bernstein's love theme, with a muted trumpet handling the melody. "That's a pretty tune," remarks Edie.

11. "Blue Goon Blues" (2:23). Another source-music piece from the bar band, heard as one of Friendly's hoods summons him (and he's served with a subpoena moments later), is a transformation of the violence theme in blues form. Terry, a little drunk, is heard whistling the tune as he walks home in the next scene.

12. "After Sermon" (1:11). As Father Barry concludes his impassioned remarks over Kayo Dugan's body and Terry considers his moral dilemma, Bernstein launches what he called "a dirge-like version of the fugato subject," a dark, funereal adaptation of the timpani half of the violence theme that grows even more dramatic as Barry is lifted out of the cargo hold.

13. "Roof 3" (1:29). Edie, still holding Joey's jacket, revisits the roof as Bernstein plays the love theme with a solo flute. Strings assume the melody as she holds Terry and they kiss.

14. "Confession Scene" (1:11). Edie runs away after Terry confesses the truth about Joey's murder. Shrill strings and percussion, again based on the second half of the violence theme, reflect her agitated mental state; the scene shifts to the rooftop, where Crime Commission lawyer Glover visits Terry and the mood becomes uncertain.

15. "Kangaroo Court" (0:31). Friendly's interrogation of Charley ends with a series of ascending, dramatic chords for brass and woodwinds, punctuated by rapid-fire notes in brass as he leaves the waterfront to meet Terry.

16. "Cab and Bedroom" (3:57). This is the second-longest cue in the score, encompassing both the famous dialogue between Terry and Charley during their cab ride and Terry forcing his way into Edie's apartment. The cue begins as Charley pulls a gun on Terry; the music is a subdued variation on "Kangaroo Court," and as Charley reflects on Terry's boxing career and Terry reminds him of the truth ("I coulda been a contender"). Bernstein bolsters the emotional impact of the scene with a reprise of the dirge-like music of "After Sermon." Once Terry leaves and the cabbie races off with Charley, the swirling strings and sharp brass of the violence theme return and Charley's doom is sealed. Attention shifts to Terry breaking into Edie's apartment, with an unexpectedly harsh rendition of the love theme; the violence theme returns as Terry appears threatening, until he grabs her and the music abruptly ceases.

17. "Charley's Death" (1:43). Murder is once again in the air, as Bernstein reprises the complete violence theme (timpani opening; muted trumpet replacing the alto sax of the original; heightened orchestral excitement). Tension mounts as Edie runs after Terry and the two are nearly killed by a speeding truck; the percussive nature of Bernstein's score stresses the high danger of the moment. Terry spots Charley's body, leading directly into:

18. "Accident — Coda" (2:16). In one of the saddest moments of the score, Bernstein reprises the impassioned music of Father Barry's speech as Terry and Edie slowly approach the murdered Charley and Terry pulls him down. The violence theme (a variation on the timpani part) returns as Terry vows vengeance.

19. "Throwing the Gun" (1:12). Another variation on the violence theme (this time, the second half), as Father Barry attempts to convince Terry to testify instead of taking the law into his own hands. An intense string version broadens to include the entire orchestra as Terry hurls his handgun at Friendly's framed photo in the bar.

20. "Dead Pigeons" (4:34). The longest, and most heartfelt, cue in the score opens with a string quartet and broadens into an orchestral elegy as Terry – shunned by his peers for testifying – discovers that his young protégé has killed all of the pigeons in the rooftop coop. Three minutes into the cue, the main theme returns for the first time since the start of the film: Terry spots a ship leaving the harbor while Edie begs him to leave. As Edie shouts at Terry and he decides to go down

to the waterfront, Bernstein quietly yet significantly counterpoints the main theme (French horn) with the love theme (flute), suggesting the joint destiny of the two young people.

21. "Wild Phrases" (0:28; 0:08). The main theme is reprised (in two sections) by the solo French horn as Terry stands alone on the docks, the only worker not hired for the day.

22. "The Fight" (1:20). Terry attacks Friendly to Bernstein's now-familiar fight music, the staccato brass and percussion hits that denote the rough side of the union toughs. Mournful strings and flutes suggest the worst for Terry.

23. "Terry Unconscious" (1:57). The longshoremen, realizing that the badly beaten Terry is now their best hope for regaining control of their union, beg him to help them. Bernstein quietly underscores the dialogue with unobtrusive but supportive woodwinds, and when Terry decides to take a stand, the main theme returns. This leads directly into:

24. "Walk and End Title" (2:11). As the half-dead Terry walks unsteadily up the plank and past his once-scornful colleagues, Bernstein leads with a mysterious vibraphone-and-bass version of the main theme (will he make it?). Brass and woodwinds join as Terry stumbles his way toward the giant rollup door; strings are added as the mood becomes more hopeful. No natural sound intrudes. As he stands before the boss, slightly dissonant brass chords sound ("All right, let's go to work!"). Bernstein then brilliantly combines the main theme with the love theme – a clear statement that it is Edie who has enlightened Terry and enabled him to press on – as the men follow Terry into the building, while Friendly's shouts are ignored, and Father Barry and Edie look on proudly. The main theme is once more heard in its entirety as the door closes slowly behind the men and the words "THE END" appear. The Columbia logo returns and the score concludes on a crashing, intriguingly dissonant yet triumphant orchestral statement. As Bernstein put it: "As he makes his sacrificial gesture at the end of the film, the motive of his nobility climbs in intensity, mingled now with suggestions of the love music, to the inevitable fortissimo."

Many years later, Kazan complained about some of Bernstein's choices. "I try not to bring another personality into the picture

13. Two pages of the final music cue ("Walk and End Title") in Leonard Bernstein's own hand. (From the Bernstein Collection at the Library of Congress, used by permission of Amberson, Inc.)

through the music, but there was no way to avoid that with Lenny," he said. "So you're aware of the music. It put the picture on the level of almost operatic melodrama here and there" (Young 183). For his part, Schulberg laughs when he says "At times in the movie

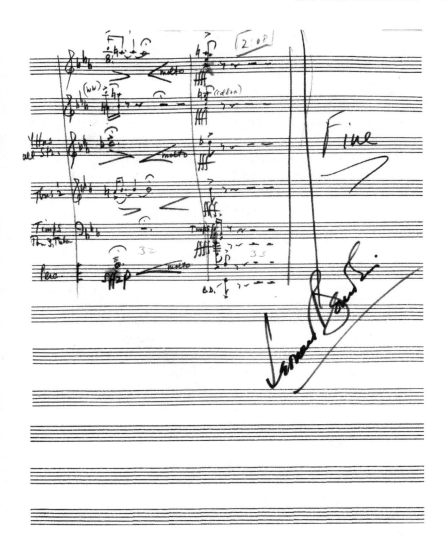

itself, I simply thought it was too loud, it was sometimes outdo-
ing the dialogue or telling too much. But that doesn't detract from
the work itself. It is a marvelous score, a wonderful piece of musical
writing."

What was "operatic melodrama" to Kazan was "very imagina-
tive and unusual psychological use of the sound track" to Laurence
Rosenthal, the widely respected composer of such scores as *The
Miracle Worker* and *Becket*. In an essay for the landmark 1973 study

Music for the Movies, Rosenthal praised Bernstein's device of "obscuring with music certain lines of dialogue, emphasizing their intended banality. Here the emotional line of the music tells much more than would the obliterated words."[19]

Elmer Bernstein – no relation to Leonard – who is one of the most honored composers of contemporary film music (having written such classics as *To Kill a Mockingbird, The Magnificent Seven*, and *The Ten Commandments*), declares "I think it's one of the great scores ever written in Hollywood, because of its tremendous energy. It energized the film. It lent a dignity to the love interest instead of trivializing it. And forgetting everything else, it was just superior music on its own."[20]

POSTLUDE

From the very beginnings of film criticism, the contribution of music has often been ignored for a variety of reasons, most of them shockingly mundane. Critics tend to be overly enamored of the image at the expense of sound; don't fully understand how movies are made and therefore discount the often subtle role that music plays; have no musical training and fear looking foolish writing about it; or simply don't notice the score.

On the Waterfront met with glowing reviews but, as usual, the composer was largely left out of the lavish praise.

A handful of critics did mention the music. On July 19, *Life* magazine labeled the film "brilliant" and noted: "Its somber mood, created at the outset by a chilling musical score by Leonard Bernstein. . . ." *The New York Times*, in its July 29 review (included in this volume) lumped the composer with the rest of the principal creative collaborators as having "convincingly . . . illustrated the murder and mayhem of the waterfront's sleazy jungles." *The New Yorker*, on July 31, said Bernstein's work was "at once pertinent and unobtrusive, and always serves to step up the dramatic points the film is making."

On Aug. 9, *Newsweek* combined its praise of composer and cinematographer: "The pitch of Leonard Bernstein's score and the chiaroscuro of Boris Kaufman's study of the Hoboken docks and tenements have a way of making the story and its actors into dramatic universals." *Time*, curiously, failed to mention the composer in its

Aug. 2 review but caught up three years later in a cover story about Bernstein: "In his score for the movie *On the Waterfront*, some critics heard a new note in Bernstein's music, a curiously piercing purity that seemed to burst from a hot core of originality" (February 4, 1957).

Columbia's Morris Stoloff wrote the composer on Aug. 21: "I am very happy about the impact of your score on both musicians and public alike." He continued. "I must tell you that, particularly in Hollywood, there have been tremendous comments on it," adding that RKO's musical director, Constantin Bakaleinikoff, "seems anxious to have you do a score for one of their biggest pictures."[21]

If a formal offer ever came, it wasn't accepted. Bernstein was busy in Martha's Vineyard, Massachusetts, first writing his "Serenade" for solo violin, strings, harp and percussion, then devoting full time to his *Candide* project with Lillian Hellman and lyricist John Latouche (who had collaborated with Vernon Duke on *Cabin in the Sky* and Jerome Moross on *The Golden Apple*).

Latouche, probably at Bernstein's suggestion, penned a lyric to the love theme of *On the Waterfront*, and it was published by J. J. Robbins later that year in a nicely appointed edition featuring the movie art on its cover. The lyric was uninspired ("I wait on the waterfront / the harbor lights are burning low … ") and the tune failed to make the pop charts.

"Serious" music critics paid little or no attention to film music in that era, although a handful of music professionals did. The leading publication of its time, *Film Music*, published by the National Film Music Council in New York, made *On the Waterfront* its cover story in the September – October 1954 issue. At Stoloff's suggestion, Bernstein provided editor William Hamilton with copies of "conductor parts" – a condensed version of the score for each cue – from which he penned a scholarly discussion.

"In spite of all the fabled terrors of film-score composition, Leonard Bernstein's first try at it has succeeded with the éclat so characteristic of him," Hamilton wrote, citing the "boldness" of its structure and noting that "the purposeful unity of the whole work is one of its strongest features."[22]

A few months later, Austrian critic Hans Keller, writing in the English periodical *The Score*, declared that "Leonard Bernstein's music is about the best film score that has come out of America." Keller cited its "sheer professional skill" and believed that "in textural style and harmonic idiom it is more daring than many more individual film scores by our own leading composers.... It is clear that Bernstein is determined to subject the Hollywoodian sound track to a radical spring cleaning."

On Feb. 12, 1955, the Academy of Motion Picture Arts and Sciences announced its nominations for the 1954 Academy Awards. Among the 12 Oscar nominations accorded *On the Waterfront*, one was for Leonard Bernstein in the category of "scoring of a dramatic or comedy picture."

Sam Spiegel pulled out all the stops to win for his movie. He took out full-page advertisements extolling the merits of his cast and crew, including one in *The Hollywood Reporter* (March 4) and another in *Daily Variety* (March 9) specifically designed to remind Academy members of Bernstein's musical accomplishment.

The 27th annual Academy Awards ceremonies were held March 30, 1955, in two locations: the RKO Pantages Theatre in Hollywood and the NBC Century Theatre in New York. Bernstein did not attend; he was conducting opera at La Scala in Milan, Italy (Burton 243–6). The film won eight Oscars, but music honors were not among them. Bernstein lost to perennial Hollywood favorite Dimitri Tiomkin for the music of the John Wayne thriller *The High and the Mighty*, whose whistled theme had been a giant hit on records the previous summer.

Columbia music director Morris Stoloff, on June 22, wrote "Although the Academy may not have shown its appreciation, I personally value your music highly and I can speak as well for my company." Stoloff sent along the original scores for *On the Waterfront*, which Bernstein was then adapting into a 20-minute, single-movement symphonic suite for performance that summer in Tanglewood.

The suite was a convenient way for Bernstein to ensure that his music would live on in a more musically coherent form and an arguably more dignified concert hall setting (à la Sergei Prokofiev's *Alexander Nevsky*, Sir William Walton's *Henry V*, and Aaron Copland's *The Red Pony*, movie scores by "serious" composers turned into concert works). It was premiered by the Boston Symphony Orchestra on August 11, 1955; the composer recorded it with the New York Philharmonic on May 16, 1960.[23]

12 AWARD NOMINATIONS

By the Academy of Motion Pictures Arts and Sciences

ON THE WATERFRONT

A HORIZON PICTURE
A Columbia Release

Best Musical Score
LEONARD BERNSTEIN

BEST MOTION PICTURE *"ON THE WATERFRONT"*			BEST ACHIEVEMENT IN ART DIRECTION *(Black and White)* *RICHARD DAY*
BEST PERFORMANCE BY AN ACTOR *MARLON BRANDO*	BEST PERFORMANCE BY AN ACTRESS IN A SUPPORTING ROLE *EVA MARIE SAINT*	BEST STORY AND SCREENPLAY *BUDD SCHULBERG*	BEST ACHIEVEMENT IN FILM EDITING *GENE MILFORD*
BEST PERFORMANCE BY AN ACTOR IN A SUPPORTING ROLE *LEE J. COBB* *KARL MALDEN* *ROD STEIGER*	BEST ACHIEVEMENT IN DIRECTION *ELIA KAZAN*	BEST MUSICAL SCORE FOR A DRAMATIC PICTURE *LEONARD BERNSTEIN*	BEST ACHIEVEMENT IN CINEMATOGRAPHY *(Black and White)* *BORIS KAUFMAN*

14. Advertisement from *The Hollywood Reporter*, March 9, 1955. (Courtesy of the Academy of Motion Picture Arts and Sciences, Los Angeles)

Leonard Bernstein would never again compose for the movies. During the dubbing of *On the Waterfront*, he told the *Los Angeles Times* that he was no longer interested in writing "background" music. Charlie Harmon adds: "He always claimed that he didn't do another film because he was so upset at the cutting and editing process over which he had no control."

Nearly 50 years later, Bernstein's music for *On the Waterfront* continues to stir audiences and deepen the impact of the film. Music critic Clifford McCarty's commentary, written in 1955, is equally valid today: "So fresh and powerful is Bernstein's music, and in so personal an idiom, that it at once sets itself apart from the more conventional 'Hollywood' scores" (Grunfeld 213–14). Sam Spiegel may have hired Bernstein solely for marquee value, but the music that he wrote captured the energy of the locale, the passion of young lovers, the danger of the moment, and the ultimate victory of one man over a corrupt system. It was more than many film scores ever accomplish, written by one of the century's most original musical voices. What a shame that Leonard Bernstein composed only one movie score – but what good fortune that it happened to be for *On the Waterfront.*

NOTES

1   Background on Bernstein is drawn from Stanley Sadie, Nicolas Slonimsky, Steven Suskin, and the several Bernstein biographies cited.
2   This and subsequent Schulberg quotations are from a telephone interview conducted with him on January 11, 2000.
3   Alex North's widow, Anne Marie North, confirmed this conclusion in an informal interview in January 2000.
4   These names are found in Kazan's production notebook for the film, among the Kazan papers at Wesleyan University. There are also fleeting references to Irish folk tunes that he intended to use ("Galway Bay," "I'll Take You Home Again Kathleen"), apparently to establish the ethnic background of many of the waterfront workers; none were used.
5   Burton's biography is the best and most reliable of the several available by virtue of his broad and unprecedented access to the composer's private papers.
6   All contract details are drawn directly from Bernstein's contract, which is in the music files of Columbia Pictures, now a part of Sony Pictures Corporation.
7   Goldberg. "Cue sheets" in this case refers to the music editor's second-by-second descriptions of the action happening on screen; "cutter" refers to the music editor; and "converter table" could mean several things but most likely refers to the conversion of musical tempi into time, in fractions of seconds.
8   Interview with Charlie Harmon, June 25, 1999.
9   Both composer and musician – the latter of whom played on the recording sessions – asked for anonymity in discussing the score, not wishing to

denigrate publicly Bernstein or his memory. Both otherwise expressed great admiration for the composer.

10   Their orchestration bills, specifying which cues they handled and how much they were paid, are in the music files at Columbia/Sony.

11   This item appeared in Mike Kaplan's "Clef Dwellers" column in *Daily Variety*, May 4, 1954.

12   Orchestra size, payment information, and recording dates are based on recording logs in the Columbia files and the archives of Local 47, American Federation of Musicians, in Los Angeles.

13   Stoloff background is based on his file at the Margaret Herrick Library. Oscar data are from Richard Shale, *Academy Awards*.

14   This and subsequent Gilbert quotations are from an interview with the composer, January 6, 2000.

15   Interview with George Duning, December 1, 1999. The Previn anecdote is in Burton, 237.

16   Interview with James Decker, January 8, 2000.

17   Interview with George Greeley, January 7, 2000.

18   Bernstein's program notes for the symphonic suite were his only public comments about the construction of the score. They are preserved, in his own hand, among the Bernstein papers at the Library of Congress; they were also published under the composer's byline in the *Berkshire Evening Eagle*, August 10, 1955.

19   His essay is whimsically titled "Laurence Rosenthal on the Aesthetics of Scoring Films. Or, Old Composers Never Die, They Simply Fade Away in the Dubbing Room," in Thomas, 33–6.

20   Interview with Elmer Bernstein, January 20, 2000.

21   Stoloff's two letters to Bernstein are in the composer's papers at the Library of Congress.

22   Kenneth R. Hey, one of few scholars seriously to examine the Bernstein score, draws heavily on Hamilton's analysis.

23   The performance was reviewed by "H.T." in *The New York Times* on August 12, 1955. Recording date for the suite is noted in Sony Classical's 1997 reissue of the work on compact disc (SMK 63085).

Selected Reviews and Commentary

WATERFRONT: FROM DOCKS TO FILM

Budd Schulberg

(*New York Times*, July 11, 1954)

Reprinted with permission of the author.

Some four years ago – it seems more like forty – men from a new film company came to me with the idea of doing a picture based on Malcolm Johnson's Pulitzer Prize – winning report of New York waterfront conditions. The epic scale of the corruption and violence intrigued me. Only a few blocks from Sardi's and Shor's and other places where itinerant social philosophers assemble to discuss the problems of the day, guys who said no to industrial feudalism were getting clobbered and killed. The waterfront, Johnson had written, was a lawless frontier where men for generations had taken power into their own hands.

I decided to take the plunge. But before I could write it I had to move from Johnson's vivid reporting to some first-hand knowledge of my own. One of the first things that caught my imagination was the contribution being made by waterfront priests. A number of them, from old Father Monaghan on Staten Island to young Father John Corridan of the lower West Side, had championed the men who had been forsaken on the docks.

Evil

There was a system of hiring called the shape-up, which had been outlawed in England a century ago as inhuman, degrading and wasteful of manpower. These priests saw the immorality of the shape-up: five or six hundred men standing around a hiring boss, often a Sing-Sing old grad, who taps the two hundred or so he wants that day. There was hardly an evil in the harbor, said the waterfront priests, not directly traceable to the shape-up.

I got to know Father Corridan, a rangy, fast-talking, chain-smoking West Side product who talks the darndest language I ever heard, combining the gritty vocabulary of the longshoremen with mob talk, the statistical findings of a trained economist and the teachings of Christ.

I also got to know some longshoremen. A lot of research, it should be confessed, was conducted in the waterfront bars, for the saloons have a special significance around the harbor. One will be the hangout of a particular waterfront mob, another the gathering place of the "insoigents" trying to get the boys off their necks. In some of these bars my dockworker guides were warmly welcomed. In others, there would be ominous silence and a lot of cold-eyed staring. In the hostile pubs it was wiser for a longshoreman and a reporter or any kind of writer not to be seen together.

A few months later, in the early spring of 1951, my script was finished. Robert Siodmak, who was to direct it, seemed happy about it, and I thought my days on the waterfront were done. But the months melted away without production. The little film company was something less than a financial rock. In fact, it was unable to get up the "scratch." The subject matter was a little too hot to handle. If the longshoremen's locals were gangster run, how could our picture company get on the docks? Why not make a nice Western or musical? Prospective backers backed away.

Another year passed. Now the rights to the script had reverted to me. And, when Johnson's option with the original company lapsed, I took plunge number two, and bought his material. Truth was, I couldn't get the waterfront out of my mind.

One day I got a letter from Elia Kazan. Something on his mind, he wrote. How about lunch? We met for the first time and he told me a notion he had for a picture to be made in the East. Not the waterfront. Something to do with the strange ways of justice in a town I knew. I thought it had something but there was my waterfront frustration. Why not my script first? The other project some later day? Oddly enough, Kazan said, he had tried to do a waterfront story at the same time that I had been pushing mine. His had also fallen through.

So we made a new start. Time had changed the waterfront scene and we needed a new story, a stronger approach. Our script was finished in the spring of 1953. A year ago we went out to Hollywood in high spirits. A major studio was willing to give our brainchild a home. Hollywood has done realistic, hard-hitting stories particularly well in the past and we were hopeful of reviving a healthy tradition.

Stymie

Our exuberance was short-lived. The head of the studio had changed his mind, waterfront wouldn't fit in with the program of costumed horse operas he was lining up. That was stone wall number 1, and 2 and 3, 4 and 5 were right behind it. The picture was still too controversial, we were told. Too grim, too shocking. And would the people care about the struggle on the docks?

For an embattled week Kazan and I could not seem to convince anyone else but each other. In our hotel was a wandering film man, Sam Spiegel, the erstwhile S. P. Eagle, a truly international character and an independent producer. Once in a while our doors would open at the same time and we could look briefly into each other's apartments and lives.

One morning I went across the hall at my neighbor's invitation and paced up and down in front of Sam's bed. In Hollywood we have a rather charming tradition whereby writers rise early and tell stories to producers in their bedrooms or while they are shaving. Anyway, I did, and the rest is history or, at least, the next best thing, a completed motion picture. Sam heard me out and said, "I will do the picture."

That wasn't the end of our adventure – really only a new beginning. Between June, 1953, and last February, when the final shot went into the can, we faced stone walls 6, 7, 8, and 9. But somehow, with a scratch here and a rip there, we got over all of them, and here we are, four years and at least eight full scripts later, ready to show a picture a lot of people told us could never be made on the docks of New York.

THE SCREEN: ASTOR OFFERS *ON THE WATERFRONT*

A. H. Weiler

(*New York Times*, July 29, 1954)

A small but obviously dedicated group of realists has forged artistry, anger and some horrible truths into "On the Waterfront," as violent and indelible a film record of man's inhumanity to man as has come to light this year. And while this explosive indictment of the vultures and the meek prey of the docksides, which was unveiled at the Astor yesterday, occasionally is only surface dramatization and an oversimplification of the personalities and evils of our waterfront, it is, nevertheless, an uncommonly powerful, exciting and imaginative use of the screen by gifted professionals.

Although journalism and television already have made the brutal fascination of the wharves a part of current history, "On the Waterfront" adds a graphic dimension to these sordid pages. Credit for this achievement cannot be relegated to a specific few. Scenarist Budd Schulberg, who since 1949, has lived with the story stemming from Malcolm Johnson's crusading newspaper articles; director Elia Kazan; the principals headed by Marlon Brando; producer Sam Spiegel; Columbia, which is presenting this independently made production; Leonard Bernstein, who herein is making his debut as a movie composer; and Boris Kaufman, the cinematographer, convincingly have illustrated the murder and mayhem of the waterfront's sleazy jungles.

They also have limned a bestial and venal boss longshoreman; the shape-up by which only his obedient, mulct, vassals can earn a day's pay; the hard and strange code that demands that these sullen men die rather than talk about these injustices and a crime commission that helps bring some light into their dark lives.

Perhaps these annals of crime are too labyrinthine to be fully and incisively captured by cameras. Suffice it to say, however, that while Mr. Kazan and Mr. Schulberg have not dug as deeply as they might, they have chosen a proper and highly effective cast and setting for their grim adventure. Moving cameras and crews to the crowded rookeries of Hoboken's quayside, where the film was shot in its entirety, they have told with amazing speed and force the story of Terry Malloy, ex-prize fighter and inarticulate tool of tough, ruthless and crooked labor leader, Johnny Friendly. The labor leader is an absolute unregenerated monarch of the docks who will blithely shake down his own men as well as ship owners; he will take cuts of pay envelopes and lend his impecunious union members money at usurious rates and he will have his pistol-toting goons dispatch anyone foolish enough to squeal to the crime commission attempting to investigate these practices.

It is the story also of one of these courageous few about to "sing" to the commission – a luckless longshoreman unwittingly set up for the kill by Terry Malloy, who is in his soft spot only because his older brother is the boss' slick right-hand man. It is the tale of Terry's meeting with the dead man's agonized sister and a fearless, neighborhood priest, who, by love and reason, bring the vicious picture into focus for him. And, it is the account of the murder of Terry's brother; the rampaging younger man's defiant testimony before the commission, and the climactic bloody battle that wrests the union from the boss' tenacious grasp.

Journalism may have made these ingredients familiar and certainly more inclusive and multi-dimension[al] (sic), but Mr. Kazan's direction, his outstanding cast, and Mr. Schulberg's pithy and punchy dialogue give them distinction and terrific impact. Under the director's expert guidance, Marlon Brando's Terry Malloy is a shatteringly poignant portrayal of an amoral, confused, illiterate citizen of the lower depths who is goaded into decency by love, hate, and murder. His groping for words, use of the vernacular, care of his beloved pigeons, pugilist's walk and gestures and his discoveries of love and the immensity of the crimes surrounding him are highlights of a beautiful and moving portrayal.

In casting Eva Marie Saint – newcomer to movies from TV and Broadway – Mr. Kazan has come up with a pretty and blond artisan who does not have to depend on these attributes. Her parochial school training is no bar to love with the proper stranger. Amid scenes of carnage, she gives tenderness and sensitivity to genuine romance. Karl Malden, whose importance in the scheme of this drama seems overemphasized, is, however, a tower of strength as the militant man of the cloth. Rod Steiger, another newcomer to films, is excellent as Brando's fearful brother. The pair have a final scene that is a harsh and touching revelation of their frailties.

Lee J. Cobb is muscularly effective as the labor boss. John Hamilton and Pat Henning are typical "longshoremen," gents who look at home in a hold, and Tony Galento, Tami Mauriello, and Abe Simon – erstwhile heavyweight boxing contenders who portray Cobb's chief goons – are citizens no one would want to meet in a dark alley. Despite its happy ending; its preachments and a somewhat slick approach to some of the facets of dockside strife and tribulations, "On the Waterfront" is moviemaking of a rare and high order.

THE BIG SELL: A REVIEW

Mr. Harper

(*Harper's*, August 1954)

Whether an American movie should try to deal soberly and accurately with American life is a question that has to be asked – and periodically answered Yes in general terms and No in particular ones. "On the Water-front" with Marlon Brando, is the most recent among the discouraging exhibits of how far wrong you can go with the best of intentions. It is a film with every virtue except the one which would have redeemed it even had it lacked the others, which is justice. For the most part it is beautifully acted, beautifully directed, and beautifully photographed – and in total it is an obnoxious fake: false to the longshoremen whose lot it purports to depict, false to the dedicated individuals who have tried to improve that lot, and ultimately false to itself.

Movie-makers of the caliber of Mr. Brando and Elia Kazan (who is his director here) obviously aim for significance and distinction. One can see how this project must have attracted them; it was a chance to work with realism and respect within an important, glamorous, and cinematically untouched area of national life; to say something relevant about an issue which had been but recently in the headlines; and to handle the dramatic materials of American low life with that caressing tenderness that is mis-named "documentary." At this point all the forces undoubtedly came into action which are supposed to keep American movies from offend-ing anyone powerful enough to afford a Los Angeles office: and there took place the usual struggle to save what would be saved, to conceal in subtleties what could not be left explicit, and to achieve a compromise that was not one of the spirit.

Everyone does this: there is no other way to make big-company movies, and no reason why there should be another way. The things movies "say" are so much better stated through indirect suggestion, and Hollywood has developed so many techniques of skillful evasion, that the burden of censorship and the pressure groups has always been more apparent than real. Art thrives on limitations. For the classic French dramatists the three unities of time, place, and action (plus the whimsical sensitivities of a monarchical court) must have been continuously irritating, but they were no obstacle to greatness. The audiences of any age make certain demands about the stories they are willing to listen to, demands that are always observed even when they are circumvented. What is interesting about the artist's compromise, in the movies as elsewhere, is what he chooses to conserve and what he chooses to sacrifice.

For the sake of a hollow fidelity to the brooding atmosphere of violence and venality around the New York docks, "On the Waterfront" gives up any sense whatever of responsible judgment. It is a charming and fitfully naturalistic vignette, a safely sterilized and hygienic slumming expedi-tion, which allows the spectator all the satisfaction of sharing life in the raw without having to do, or even think, anything about it. This movie first engages your attention and sympathy by saying things that are true – things drawn from the long roster of evidence that the waterfront has in fact been in the grip of thieves and murderers – and then resolves its own comparatively simple dramatic conflicts by saying what is not only untrue but insulting to the honest men who have truly fought, and bled, and died "on the waterfront." As a memorial, this film is respectful neither to their motives, nor to their difficulties, nor to their good sense.

"On the Waterfront" is not circumscribed by an inability to distribute blame; if anything, it manages to blame everyone but Marlon Brando. The majority of the longshoremen are represented as weak and befuddled by the threats of their leaders. The Church is represented as aggressively indifferent, except in the person of a single sympathetic but naive priest. The unions are represented only by one "pistol local," which is made to seem uniquely vicious and whose leader, in a grotesque parody, utters the only defense of the laboring man's economic aspirations which the film contains. There is a sly but inconclusive insinuation that he is covertly in league with the stevedoring bosses, but otherwise "On the Waterfront" leaves you with the vaguely confusing impression that no one union is really like this but that all of them are a little. A "crime commission" makes a brief appearance but mainly as a setting for Mr. Brando's crucial decision to "call copper" and tell all. In the end there is a fist fight, the Bad Mans [sic] gets tossed in the water, and everyone goes happily back to work. Thus we leave beautiful Hell's Kitchen.

For the rest, it is all Brando – the infinitely slow penetration of an idea into his head and the incredible pressures required to overcome his natural inertia. He plays the part well – nonsense, he plays it perfectly, with that cat-like confidence that comes from knowing an Academy Award role when he sees it. As the punchy ex-pug, the teen-ager's idol, the mob's boy with the good heart, Mr. Brando seems to savor his own performance with the same relish he gets from turning over on his tongue the stereotyped nasal idiom of the underprivileged – "He was a good kid, dat Joey" (this of a man he has just sent to die). There are other fine performances, among them Karl Malden's as the priest, with a face of individualistic dignity that is much more impressive than the lines he is given to speak. But for the rest, it is all Brando – his divided loyalties, his soul-searching, his sacrifice, his sufferings, and his wholly ambiguous triumph.

The point of the picture, if there is a point (and the concluding sequences are all of a rush, as though no one knew quite how to stop it but wanted to get everything in first), is that Mr. B., a convinced thug, is led by a dawning awareness of wrong into personal conflict with his villainous colleagues. His first impulse is to precipitate a gun-fight in which he would obviously be killed. Reason (in the person of the priest) prevails, and he takes the "harder" step of breaking the waterfront code of silence on the witness stand – thus alienating himself from his society but so weakening it that he can then have his fight without guns and merely be beaten to a pulp.

Bloody but unbowed – and reinstated in the eyes of the community – he subsequently shows by his survival that the power of the corrupt union is broken, thus averting a wildcat strike and presumably falling prostrate at the feet of a towering white-haired figure who symbolizes Company Authority. Several interpretations of this little scenario are possible, but it would be difficult to say which is the most nauseating.

Understandably, drama must convert abstract issues into human ones. It would be asking too much of "On the Waterfront" that it cope effectively with the complex triangular relationship between the International Longshoremen's Association, the shipping companies, and the mobsters which one investigating group after another have over the years sought to unravel. It might even be asking too much of a movie that it pay just attention to the courage and intelligence of men like Father John Corridan of the St. Francis Xavier Labor School, who must go on being calm, persuasive, and patient after the "crime commissions" go home and the public turns to other sources of titillating scandal. But it is not asking too much to demand of films with pretensions to being serious and moving that they do not exploit, do not ridicule, and do not falsify the "reality" on which they are based. If there is no alternative, then the picture should not have been made – not by men who can afford to be choosy, like Mr. Brando, Mr. Kazan, and Mr. Budd Schulberg, the film's writer.

It is the practice these days of such "liberal" highbrows as Mr. Brando to complain about the predominance in American life and letters of the passive, blundering, masochistic hero made immortal by Mickey Spillane – his modern crusader with no motives, no emotions, no morals, and no end in view, whose sole function is to move inexorably through a perverse and chaotic world, precipitating violence and winning only by being alive at the end of the last chapter.

It is a sinister archetype for any literature, but even more sinister is its penetration into the dramatic sermonizing of intelligent and well-intentioned people who know better. If the makers of "On the Waterfront" had chosen to have it merely a decadently sophisticated underworld travelogue – a kind of American "*Quai des Brumes*" – they would have been truer to themselves, their subject, and their art. Still better, they could of stood in bed.

MAN'S HOPE: A REVIEW

Philip T. Hartung

(*Commonweal*, August 20, 1954)

© 1954 Commonweal Foundation. Reprinted by permission.

It is so seldom that an American film spends most of its footage considering the basic dignity of man (as did the "Italian Bicycle Thief" and the French "Diary of a Country Priest") that we have twofold reason for welcoming "On the Waterfront." It is, in the first place, extraordinarily successful as a movie. Under the direction of Elia Kazan the action moves along at a fast pace in telling a story of violence and passion on the New York waterfront. Most of the picture was beautifully photographed in Hoboken, New Jersey, with the Hudson River, the New York skyline, the Hoboken piers, saloons, tenements, and one Catholic church in particular as background, and it effectively uses these real scenes as part of the story, and the setting becomes almost as important as the actors.

"On the Waterfront" is an excellent example of cooperation in picture making; for that reason it is difficult to spotlight any one person in the credits. Sam Speigel's excellent production with emphasis on quality all down the line; Budd Schulberg's well-written screenplay which stems from Malcolm Johnson's series of newspaper articles (which won a Pulitzer prize in 1949) and from interviews Schulberg had with various dock leaders and workers, especially Father John M. Corridan, assistant director of the Xavier Labor School; the musical score by Leonard Bernstein which highlights the action and mood and serves as an asset, never as a scene stealer; and Director Elia Kazan's thoughtful handling of the unusual cast which includes professionals, non-professionals and some newcomers, all result in a total effect which brilliantly conveys the desperate situation on the waterfront.

Kazan should also get a hand for guiding Marlon Brando in the finest performance of his distinguished movie career. Brando plays an ex–prize fighter who is little more than an errand boy for the waterfront union's crooked boss (Lee J. Cobb). The young man is tolerated by this moneyed big shot only because his brother (Rod Steiger) is the boss' right hand. Brando knows that the boss' goon killed a young fellow who was going to break the waterfront code by testifying to the Crime Commission. Brando is almost indifferent to his very small part in the murder until the dead boy's sister and the parish priest work on him to tell what he knows. Schulberg has written the role with understanding and Brando plays it with equal understanding: there is a touch of the usual Brando toughness and every-man-for-himself attitude, but this is really a portrait of change, of regeneration, and Brando is magnificent in the scenes in which he becomes convinced by the girl and the priest – as well as by the act of extreme violence in which the mugs kill his brother – that the only way he can fight back and save his own integrity is by testifying in the courtroom.

Karl Malden's portrayal of the courageous priest is as outstanding as the author's characterization of the part. The selection of the lovely Eva Marie Saint for the role of the convent-raised girl who sways Brando through her gentle loveliness as well as her principles was one of the wisest decisions of the film. The scenes between her and Brando have a haunting beauty.

But it is the picture's dignity you will remember the longest: the portrait of a young man who struggles through a seemingly hopeless situation. "On the Waterfront" has weaknesses – particularly in the simplification of the waterfront mess and its inability to make clear the loyalty of men to an organization that allows their loved ones to be destroyed. But as a drama of man's victory and rise from low estate, "On the Waterfront" is a film to stand with the best. The final scenes have the quality of the making of a saint. In this man's triumph is visualized and felt the final victory of all men.

ON THE WATERFRONT: A REVIEW

Penelope Houston

(*Sight & Sound*, October/December 1954)

Taken from *Sight and Sound*, 24.2 (October/December 1954) © *Sight and Sound*/British Film Institute, all rights retained.

Elia Kazan's "On the Waterfront" (Columbia) is a significant, almost a definitive, example of a type of film which traditionally finds Hollywood at its most expert: the melodrama with a stiffening of serious ideas, the journalistic exposé of crime and corruption. Its subject harks back to the racket-smashing thrillers of the 'thirties; its style – location shooting, conscientious concern with surface realism – belongs to the present decade; its pretensions, the attempt to build authentic drama out of an investigation of waterfront gangsterism, are characteristic not only of the director but of a whole school of Hollywood thought.

The film's central character, Terry Malloy (Marlon Brando), is a young man in his late twenties, once a boxer, now an aimless hanger-on in the retinue of Johnny Friendly (Lee J. Cobb), the corrupt union boss who imposes gangster law on the New York waterfront. Terry is involved in the murder of a recalcitrant docker who has threatened to speak out against Friendly; he falls in love with the victim's sister; a Catholic priest works, deliberately, on his slowly awakened conscience; the murder of his brother, Friendly's lieutenant, gives him a motive of personal revenge, and he agrees to testify before the Crime Commission. The sequel to this action is a savage beating up and an almost symbolic conclusion, as the dockers wait for Terry – his face smashed in, his walk a blind, lurching shamble – to lead them back to work. Taking his background material from Malcolm Johnson's Pulitzer Prize winning articles, Budd Schulberg has written a script which is vigorous, credible at times (in the scenes between Terry and the girl) authentically touching, and which, though it has its over-conventional elements in the characterization of Friendly and of the priest, never falls into the familiar, specious habit of "dignifying" its working class characters by making them speak in pseudo-Biblical language.

The script, in fact, contains the basis for a sharply observed journalistic investigation of a man's slow realisation of the truth about his environment, and Marlon Brando's playing gives the film the opportunity to become something rather more than this. This is a strong, confident performance, wholly contemporary in feeling and taking us right away from the old, chip on the shoulder thug-hero on the Hemingway model. The battered prize fighter's face, the slouching walk, the shoulder-shrugging gestures completing half-spoken sentences, the cocksure, gum-chewing arrogance and the gentle, uncertain half-smile are all used to unerring effect; as he walks in the park with the girl, aimlessly pulling on her glove while they talk, or makes it clear to his brother (admirably played by Rod Steiger) that his betrayal of the gang is irrevocable, relationships are crystallised, situations exist, as it were, outside their screen context. Although the playing otherwise is less satisfactory – Eva Marie Saint is gauche and adequately appealing as the wanly courageous heroine, but Karl Malden gives a strident, unrelaxed performance as the priest, and Lee J. Cobb's blustering gang leader is a conventionally overdrawn figure – Brando's performance gives the film a wonderfully firm centre.

Kazan, however, not content to let the story develop its own impetus, tends to over-inflate the simplest situation, to build up an atmosphere of artificial tension and urgency. Abetted by Leonard Bernstein's score, which undoubtedly contributes forcefully to the mood of the film, he has gone all out for the raucous, aggressive, showy effect. The virtuosity of Kazan's handling, the skill with which he sets a scene of violence, are not in doubt; one does, however, question the validity of his methods and of his approach. This seems to derive directly from the Group Theatre tradition (it is worth recording, incidentally, that Kazan, Karl Malden, and Lee J. Cobb all appeared in the Theatre's 1937 production of *Golden Boy*), from the depression period of the 'thirties when the New York stage discovered "realism" and playwrights such as Odets created the man-in-the-street hero, semi-articulate, inevitably victimised, reaching vaguely for higher and gentler things. (The Golden Boy had his violin; Terry, the reluctant thug, keeps pigeons.) The influence, now more than a little jaded, persists in the attitude to character, in the insistence that ordinary people are remarkable and must somehow be made to appear so, in the sentimentalising of the tough guy. (Schulberg, too, has always a soft spot for the broken-down boxer.)

During recent years, Hollywood "realism" has developed its own immediately recognisable conventions and attitudes. A now familiar technique of handling actors demands those mannerisms – Karl Malden's check in mid-speech, for instance – always just a little too studied for naturalism. There is the cunningly employed under-statement, so that a scene of violence and tension ends with the priest demonstrating the human touch by ordering a glass of beer. And it seems symptomatic that, as in the Hollywood-influenced *Terminal Station*, location shooting no longer guarantees an appearance of actuality. In spire of Boris Kaufman's beautifully atmospheric camerawork, recording the pale, cold early morning light on the docks, the depressed back streets and dismal little parks, the scenes are so carefully set, the characters so deliberately grouped (as in the saloon interior, with the two comatose down-and-outs propped picturesquely against the staircase), that we seem to have reached a point halfway between the studio and the real. It is a long way from the rougher idioms of *The Naked City*, though perhaps Kazan's own *Panic in the Streets* was already moving in this direction.

Primarily, however, one distrusts this sort of convention because, in making it too easy to create a plausible seeming surface, a set of characters who will be accepted for their familiarity, it inevitably encourages evasion. In "On the Waterfront", there is a scene in which Terry has to tell the girl of his part in her brother's murder: as they speak, their voices are drowned by a bellowing ship's siren. If the picture were presented as no more than melodrama, the trick would seem acceptable enough; but in building up his subject as he has, Kazan has foregone his right to evade so crucial a stage in this particular relationship. In a sense, the incident may be taken to sum up the film: excitement is whipped up, attitudes are struck, but the incidental detail blots out the human situation and – though it is not for want of trying – the transition from melo-drama to drama is never made.

AN INTERVIEW WITH BORIS KAUFMAN

Edouard L. de Laurot and Jonas Mekas

(*Film Culture*, 1.4 Summer 1955)

Reprinted with permission.

Camera on Location

You have recently received an award for your camera work for "On the Water-front" and, in view of the fact that this was the first feature that you have made in the United States with a large company, we would like you to tell us what difference you found between this type of work and the work you have done with Jean Vigo in France. Did you find that you had more latitude, more freedom in working on documentary film? Or did you, in the case of "On the Waterfront," have as much freedom to introduce your own ideas and approaches and to develop them?

I found that there was not much difference. Whenever it is a matter of expressing an idea, an action, a situation or a mood, size is a secondary thing. In "On the Waterfront", I was lucky to have quite a lot of freedom, that is to say, trust. I was free to contribute to the interpretation.

What in your experience are the temperamental differences between Kazan and Vigo? Can't it be said that Vigo was concentrating more on subtle detail, and Kazan on violent action; thus the requirements these two directors put on you were accordingly different?

They have similarities and dissimilarities, of course. I think that Kazan can be violent and tender – both styles are present in *On the Waterfront*. Critics who are reproaching *On the Waterfront* try to find a story that wasn't there.

Many criticized "On the Waterfront" in Europe for inadequately presenting a problem that it purported to present fully.

Because, naturally, in Europe they expected solutions. But this was not the scope of the picture. It exposed the problem instead of giving a *cliché* solution.

I think that most of the critics did not expect a cliché solution, but they were agreed that Kazan did not expose these problems fully.

Could you tell us in what way your previous work was different from your work on "On the Waterfront?"

Yes. It was the first picture of a large size that I had to shoot without a studio at all. When one confronts physical conditions on a given location, one has to be pliable enough to adapt oneself to existing physical shapes. In the studio, one can start from complete darkness and create all the light and shadow one wants. But one cannot do this on location. One is faced with something that exists, and one can only modify or distort it in a certain way. In *On the Waterfront* I had to face two and a half months of shooting in most unfavorable conditions, worst months of the year – with rain, fog, and sunshine – and maintain uniformity throughout the film. This was another challenge and had to be approached either with despair or with positive thinking. Almost every scene has been at least in part improvised because the writer could not, of course, visualize the conditions under which the film was to be shot.

It would be interesting if you could recall some concrete examples of how you adjusted your camera work to the existing conditions on location, through experimenting.

On the rooftops, for instance, in the scene with the pigeons, I had to shoot against black tar paper, black hatches, black dull metal, soot-covered pigeon coops, some TV antennas, and chimneys. So to bring it to life, I used smoke, water, and a little paint – the last in order to break this blackness and bleakness of tar paper. I also employed unusual filters and diffusion to maintain consistency within the changing conditions. Another example was the scene in the park. There were some leaves burning in the basket when we arrived. So I seized it as a possible source of drifting smoke. I sent for some smoke-pots and I let artificial smoke drift across the field. This device enabled me to continue the sequence through a different park which followed the first one, and to make it flow. In other words, I tied the smoke over, and I cleared only when we came to the iron fence facing the river. This is an example of positive exploitation of conditions. I used the smoke not as an artifice but because I found justification for it: the mood of the scene and the need for maintaining continuity. Also some interiors made in small tenement apartments were a challenge because of the physical smallness of the place into which my crew, the sound crew, and the actors had to be squeezed. The camera had to be mobile and the lighting keyed with precision.

IMAGE AND THEME

And apart from such specific examples, could you tell us what in your opinion have been your main individual contributions to camera art as such?

It is difficult for me to judge myself. I think I have always tried to maintain integrity. I avoid the spectacular; I reject whatever is not dramatically justified, and I try to develop a permanent style, a standard of good photography which will fit any subject. Every subject matter calls for a new and different approach. I try to start from scratch, rejecting my own language of experience – all that interferes with spontaneity.

You mean that to a large extent there should be a unity between content and form in the scene so that if a new content has to be expressed, then form should not be artificially imposed because of the particular preference the cameraman may have for a previously developed style.

Yes; in my opinion, the essence of film-making is a fusion of conceptions. I try to fuse my style with the final expression. One must also have the ability to visualize the scene that is being shot as it will exist on the screen in the final form, otherwise there is no way to judge what dramatic intensity is required. You have to feel the pulse of the scene and its relative value in the sequence. This feeling is necessary for the director as well as for the cameraman. And this is why the work with Kazan was so rewarding.

Filmographies and Bibliographies of Kazan and Schulberg

Elia Kazan as Film Director

THE PEOPLE OF THE CUMBERLANDS (1937)
Although this documentary is often credited to Kazan, he is listed on the credits as an "assistant," along with William Watts.

DIRECTION: Robert Stebbins and Eugene Hill [pseudonym for Sidney Meyers]
SCREENPLAY: Elia Kazan
CINEMATOGRAPHY: Ralph Steiner
PRODUCTION: Frontier Films
RUNNING TIME: 20 minutes

IT'S UP TO YOU (1941)
Kazan is sometimes credited as the film director for this Federal Theatre mixed media project that includes both film and dance.

WRITTEN BY: Arthur Arent
PRODUCTION: U.S. Department of Agriculture

A TREE GROWS IN BROOKLYN (1945)
SCREENPLAY: Tess Slesinger and Frank Davis, based on the novel by Betty Smith
CINEMATOGRAPHY: Leon Shamroy
EDITING: Dorothy Spencer
MUSIC: Alfred Newman
PRODUCER: Louis D. Lighton
RELEASED BY: Twentieth Century-Fox
RUNNING TIME: 128 minutes

PRINCIPAL CAST: Dorothy McGuire (Katie Nolan), Joan Blondell (Aunt Sissy), James Dunn (Johnny Nolan)

THE SEA OF GRASS (1947)

SCREENPLAY: Marguerite Roberts and Vincent Lawrence, based on the novel by Conrad Richter
CINEMATOGRAPHY: Harry Stradling
EDITING: Robert J. Kern
MUSIC: Herbert Stothart
PRODUCER: Pandro S. Berman
RELEASED BY: MGM
RUNNING TIME: 131 minutes
PRINCIPAL CAST: Spencer Tracy (Jim Brewton), Katharine Hepburn (Lutie Cameron), Melvyn Douglas (Brice Chamberlain)

BOOMERANG! (1947)

SCREENPLAY: Richard Murphy, based on a *Reader's Digest* article, "The Perfect Case" (December 1945), by Anthony Abbott (Fulton Oursler)
CINEMATOGRAPHY: Norbert Brodine
EDITING: Harmon Jones
MUSIC: David Buttolph
EXECUTIVE PRODUCER: Darryl F. Zanuck
PRODUCER: Louis de Rochemont
RELEASED BY: Twentieth Century-Fox
RUNNING TIME: 88 minutes
PRINCIPAL CAST: Dana Andrews (Henry L. Harvey), Jane Wyatt (Mrs. Harvey), Lee J. Cobb (Chief Robinson)

GENTLEMEN'S AGREEMENT (1947)

SCREENPLAY: Moss Hart, based on the novel by Laura Z. Hobson
CINEMATOGRAPHY: Arthur Miller
EDITING: Harmon Jones
MUSIC: Alfred Newman
PRODUCER: Darryl F. Zanuck
RELEASED BY: Twentieth Century-Fox
RUNNING TIME: 118 minutes
PRINCIPAL CAST: Gregory Peck (Phil Green), Dorothy McGuire (Kathy), John Garfield (Dave Goldman), Celeste Holm (Anne), Jane Wyatt (Jane), Dean Stockwell (Tommy Green), Sam Jaffee (Professor Lieberman)

PINKY (1949)
SCREENPLAY: Philip Dunne and Dudley Nichols, based on the novel
   Quality by Cid Ricketts Sumner
CINEMATOGRAPHY: Joe MacDonald
EDITING: Harmon Jones
MUSIC: Alfred Newman
PRODUCER: Darryl F. Zanuck
RELEASED BY: Twentieth Century-Fox
RUNNING TIME: 102 minutes
PRINCIPAL CAST: Jeanne Crain (Pinky Johnson), Ethel Barrymore
   (Miss Em), Ethel Waters (Aunt Dicey)

PANIC IN THE STREETS (1950)
SCREENPLAY: Richard Murphy, based on a story by Edna and
   Edward Anhalt
CINEMATOGRAPHY: Joe MacDonald
EDITING: Harmon Jones
MUSIC: Alfred Newman
PRODUCER: Sol C. Siegel
RELEASED BY: Twentieth Century-Fox
RUNNING TIME: 96 minutes
PRINCIPAL CAST: Richard Widmark (Dr. Clinton Reed), Paul Douglas
   (Police Captain Warren), Barbara Bel Geddes (Nancy Reed), Walter
   Jack Palance (Blackie), Zero Mostel (Raymond Fitch)

A STREETCAR NAMED DESIRE (1951)
SCREENPLAY: Tennessee Williams, based on his own play
CINEMATOGRAPHY: Harry Stradling
EDITING: David Weisbart
MUSIC: Alex North
PRODUCER: Carles K. Feldman
RELEASED BY: Group Productions
RUNNING TIME: 122 minutes
PRINCIPAL CAST: Vivien Leigh (Blanche DeBois), Marlon Brando
   (Stanley Kowalski), Kim Hunter (Stella Kowalski), Karl Malden (Mitch)

VIVA ZAPATA! (1952)
SCREENPLAY: John Steinbeck
CINEMATOGRAPHY: Joe MacDonald
EDITING: Barbara McLean
MUSIC: Alex North

PRODUCER: Darryl F. Zanuck
RELEASED BY: Twentieth Century-Fox
RUNNING TIME: 113 minutes
PRINCIPAL CAST: Marlon Brando (Emiliano Zapata), Jean Peters (Josefa), Anthony Quinn (Eufemio)

MAN ON A TIGHTROPE (1953)

SCREENPLAY: Robert Sherwood, based on the story "International Incident" by Neil Paterson
CINEMATOGRAPHY: Georg Krause
EDITING: Dorothy Spencer
MUSIC: Franz Waxman
PRODUCER: Robert L. Jacks
RELEASED BY: Twentieth Century-Fox
RUNNING TIME: 105 minutes
PRINCIPAL CAST: Frederic March (Karel Cernik), Terry Moore (Tereza Cernik), Gloria Graham (Zama Cernik), Adolphe Menjou (Fesker), Cameron Mitchell (Joe Vosdek)

ON THE WATERFRONT (1954)

SCREENPLAY: Budd Schulberg, based upon his original story and suggested by articles by Malcolm Johnson
CINEMATOGRAPHY: Boris Kaufman
EDITING: Gene Milford
MUSIC: Leonard Bernstein
PRODUCER: Sam Spiegel
RELEASED BY: Columbia
RUNNING TIME: 108 minutes
PRINCIPAL CAST: Marlon Brando (Terry Malloy), Eva Marie Saint (Edie Doyle), Karl Malden (Father Barry), Lee J. Cobb (Johnny Friendly), Rod Steiger (Charley Malloy)

EAST OF EDEN (1955, also produced)

SCREENPLAY: Paul Osborn, based on the novel by John Steinbeck
CINEMATOGRAPHY: Ted McCord
EDITING: Owen Marks
MUSIC: Leonard Rosenman
PRODUCER: Elia Kazan
RELEASED BY: Warner Brothers
RUNNING TIME: 115 minutes
PRINCIPAL CAST: Julie Harris (Abra), James Dean (Cal Trask), Raymond

Massey (Adam Trask), Richard Davalos (Aron Trask), Burl Ives (Sam, the sheriff)

BABY DOLL (1956, also produced)
SCREENPLAY: Tennessee Williams, based upon his one-act plays, *27 Wagons Full of Cotton* and *The Unsatisfactory Supper* (also called *The Long Stay Cut Short*)
CINEMATOGRAPHY: Boris Kaufman
EDITING: Gene Milford
MUSIC: Kenyon Hopkins
PRODUCER: Elia Kazan
RELEASED BY: Warner Brothers
RUNNING TIME: 114 minutes
PRINCIPAL CAST: Carroll Baker (Baby Doll Meighan), Karl Malden (Archie Lee Meighan), Eli Wallach (Silva Vacarro)

A FACE IN THE CROWD (1957, also produced)
SCREENPLAY: Budd Schulberg, based on his short story, "Your Arkansas Traveller," from his book *Some Faces in the Crowd*)
CINEMATOGRAPHY: Harry Stradling, Gene Rescher
EDITING: Gene Milford
MUSIC: Tom Glazer
PRODUCER: Elia Kazan
RELEASED BY: Warner Brothers
RUNNING TIME: 126 minutes
PRINCIPAL CAST: Andy Griffith (Lonesome Rhodes), Patricia Neal (Marcia Jefferies), Anthony Franciosa (Joey Kieley), Walter Matthau (Mel Miller)

WILD RIVER (1960, also produced)
SCREENPLAY: Paul Osborne, based on the novel *Mud on the Stars* by William Bradford Huie and *Dunbar's Cove* by Borden Deal
CINEMATOGRAPHY: Ellsworth Fredericks
EDITING: William Reynolds
MUSIC: Kenyon Hopkins
PRODUCER: Elia Kazan
RELEASED BY: Twentieth Century-Fox
RUNNING TIME: 109 minutes
PRINCIPAL CAST: Montgomery Clift (Chuck Glover), Lee Remick (Carol Garth), Jo Van Fleet (Ella Garth)

SPLENDOR IN THE GRASS (1961, also produced)
SCREENPLAY: William Inge
CINEMATOGRAPHY: Boris Kaufman
EDITING: Gene Milford
MUSIC: David Amram
PRODUCER: Elia Kazan
RELEASED BY: Warner Brothers
RUNNING TIME: 124 minutes
PRINCIPAL CAST: Natalie Wood (Deanie Loomis), Warren Beatty (Bud
    Stamper), Pat Hingle (Ace Stamper)

**AMERICA AMERICA (1963, also wrote and produced from his
autobiographical novel)**
SCREENPLAY: Elia Kazan, based on his own novel and an unpublished
    story "Hamal"
CINEMATOGRAPHY: Haskell Wexler
EDITING: Dede Allen
MUSIC: Manos Hadjidakis
PRODUCER: Elia Kazan
RELEASED BY: Warner Brothers
RUNNING TIME: 168 minutes
PRINCIPAL CAST: Stathis Giallelis (Stavros Topouzoglou), Frank Wolff
    (Vartan Damadian), Harry Davis (Isaac Topouzoglou)

**THE ARRANGEMENT (1969, also wrote and produced from his
own novel)**
SCREENPLAY: Elia Kazan, based on his own novel
CINEMATOGRAPHY: Robert Surtees
EDITING: Stefan Arnsten
MUSIC: David Amram
PRODUCER: Elia Kazan
RELEASED BY: Warner Brothers
RUNNING TIME: 125 minutes
PRINCIPAL CAST: Kirk Douglas (Eddie Anderson), Faye Dunaway
    (Gwen), Deborah Kerr (Florence Anderson), Richard Boone (Sam
    Anderson), Hume Cronyn (Arthur)

THE VISITORS (1972)
SCREENPLAY: Chris Kazan
CINEMATOGRAPHY: Nick Proferes
EDITING: Nick Proferes

MUSIC: Bach's Suite No. 1 for lute played on the guitar by
  William Matthews
PRODUCERS: Chris Kazan and Nick Proferes
RELEASED BY: United Artists
RUNNING TIME: 90 minutes
PRINCIPAL CAST: Patrick McVey (Harry Wayne), Patricia Joyce
  (Martha Wayne), James Woods (Bill Schmidt)

THE LAST TYCOON (1976)
SCREENPLAY: Harold Pinter, from the novel by F. Scott Fitzgerald
CINEMATOGRAPHY: Victor Kemper
EDITING: Richard Marks
MUSIC: Maurice Jarre
PRODUCER: Sam Spiegel
RELEASED BY: Paramount
RUNNING TIME: 122 minutes
PRINCIPAL CAST: Robert DeNiro (Monroe Stahr), Tony Curtis
  (Rodriguez), Robert Mitchum (Pat Brady), Jeanne Moreau (Didi),
  Jack Nicholson (Brimmer), Donald Pleasance (Boxley), Ray Milland
  (Fleishacker), Ingrid Boulting (Kathleen Moore)

Elia Kazan as Author (Books)

Act of Love. New York: Alfred A. Knopf, 1978.
America America, with an Introduction by S. N. Behrman.
  New York: Stein and Day, 1962.
The Anatolian. New York: Alfred A. Knopf, 1982.
The Arrangement. New York: Stein and Day, 1967.
The Assassins. New York: Stein and Day, 1971.
Beyond the Aegean. New York: Alfred Knopf, 1994.
Elia Kazan: A Life. New York: Alfred A. Knopf, and London:
  Andre Deutsch, 1988.
Kazan on Kazan. New York: Viking Press, 1974.
The Understudy. New York: Stein and Day, 1975.

Budd Schulberg as Screenwriter

A STAR IS BORN (1937, additional dialogue only)
SCREENPLAY: William A. Wellman (story), Robert Carson (story),
  Dorothy Parker, Alan Campbell; [uncredited] Budd Schulberg,
  Ring Lardner, Jr., John Lee Mahin, David O. Selznick

DIRECTOR: William A. Wellman
CINEMATOGRAPHY: W. Howard Greene
EDITING: James E. Newcom
MUSIC: Max Steiner
PRODUCER: David O. Selznick
RELEASED BY: United Artists
RUNNING TIME: 111 minutes
PRINCIPAL CAST: Janet Gaynor (Esther Blodgett/Vicki Lester), Frederic
    March (Norman Maine), Adolphe Menjou (Oliver Niles)

NOTHING SACRED (1937, uncredited)
SCREENPLAY: Ben Hecht, James H. Street (story), [uncredited]
    Budd Schulberg, Ring Lardner, Jr.
DIRECTOR: William A. Wellman
CINEMATOGRAPHY: W. Howard Greene
EDITING: James E. Newcom
MUSIC: Oscar Levant
PRODUCER: David O. Selznick
RELEASED BY: United Artists
RUNNING TIME: 75 minutes
PRINCIPAL CAST: Carole Lombard (Hazel Flagg), Frederic March (Wally
    Cook), Walter Connolly (Oliver Stone)

LITTLE ORPHAN ANNIE (1938)
SCREENPLAY: Endre Bohem and Samuel Badisch Ornitz (story), Budd
    Wilson Schulberg
·DIRECTOR: Ben Holmes
CINEMATOGRAPHY: Frank Redman
EDITING: Robert Bischoff
MUSIC: Louis Forbes
PRODUCER: John Speaks
RELEASED BY: Paramount
PRINCIPAL CAST: Ann Gillis (Little Orphan Annie), Robert Kent (Johnny
    Adams), June Travis (Mary Ellen), Ian Maclaren (Soo Long)

WINTER CARNIVAL (1939)
SCREENPLAY: Budd Schulberg, Lester Cole, Maurice Rapf
DIRECTOR: Charles Reisner
CINEMATOGRAPHY: Merritt B. Gerstad
EDITING: Dorothy Spencer
MUSIC: Werner Janssen
PRODUCER: Walter Wanger

RELEASED BY: United Artists
RUNNING TIME: 105 minutes
PRINCIPAL CAST: Ann Sheridan (Jill Baxter), Richard Carlson
(John Weldon), Marsha Hunt (Lucy Morgan)

FOREIGN CORRESPONDENT (1940, uncredited)

SCREENPLAY: Robert Benchley, Charles Bennett, Joan Harrison, James
Hilton, Richard Maibaum, [uncredited] Budd Schulberg, Harold
Clurman, Ben Hecht, John Howard Lawson, John Lee Mahim
DIRECTOR: Alfred Hitchcock
CINEMATOGRAPHY: Rudolph Maté
EDITING: Dorothy Spencer
MUSIC: Alfred Newman
PRODUCER: Walter Wanger
RELEASED BY: United Artists
RUNNING TIME: 119 minutes
PRINCIPAL CAST: Joel McCrea (Johnny Jones), Laraine Day
(Carol Fisher), Herbert Marshall (Stephen Fisher), George Sanders
(Scott Folliott), Robert Benchley (Stebbins)

WEEKEND FOR THREE (1941, story only)

SCREENPLAY: Alan Campbell, Dorothy Parker, Budd Schulberg (story)
DIRECTOR: Irving Reis
CINEMATOGRAPHY: Russell Metty
EDITING: Desmond Marquette
MUSIC: Roy Webb
PRODUCER: Tay Garnett
RELEASED BY: RKO
RUNNING TIME: 65 minutes
PRINCIPAL CAST: Dennis O'Keefe (Jim Craig), Jane Wyatt (Ellen Craig),
Edward Everett Horton (Fred Stonebraker), ZaSu Pitts (Anna)

FIVE WERE CHOSEN (1942, story)

SCREENPLAY: Budd Schulberg (story)
DIRECTOR: Herbert Kline
RELEASED BY: Clasa-Mohme, Inc.
RUNNING TIME: 82 minutes
PRINCIPAL CAST: Ricardo Montalban, Victor Kilian, Howard Da Silva,
Leonid Kinskey

DECEMBER 7th (1943)
SCREENPLAY: Budd Schulberg (uncredited)
DIRECTORS: John Ford and Gregg Toland
CINEMATOGRAPHER: Gregg Toland
EDITOR: Robert Parrish
MUSIC: Alfred Newman
PRODUCER: John Ford
PRINCIPAL CAST: Walter Huston, Harry Davenport, Dana Andrews

GOVERNMENT GIRL (1943)
SCREENPLAY: Budd Schulberg, Dudley Nichols, and Adela Rogers
   St. Johns (story)
DIRECTOR: Dudley Nichols
CINEMATOGRAPHY: Frank Redman
EDITING: Roland Gross
MUSIC: Leigh Harline
PRODUCERS: Dudley Nichols, Edward Donahue (Assoc.)
RELEASED BY: RKO
RUNNING TIME: 94 minutes
PRINCIPAL CAST: Olivia de Havilland (Elizabeth "Smokey" Allard),
   Sonny Tufts (Ed Browne), Paul Stewart (Branch), Agnes Moorehead
   (Mrs. Wright), Sig Ruman (Ambassador)

CITY WITHOUT MEN, aka PRISON FARM (1943)
SCREENPLAY: Martin Berkeley (story), Budd Schulberg (story), Samuel
   Bronston, Donald Davis, W. L. River, George Sklar
DIRECTOR: Sidney Salkow
CINEMATOGRAPHY: Philip Tannura
EDITING: Al Clark
MUSIC: David Raksin, Morris Stoloff
PRODUCER: B. P. Schulberg
RELEASED BY: Columbia
RUNNING TIME: 75 minutes
PRINCIPAL CAST: Linda Darnell (Nancy Johnson), Edgar Buchanan
   (Michael T. Mallory), Michael Duane (Tom Adams), Glenda Farrell
   (Billie LaRue)

CINCO FUERON ESCOGIDOS (1943, story)
SCREENPLAY: Rafael M. Muñoz, Xavuer Villaurrutia, Budd Schulberg
   (story). Spanish-language version of *Five were chosen*
DIRECTOR: Agustin P. Delgado, Herbert Kline

CINEMATOGRAPHY: Jack Draper
MUSIC: Raûl Lavista
RELEASED BY: Alpha Films
PRINCIPAL CAST: Ricardo Montalban, Rafael Icardo, Antonio Bravo,
Maria Elena Marqués, Julio Vallarreal

THE NAZI PLAN (1945 documentary)
SCREENPLAY: Budd Schulberg
DIRECTOR: George Stevens
EDITOR: Robert Parrish

THE PHARMACIST'S MATE (1950, TV, for Pulitzer Prize Playhouse)
TELEPLAY: Budd Schulberg, based on Pulitzer Prize article by
George Weller
PRINCIPAL CAST: Gene Raymond, Brian Donlevy

PASO DOBLE **(1954, TV, for Omnibus, CBS-TV)**
TELEPLAY: Budd Schulberg
PRINCIPAL CAST: Kim Stanley, John Cassavettes

ON THE WATERFRONT **(1954)**
SCREENPLAY: Budd Schulberg, based upon his original story and
suggested by articles by Malcolm Johnson
[for credits see above under "Kazan"]

THE HARDER THEY FALL (1956, novel basis only)
SCREENPLAY: Budd Schulberg (novel), Philip Yordan
DIRECTOR: Mark Robson
CINEMATOGRAPHY: Burnett Guffey
EDITING: Jerome Thoms
MUSIC: Hugo Friedhofer
PRODUCER: Philip Yordan
RELEASED BY: Columbia
RUNNING TIME: 109 minutes
PRINCIPAL CAST: Humphrey Bogart (Eddie Willis), Rod Steiger
(Nick Benko), Jan Sterling (Beth Willis), Mike Lane (Toro Moreno)

A FACE IN THE CROWD (1957)
SCREENPLAY: Budd Schulberg, based on his short story, "Your Arkansas
Traveller," from his book *Some Faces in the Crowd*
[for credits see above under "Kazan"]

WIND ACROSS THE EVERGLADES (1958)
SCREENPLAY: Budd Schulberg
DIRECTOR: Nicholas Ray, Budd Schulberg (uncredited)
CINEMATOGRAPHY: Joseph C. Brun
EDITING: George Klotz, Joseph Zigman
SONGS: Budd Schulberg
PRODUCER: Stuart Schulberg
RELEASED: in Finland, March 1959
RUNNING TIME: 93 minutes
PRINCIPAL CAST: Burl Ives (Cottonmouth), Christopher Plummer (Walt
 Murdock), Chana Eden (Naomi), Gypsy Rose Lee (Mrs. Bradford),
 Emmett Kelly (Bigamy Bob), Peter Falk (Writer)

WHAT MAKES SAMMY RUN? PARTS I AND II (1959, NBC)
TELEPLAY: Budd Schulberg and Stuart Schulberg, based on short stories
 from *Some Faces in the Crowd*
DIRECTOR AND PRODUCER: Delbert Mann
PRINCIPAL CAST: Larry Blyden (Sammy), Barbara Rush (Kit), John
 Forsythe (Al)

MEMORY IN WHITE (1961, TV, for G.E. Playhouse)
TELEPLAY: Budd Schulberg
PRINCIPAL CAST: Sammy Davis Jr., Charles Bronson

THE LEGEND THAT WALKS LIKE A MAN (1961, TV, for
G.E. Playhouse)
TELEPLAY: Budd Schulberg
PRINCIPAL CAST: Ernest Borgnine, William Schallert, Zsa Zsa Gabor

THE MEAL TICKET (1964, TV, The Bob Hope Chrysler Theatre)
TELEPLAY: Budd Schulberg
PRINCIPAL CAST: Cliff Robertson, Janice Rule, Broderick Crawford

A QUESTION OF HONOR (1982, TV, EMI Television Programs, Inc
and CBS)
TELEPLAY: Budd Schulberg and Stan Silverman
DIRECTOR: Jud Taylor
PRODUCER: Tony Converse, Roger Gimbel
RELEASED BY: Marquee Entertainment, Inc.
RUNNING TIME: 2 hours with commercial breaks

PRINCIPAL CAST: Danny Aiello (Martelli), Ben Gazzara (Detective Joe DeFalco), Tony Roberts (Marlowe), Carol Eve Rossen (Jeannie DeFalco), Paul Sovino (Carlo Danzie)

PRISONER WITHOUT A NAME, CELL WITHOUT A NUMBER (1983, TV, NBC Sunday Night Movie)
TELEPLAY: Oliver P. Drexel, Jr. [pseudonym for Budd Schulberg] and Jonathan Platnick
DIRECTOR AND PRODUCER: Linda Yellen
PRINCIPAL CAST: Liv Ullman, Roy Scheider

JOE LOUIS: FOR ALL TIME (1984 documentary, also produced)
SCREENPLAY: Budd Schulberg
DIRECTOR: Peter Tatum
PRODUCERS: Budd Schulberg and Jim Jacobs
RELEASED BY: ABC Enterprises
RUNNING TIME: 90 minutes
NARRATION BY: Brock Peters

A TABLE AT CIRO'S (1987, TV, WNET New York)
TELEPLAY: Budd Schulberg and Stan Silversman (story, "A Table at Ciro's" from *Some Faces in the Crowd*).
DIRECTORS: Leon Ichaso and Paul Bogart
CINEMATOGRAPHY: Newton Thomas Sigel
EDITOR: Ed Rothkowitz
MUSIC: John Corigliano and Dick Hyman
PRODUCER: David R. Loxton
RELEASED BY: Zenith Productions
RUNNING TIME: one hour
PRINCIPAL CAST: Darren McGavin (A. D. Nathan), Lois Chiles, Stella Stevens

WHAT MAKES SAMMY RUN? (2003)
Based on the novel, *What Makes Sammy Run?* In preproduction at press time.
DIRECTOR: Ben Stiller

Budd Schulberg as Author (Books)

Across the Everglades: A Play for the Screen. New York: Bantam Books, 1958.
The Disenchanted. New York: Random House, 1950.

Everything That Moves. Garden City, New York: Random House, 1980.

A Face in the Crowd: A Play for the Screen. New York: Bantam Books, 1957.

The Four Seasons of Success. Garden City, New York: Doubleday, 1972.

From the Ashes: Voices of Watts, ed. New York: New American Library, 1967.

La forêt interdite, including "Dialogue in Black and White with James Baldwin." Paris: Éditions Payot & Rivages, 1997.

The Harder They Fall. New York: Random House, 1947.

Loser and Still Champion: Muhammad Ali. Garden City, New York: Doubleday, 1972.

Love, Action, Laughter, and Other Sad Tales. New York: Random House, 1989.

Moving Pictures: Memories of a Hollywood Prince. New York: Stein and Day, 1981.

On the Waterfront: The Play, with Stan Silverman. Chicago: I. R. Dee. 2001.

On the Waterfront: A Screenplay. Carbondale: Southern Illinois Univ. Press, 1980 and London: Allison & Busby, 1992.

Sanctuary V. New York: New American Library, 1969.

Some Faces in the Crowd, Short Stories. New York: Random House, 1953.

Sparring with Hemingway: And Other Legends of the Fight Game. Chicago: I. R. Dee, 1995.

Swan Watch. New York: Delacorte Press, 1975.

Waterfront, A Novel. New York: Random House, 1955.

What Makes Sammy Run? New York: Random House, 1941.

What Makes Sammy Run? A New Musical with Stuart Schulberg. Music and Lyrics by Ervin Drake. New York: Random House, 1964.

Writers in America: The Four Seasons of Success. Garden City, New York: Stein and Day, 1981.

Selected Critical Bibliography

ON THE FILM

Anderson, Lindsay. "The Last Sequence of *On the Waterfront*." *Sight and Sound* 24:3 (1955): 127–130.

Anon. "The Beat of a Pulse." *Newsweek* 44 (August 2, 1954): 78.

Bernstein, Leonard. "Notes Struck at Upper Dubbing, California." *The New York Times* (May 30, 1954).

Biskind, Peter. "On Movies, Money and Politics." *The Nation* (April 5–12, 1999): 16.

———. "*On the Waterfront*." In *Seeing is Believing*. New York: Pantheon Books, 1983.

———."The Politics of Power in *On the Waterfront*." *Film Quarterly* 29 (Fall 1975): 25–38.

———. "When Worlds Collide." *The Nation* (April 5–12, 1999): 12.

Brando, Marlon. *Songs My Mother Taught Me*. New York: Random House, 1994.

Braudy, Leo. "No Body's Perfect: Method Acting and '50's Culture." In *The Movies: Texts, Receptions, Exposures*. Laurence Goldstein and Ira Konigsberg, eds. Ann Arbor: University of Michigan Press, 1996.

De Laurot, Edouard L., and Jonas Mekas. "An Interview with Boris Kaufman." *Film Culture* 1 (1955): 4–6.

Georgakas, Dan. "*Waterfront*." *Cineaste* 4:56 (1982).

Godbout, Oscar. "An Acting Saint' States Her Case." *New York Times* (August 1, 1954).

Goldberg, Albert. "Bernstein Writes Initial Film Score." *Los Angeles Times* (May 9, 1954).

Hamilton, William. "*On the Waterfront* (with musical examples)." *Film Music* (September–October 1954).

Hey, Kenneth R. "Ambivalence as a Theme in *On the Waterfront* (1954): An Interdisciplinary Approach to Film Study." In *Hollywood as Historian: American Film in a Cultural Context*. Peter C. Rollins, ed. Lexington, Ky.: University Press of Kentucky, 1983: 159–189.

Hughes, Robert. "*On the Waterfront*: A Defense." *Sight and Sound* 24:4 (1955).

Kazin, Alfred. *"On the Waterfront." Esquire* 97 (1982).

Keller, Hans. *"On the Waterfront." The Score* (London, June, 1955).

Lawson, John Howard, "Hollywood on the Waterfront: Union Leaders are Gangsters, Workers are Helpless." *Hollywood Review* 1.6 (November/December 1954): 1, 3–4.

Lumenick, Lou. *"Waterfront in Home Port." New York Post* (Sunday, July 23, 2000).

Mallazzi, Vincent M. "Theater: Taking Drama to the Docks Where It Was Filmed." *New York Times* (July 30, 2000): Sec. 14NJ.11

McCarten, John. "Good Tough Stuff." *The New Yorker* 30 (July 31, 1954): 52–53.

Murray, Edward. *"On the Waterfront."* In *Ten Film Classics: A Re-Viewing.* New York: Frederick Ungar, 1978.

Naremore, James. "Marlon Brando in *On the Waterfront* ." In *Acting in the Cinema.* Berkeley: University of California Press, 1988.

Neve, Brian. "The 1950s: The Case of Elia Kazan and *On the Waterfront.*" In *Cinema, Politics, and Society in America.* Philips Davies and Brian Neve, eds. New York: St. Martin's Press, 1981.

———. "Being a Contender." *Journal of American Studies* 23 (1989).

———. *"On the Waterfront:* American Society and Politics in the McCarthy Era." *History Today* 45 (1995).

Raymond, Allen. *Waterfront Priest.* New York: Henry Holt, 1955.

Rogow, Lee. "Brando on the Waterfront." *The Saturday Review* 37 (July 24, 1954): 25–26.

Reeves, Saskia. *"On the Waterfront." Sight and Sound* 6:2 (1996).

Sayre, Nora. *Running Time: Films of the Cold War.* New York: Dial Press, 1982.

Schickel, Richard. "Marlon Brando and the 50s – Why Both Still Matter." *Film Comment* 27:4 (1994).

Schulberg, Budd. "Waterfront Priest." *Commonweal* 52.26 (April 3, 1953): 643–46.

———. "How One Pier Got Rid of the Mob." *New York Times Magazine* (September 27, 1953): 17, 58–60.

———. "Drama in Hoboken." *Holiday* (August 1954): 82–85.

———. "The Inside Story of *Waterfront.*" *The New York Times Magazine* (January 6, 1980): 28–30, 32–34, 36.

———. " 'Waterfront' – More Than a 90-Minute Movie." *New York Times Book Review 7* (April 26, 1987): 1, 38.

———. Hoboken Orphans in Hollywood Storm: How *On the Waterfront* came to the Screen, Finally. *Variety* (January 1999): 40–41, 56, 58.

Welsh, Jim. *"On the Waterfront:* The Screenplay." *Literature/Film Quarterly* 9:4 (1981).

ON KAZAN:

Anon. "Dialogue on Film: Elia Kazan." *American Film* 1 (1972).

Archer, Eugene. "Elia Kazan – The Genesis of a Style." *Film Culture* 2:5–7 (1956).

Baer, William. *Elia Kazan: Interviews.* Jackson: University Press of Mississippi, 2000.

Bassinger, Jeanine, John Fraser, and Joseph W. Reed, Jr., eds. *Working with Kazan.* Middletown, Conn.: Wesleyan University Press, 1973.

Bosworth, Patricia. "Kazan's Choice." *Vanity Fair* (September 1991): 164–184

Butler, Terence. "Polonsky and Kazan: HUAC and the Violation of Personality." *Sight and Sound* 57 (1988).

Ciment, Michel, ed. *Elia Kazan: An American Odyssey*. London: Bloomsbury, 1988.

———. *Kazan on Kazan*. London: Secker and Warburg/BFI, 1973 and New York: Viking, 1974.

Cook, Christopher. "An Interview with Elia Kazan." *Encounter* 72 (1989).

———. Interview with Elia Kazan on the "Third Ear," BBC Radio 3 (June 3, 1988).

Collins, Gary. "Kazan in the Fifties." *Velvet Light Trap* 11 (1974).

Georgakas, Dan. "Don't Call Him 'Gadget': A Reconsideration of Elia Kazan." *Cineaste* 16:4 (1988).

Giannetti, Louis. "Elia Kazan." In *Masters of the American Cinema*. New York: Prentice Hall, 1981.

Girgus, Sam B. *Hollywood Renaissance: The Cinema of Democracy in the Era of Ford, Capra, and Kazan*. Cambridge: Cambridge University Press, 1998.

Kazan, Elia. "Dialogue on Film." *American Film* 1.5 (March 1976): 40.

———. "Notebook for *A Streetcar Named Desire*." In *Directing the Play, A Source Book of Stagecraft*. Toby Cole and Helen Krich Chinoy, eds. New York: Bobbs-Merrill, 1953.

Kitses, Jim. "Elia Kazan: A Structural Analysis." *Cinema* 7 (1972).

Michaels, Lloyd. *Elia Kazan: A Guide to References and Resources*. Boston: G.K. Hall, 1985.

———. "Elia Kazan: A Retrospective." *Film Criticism* 10:1 (1985).

Miller, Arthur. *Timebends: A Life*. New York: Grove Press and London: Metheuen, 1987.

Pauly, Thomas H. *An American Odyssey: Elia Kazan and American Culture*. Philadelphia: Temple University Press, 1983.

Reeves, Saskia. "Caged Birds." *Sight and Sound* 6 (1996).

Tailleur, Roger. "Kazan and the House Un-American Activities Committee." *Film Comment* 4:1 (1966).

Young, Jeff. *Kazan: The Master Director Discusses His Films*. New York: Newmarket Press, 1999.

ON SCHULBERG:

Beck Nicholas. *Budd Schulberg: A Bio-Bibliography*. Lanham, Maryland and London: Scarecrow Press, 2001.

Eskenazi, Michael. "What Makes Budd Schulberg Run?" *The New York Times* (March 25, 2001): Section 14L1.1.

Georgakas, Dan. "The Screen Playwright as Author: An Interview with Budd Schulberg." *Cineaste* 11.4 (1982): 7–15.

Gross, Ken. "Budd Schulberg." *People* 25 (December 18, 1989): 93–94, 99.

Mallozi, Vincent M. "Theater: Taking a Drama to the Docks Where It Was Filmed." *New York Times* (New Jersey Weekly Desk) (July 30, 2000).

Newfield, Jack and Mark Jacobson. "An interview with Budd Schulberg." *Tikkun* 15.3 (May/June 2000): 9–12.

Nichols, Lewis. "Talk with Budd Schulberg." *New York Times Book Review* (May 24, 1953).

Rowe, Claudia. "Two Boxing Fans Sure They're Doing the Right Thing." *New York Times* (December 4, 2001): E.5.

Schulberg, Budd. "*Waterfront*: From Docks to Film." *New York Times* (July 11, 1954): Sec. 2, 5.

———— "Why Write It When You Can Sell It to the Pictures?" *Saturday Review* (September 3, 1955): 5–6, 27.

Spiegel, Maryln. "Schulberg Tackling Fitzgerald Play Anew." *New York Times* (December 1, 1996): Sec. 13L1.8.

Steglitz, JoAnne. "*On the Waterfront* Screenwriter Budd Schulberg." *Hoboken Current* (July 27–August 2, 2000): 3–4.

OTHER WORKS CITED:

Aristotle. *Poetics*. S. H. Butcher, transl. with an introduction by Francis Fergusson. New York: Hill and Wang, 1995.

Aronowitz, Stanley. *False Promises: The Shaping of Working Class Consciousness*. New York: McGraw-Hill, 1973.

Bentley, Eric. *Thirty Years of Treason, Excerpts from Hearings before the House Committee on Un-American Activities, 1938–1968*. New York: Viking, 1972.

Bernstein, Leonard. "Bernstein Expounds on Music for Movies." *Berkshire Evening Eagle* (Aug. 10, 1955).

————. *The Joy of Music*. New York: Simon and Schuster, 1959.

Bernstein, Walter. *In Side Out: A Memoir of the Blacklist*. New York: Alfred A. Knopf, 1996.

Brando, Marlon. *Songs My Mother Taught Me*. New York: Random House, 1994.

Brustein, Robert. *Revolt of the Theatre*. Boston, Toronto: Little, Brown, 1964.

Burton, Humphrey. *Leonard Bernstein*. New York: Doubleday, 1994.

Campbell, Joseph. *The Hero With a Thousand Faces*. Princeton: Princeton University Press, Bollingen Series XVII, Third Printing, 1973.

Carney, Raymond. *American Vision: The Films of Frank Capra*. Cambridge: Cambridge University Press, 1986.

Clurman, Harold. *The Fervent Years*. New York: Alfred A. Knopf, 1945.

Denning, Michael. *The Laboring of American Culture in the Twentieth Century*. London: Verso, 1996.

Erikson, Erik. "Autobiographic Notes on the Identity Crisis." *Daedalus* 99.4 (Fall 1970): 747.

Georgakas, Dan, and Lenny Rubenstein, eds. *The Cineaste Interviews*. Chicago: Lake View Press, 1983.

————. "Radical Filmmaking, 1930s." In *The Encyclopedia of the American Left*, Paul Buhle, Mari Jo Buhle, and Dan Georgakas, eds. 2nd ed. New York: Oxford University Press, 1999.

Grunfeld, Frederic V., ed. *Music and Recordings, 1955*. New York: Oxford University Press, 1955.

Hellman, Lillian. *Scoundrel Time*. New York: Bantam Books, 1977.

Ignatiev, Noel. *How the Irish Became White*. New York: Routledge, 1995.

Johnson, Malcolm. *Crime on the Labor Front*. New York: McGraw-Hill, 1950.

Jung, Carl. R. F. C. Hull, transl. *Two Essays On Analytical Psychology*. Princeton: Princeton Univ. Press, Bollingen Series XX, 2nd ed., 1972.

Lawson, John Howard. *Film in the Battle of Ideas*. New York: Masses and Mainstream, 1953.

Lee, Lance. *A Poetics for Screenwriters*. Austin: University of Texas Press, 2001.

MacDonald, Laurence E. *The Invisible Art of Film Music*. New York: Ardsley House, 1998.

Moore, Sonia. *The Stanislavsky System*. New York: Pocket Books, 1967.

Navasky, Victor S. *Naming Names*. New York: Viking, 1980 and Penguin Books, 1981.

New York Times Directory of the Theater. New York: Arno Press, 1973.

Pells, Richard H. *The Liberal Mind in a Conservative Age: American Intellectuals in the 1940s and 1950s*. New York: Harper and Row, 1985.

Peyser, Joan. *Bernstein: A Biography*. New York: William Morrow, 1988.

Prendergast, Roy. *Film Music: A Neglected Art*, 2nd ed. New York: W.W. Norton, 1992.

Sadie, Stanley, ed. *The Norton – Grove Concise Encyclopedia of Music*. New York: W.W. Norton, 1991.

Secrest, Meryle. *Leonard Bernstein: A Life*. New York: Alfred A. Knopf, 1994.

Shale, Richard. *Academy Awards*. New York: Frederick Ungar, 1982.

Sinclair, Andrew. *Spiegel: The Man Behind the Pictures*. Boston: Little, Brown, 1987.

Slonimsky, Nicolas. *Baker's Biographical Dictionary of Musicians*. 8th ed. New York: Schirmer Books, 1992.

Smith, John M. "Three Liberal Films." *Movie* 191 (1971–2): 20.

Smith, Wendy. *Real Life, The Group Theatre and America, 1931–1940*. New York: Alfred A. Knopf, 1990.

Suskin, Steven. *Show Tunes, 1905–1991*. New York: Limelight Editions, 1992.

Thomas, Tony. *Music for the Movies*. Cranbury, N.J.: A.S. Barnes, 1973.

Truffaut, François. *The Films in My Life*. Harmonsworth: Penguin Books, 1982.

Warshow, Robert. "The Liberal Conscience in *The Crucible*." *Commentary* (March 15, 1953): 265–71.

Whitburn, Joel. *Pop Memories 1890–1954: The History of American Popular Music*. Menomonee Falls, Wisconsin: Record Research Inc., 1986.

Wiley, Mason, and Damien Bona. *Inside Oscar: The Unofficial History of the Academy Awards*. New York: Ballantine Books, 1993.

Wollen, Peter. "Never at Home." *Sight and Sound* 4.5 (May, 1994): 15.

Index